The Immigrant

One from My Four Legged Stool

written by Alfred Woollacott III

 *My Four Legged Stool*

First Myfourleggedstool Publishers Edition, November 2014
P O Box 2911 Oak Bluffs, Massachusetts 02557

Copyright © 2014 Alfred Woollacott III

All rights reserved, including the rights to reproduce this book or portions thereof in any form whatsoever.
For information address Myfourleggedstool Publishers
P O Box 2911 Oak Bluffs, Massachusetts 02557
Attn: Alfred Woollacott, III

This book is a fiction, riveted to historical times and the life of John Law. Any references to historical events, real people, or real locales are used fictitiously. Other names, characters, places and incidents may have occurred and how they are presented are products of the author's imagination, and any resemblance to actual events or locales or persons, living or dead, is entirely coincidental.

Cover and book design by Robert Kauffman

Logo Design by Russ Thomas, Creative Nation

ISBN: 978-0-9904423-3-2

Acknowledgements

"Al, you're too young to retire. What are you going to do the first day of retirement?"

"Buddy, the same thing I always have done, except not go to work."

That 2002 response to Bud La Cava didn't answer his question. How was I going to fill a 60 hour plus per week void? I love history, read virtually nothing but, and I began dabbling into my family history upon my retirement. When I read a genealogy website posting from a Charles HB Cole, wanting information on the Fitchburg Woollacotts, my dabbling began to transform into an obsession. As I trudge on through dates, locations and snippets of information, several ancestors' lives captivated me. With guidance from Helen Schatvet Ullmann, I wrote my first genealogical article in register format on John Law and his descendants. My entire working life was spent accumulating facts and reaching conclusions. Genealogical writing should be easy, so I thought. But Helen is a consummate genealogist, who tightened my documentation and writing to a much needed rigor.

But I still remained captive to these ancestors, and 'just the facts, ma'am' was not enough to release me. Furnished with facts, I began to fictionalize their lives. For this writing style, I needed considerable help. John Hough Jr, a Vineyarder, writes historical fiction. And as great a writer as he is, he is even a more accomplished instructor. He started me along the road of changing a 'just the facts, ma'am' style into a compelling narrative. Many times with hands poised over a keyboard, while trying to revise a page, John's insight would come, allowing my fingers to tap anew.

A benefit of living on an island '45 minutes from America' is you are isolated, and thus a sense of community is heightened. In addition to John, we have accomplished authors and many more aspiring ones living on Martha's Vineyard. Frequently, stories appear in the local newspapers about local authors, which helped to create my self-imposed riding crop – 'Hell, if they can do it, so can I'. Lara O'Brien Robinson, Sam Low and Rick Herrick are some of the accomplished writers that call the Vineyard home. Lara's words, 'Al, don't rush it; make sure you get it right before you publish' were sage advice. When I gave my manuscript Sam and received back so many comments that I could barely see the original, I knew I had more work to do. Rick spent countless hours with me, offered insightful comments and helped to smooth my choppy, rat-a-tat style. I am deeply indebted to Rick, a retired college professor; an apt career for a dedicated educator.

Cynthia Riggs, another local writer of Vineyard mysteries, added to my writing abilities. Early reads from Shelley Brown and early edits from Suzanna Sturgis guided me back on track. Russ Thomas of Creative Nation created the four legged stool logo, and Robert Kauffman produced the book layout and cover, and helped with the marketing effort.

'Retirement - twice as much husband, half as much money' is on a plaque given to my wife, Jill. The latter half of that quip proved to be correct. My ever active mind didn't retire when I did. Like always, whenever it races, usually in the early morning hours, I arise and engage it to be taken somewhere. So in my retirement, Jill continued to roll toward my side of the bed and reach out for me until she realized I was gone – now, not to work, but down stairs, typing. We have been married for over 40 years, and a reason for that seemingly implausible statistic is we know one another like no one could ever imagine. While Jill would no doubt relish twice as much husband, she knows I can't sit still for more than a fleeting moment. She has always supported my many endeavors and lets me go. Whatever I may have accomplished in my life, I know it would have been far less without Jill's support.

The Immigrant
One from My Four Legged Stool
About the subtitle

We all have unique four legged stools, each leg an outshoot from our grandparents who contributed to our being. At conception, our entire biology stems from our forebears, the history that preceded us. Our environment, first from within the womb then without, people and events, often beyond our control, shape us further. If history does repeat, did our forebears experience what we now are experiencing? And if so, will we react as they once did? And should our biological bonds forget, will random energy pulses trigger a memory cord? John Law, the book's protagonist, is a part of my stool leg that stems from my maternal grandmother; thus, One from My Four Legged Stool.

He was born *circa* 1635, and died 4 January 1708. Significant events, some beyond his control, occurred throughout his life. Historians have written volumes on the major players in these events; Lord Cromwell, Governor Winthrop, King Philip, even bit players are afforded ink. But John Law's life is too insignificant for the historian's lens. "The Immigrant" is riveted in history, and yet in the end, a work of fiction written by an author with a few drops of John Law's blood.

Thomas B. Macaulay said, "A people, which takes no pride in the noble achievements of remote ancestors, will never achieve anything worthy to be remembered with pride by remote descendants." This book takes Macaulay's challenge seriously.

 *My Four Legged Stool*

Many characters in this book are historical figures, and their life and times have been meticulously researched. If you desire only John Law's genealogy or historical facts about the time when he lived, you can visit my website at www.myfourleggedstool.com . If you want a fascinating historical saga, continue reading.

Contents

Chapter One 5
Chapter Two 13
Chapter Three 23
Chapter Four 31
Chapter Five 37
Chapter Six 43
Chapter Seven 49
Chapter Eight 57
Chapter Nine 67
Chapter Ten 73
Chapter Eleven 81
Chapter Twelve 87
Chapter Thirteen 93
Chapter Fourteen 103
Chapter Fifteen 109
Chapter Sixteen 117
Chapter Seventeen 125
Chapter Eighteen 131
Chapter Nineteen 137
Chapter Twenty 141
Chapter Twenty-one 149
Chapter Twenty–two 163
Chapter Twenty-three 167
Chapter Twenty–four 179
Chapter Twenty-five 185
Chapter Twenty–six 189
Chapter Twenty-seven 199
Chapter Twenty–eight 205
Chapter Twenty-nine 213

Chapter Thirty 217
Chapter Thirty-one 221
Chapter Thirty-two 231
Chapter Thirty-three 235
Chapter Thirty-four 239
Chapter Thirty-five 247
Chapter Thirty-six 253
Chapter Thirty-seven 261
Chapter Thirty-eight 271
Chapter Thirty-nine 283
Chapter Forty 289
Chapter Forty-one 295
Chapter Forty-two 301
Chapter Forty-three 307
Chapter Forty-four 317
Chapter Forty-five 321
Chapter Forty-six 327
Chapter Forty-seven 331
Chapter Forty-eight 335
Chapter Forty-nine 341
Chapter Fifty 347
Chapter Fifty-one 355
Chapter Fifty-two 367
Chapter Fifty-three 371
Chapter Fifty–four 377
Chapter Fifty-five 383
Chapter Fifty-six 387
Chapter Fifty-seven 395
Chapter fifty-eight 399
RESOURCES 403

Chapter One

*On route from Concord's North Bridge
Acton, Massachusetts, American Colonies
19 April 1775*

I've got to get home.

That recurring thought had helped to keep Reuben Law tied to reality as he returned with the Acton militia from a horrific, April 19, 1775 morning at Concord's North Bridge. The events had been too intense and had occurred in such rapid fire fashion for Reuben to process and comprehend the full meaning. He had not been so overwhelmed since his father's death years earlier. He felt as though a colossal serpent was within him and didn't know when the next undulation would roil his stomach, only that it would. But Reuben's inner essence, whose existence had been created in part from his forebears' experiences, had born witness to a similar horror over one hundred years earlier on Doon Hill at Dunbar, Scotland.[1] His soul comprehended what Reuben was still incapable of understanding on this morning.

His morning began with three reverberating musket shots rousting him from his sleep. The shots were a call to arms for the Acton Militia. He wondered if it would be just another routine alarm, or something more. As he exited the house, his mother

---

1 *The Battle of Dunbar was on September 3, 1650, where the English Parliamentarian forces defeated the Scottish Royal Forces.*

foreboded dread and pleaded with him not to go. The image of his hand wringing mother continued to haunt him as he hustled to his Captain's house in an eerie pre-dawn light. Along the way, twinkles from his favorite constellation soothed him, and when he arrived at Captain Davis's house, he was eased further. His Captain's presence reminded him of a similar calming influence he had received from his father's whenever his young world had been shaken. The marching to The Bridge with the fifing and camaraderie depleted his pent up adrenaline and emboldened him. He was inspired until he spotted a bearskin mitre cap of a Grenadier, the elite of the British troops, rising above a sea of red coats. Reuben's stomach became queasy as his serpent fluttered.

As the Acton Militia marched to the bridge and past other militia companies on the western side of the river, the harmony of warbling birds, punctuated with chirps and occasional gurgles from eddies swirling under the bridge, comforted Reuben. The water, once past the bridge, returned to a lazy flow and became soothing, a symphony, replayed every spring since creation and part of the world order. But on this April morning, the troops massed fifty yards from each other seemed out of order. A musket roared, and Reuben's serpent ripped through his stomach. Smoke billowed, muskets roared again and Captain Davis's chest exploded like a star, spewing a crimson shower of flesh. When the volleying ended, the Captain's blood flowed as effortlessly as the water beyond the bridge. The exhilarating aroma of gunpowder that had heightened the Minutemen's camaraderie as they practiced in their Captain's yard was left to bygone days. Its pungent odor now permeated Reuben's lungs as the horror at Concord's North Bridge was being seared into his soul.

His stomach became queasy again as he and Militiamen neared the Davis homestead, a two-story house with a centered chimney, a steeply pitched barn and a windowed shed nearby. Reuben had always viewed the buildings as forming a fortress that protected the inner yard, symbolic of a strong, impenetrable Captain. Now, sobbing women and befuddled children filled the yard, and the buildings didn't seem like a fortress at all.

Reuben left his comrades to speak to Hannah, his fallen Captain's wife. He focused on a levering pole used to gather well water that rose above the crowd because it diverted his attention from the curious eyes that followed him as he wended his way to Hannah. When he took hold of Hanna's hand, her head jolted up, and her sobbing ceased. He rested his other hand on their clasp as a confused Hannah waited. Reuben waited too, allowing the serpent to recede from his throat, and then he spoke. "I lost my father when I was young."

Hannah bobbed her head.

"Captain Davis was like a father to me. I cannot possibly fathom your sorrow."

"He was consumed with dread this day, but guided by God's will," said Hannah. "Now, he is with his God." She pulled her hands from Reuben and collapsed her head into them.

Reuben wondered if his words had been appropriate, and with each of Hannah's sobs, his doubts increased. He moved toward the Davis children and was attracted to young Ephraim, who was clinging to his sister's dress. Fifteen years earlier, Reuben had lost his father. Ephraim now looked like Reuben had felt back then. He put his hand on Ephraim's shoulder and knelt to be eye level with him.

"Your father was a gallant soldier. He's with God now, but he will still care for you."

Life came to Ephraim's face. Hannah raised her head, wiped her tears and listened.

"I was a young lad like you when my father went to see God. Thought I would never see him again. But a man told me, 'When the stars shine, find the Big Dipper'."

"The Big Dipper?" Ephraim turned his questioning face to his sister.

"I've seen it," she said.

Ephraim turned back to Reuben. He sniffed and wiped his nose with his index finger. "Can I see it tonight?"

Reuben glanced at the cloudless sky. "Look in the nook between the cup and handle. Your father will be sitting there."

"Does it really work?"

"Sure does. I talked with my father before dawn as I came here."

"But will it work for me?"

"If you believe, it will work for you." The two smiling children filled Reuben with an inner peace. His words for Hannah may have been lacking, but he had found the right ones for her young children.

"Reuben Law, what are you doing?"

Reuben pivoted to see a woman dressed in a full-length black dress. She wasn't smiling. A stiff collar gripped her neck and lifted her head back. She peered over flared nostrils. He arose from his crouch and said, "Telling Ephraim a story, ma'am."

"Your story is heresy. Captain Davis would never allow such a sacrilege."

"I meant no harm. Just telling a story my Uncle Titus told me when I..."

"Aha," interrupted the woman. "Your uncle has nothing but contempt for the Lord. Some say you Laws are still a bunch of Scottish heathens, surely not me, even though you shame your Captain."

"Good Lord ma'am, it's just a story to ease a troubled lad."

"God doth not reside in the Big Dipper. And you, Reuben Law, are as impudent as your uncle."

That final rebuke pierced through Reuben, and he knew it was time to leave. As he did, he caught a glimpse of a still smiling Ephraim. He winked at him, and the young lad's eyes twinkled.

Reuben caught up with his comrades and joined in the march. He had experienced many emotions this day, but his anger over being called a 'Scottish heathen' now lingered. His great grandfather's Scottish blood surged from within. *Mother is as British as that Puritan prig,* he thought. *Yet I'm a Scottish heathen? Weren't no Scotsman that killed Captain Davis.* He cocked his head skyward. *If thou art a just God, smite every Brit bastard asunder.*

Those truly blasphemous and hasty thoughts stung Reuben's conscience. He paused and inhaled to cool his ire. As his comrades moved past him, the aroma from freshly plowed farmland filled his senses. It evoked pleasing thoughts until he was reminded of this morning's promise to his mother to till the family's fields. He was sure the horror at The Bridge had reached her by now. Reuben's stomach became nauseatingly gassy as the serpent hissed. *I've got to get back to my mother.*

"We're still on alarm. Pursuing the Regulars back to Lexington and Menotomy," called out a Militiaman.

Reuben resumed marching, but his Scottish blood continued to pound. He had heard his great grandfather had fought Lord Cromwell during the Third English Civil War[2] at Dunbar on Doon Hill in Scotland. His inner being surged forth, and he now felt the same disdain for the British that his great grandfather had felt. *I with smote those British bastards for my Captain just like Great Grandfather did to those English Roundheads.*[3] *Why he killed thousands before…*

"Hey Law, stop dreaming and get moving."

Reuben continued pursuing after the British troops, without incident. By the late afternoon, the Acton Militia headed back home, and Reuben returned to his mother. He was still shaken by the events at The Bridge, but had yet to grasp its future consequences on his life.

---

2   *The Third English Civil War (1649–1651) was the last of the English Civil Wars (1642–1651), a series of armed conflicts and political machinations between English Parliamentarians under the leadership of Lord Cromwell and the Scottish Royalists.*

3   *Roundhead was the nickname given to the Parliamentarian forces during the English Civil War. It was used as a term of derision since some parliamentarians wore their hair closely cropped round the head, an obvious contrast between them and the men of courtly fashion with their long ringlets.*

The next morning, he plowed the family's fields as he had promised his mother the day before, 19 April 1775.

Chapter Two

Doon Hill, Dunbar, Scotland
1 September 1650

M*e needs to get back to me mum*, thought John Law.

"Aye Law, stop dreaming and get moving," called out a comrade.

A fourteen-year old John Law surveyed the hoof prints in the soggy ground and resumed his ascent of Doon Hill, the easternmost summit of Scotland's Lammermuir Hills. He avoided the clumps and divots kicked up by the cavalry and reached a plateau. There, he stood among other pike men while holding his pike erect. He looked down the slope and followed the Brox Burn as it slashed through the wooded glen and emptied into the Firth of Forth. On a sliver of flat land between the Doon Hill and the Firth was a salt laden golf course,[4] which was now occupied by Cromwell's English Parliamentarian army. Behind the army, the Firth flowed into the seemingly endless North Sea. The masts of the English ships, which bobbed in a stiff breeze, were as tight as a comb's teeth. John was initially frightened at the sight until he realized he was out of range of their cannons. As he thought further, he realized the English

---

4   *The course was built in 1616, and in 1640, a Presbyterian minister was disgraced when he was caught committing the unpardonable sin of playing golf*

forces were a mile and a half away and had their backs to the sea. He was out of range of their cannons, too, and Cromwell's options for movement were severely limited, which his young mind sensed was an advantage for the Scots.

He shifted his eyes further east and followed the Coxsburnpath, the main road south out of Dunbar to Berwick, England. The Scottish Royal troops were amassed on high ground, close to the road. East of the Coxsburnpath was a beach with Scottish forces on it and beyond them, the North Sea. An English retreat south seemed effectively blocked. In front of the road and nearer to John stood a few clusters of corn stalks on barren fields. John had heard the Scots had stripped the countryside bare ahead of the advancing English to limit their food supply. Now, he saw the effect of their destruction.

John rubbed his pale blue eyes to ease the sting caused by salty mist being constantly driven into them. A gust fluttered his salt laden cheek fuzz, and he brushed at the tingle it created. Annoyed, he turned out of the wind, and his red locks flew from his neck and fluttered until the gust subsided. He surveyed his more immediate surroundings as the cold wind drove into his back. He was among Scottish cavalrymen, pike men, musketeers, and a few dozen short-range cannons, which covered the hillside. He was heartened by the display of force. Scottish officers, a few garbed in black, many in scarlet with white-laced collars and cuffs trimmed with gold or silver laces, bounced in unison with their horses' prance. Some wore blue woolen brimmed hats, and others donned steel helmets imported from the Continent. Their shoulder length hair flowed in the breeze. The officers were a spectacle of wealth that impressed John and increased his confidence.

The Immigrant

The Scottish Royal forces, under the command of General Leslie, were loyal to King Charles II ever since The Covenanters[5] had proclaimed him King of Great Britain a few months earlier. The newly proclaimed King's father, Charles I, had been executed by Lord Cromwell eighteen months earlier, in January 1649, at Whitehall, London. Cromwell, commander of the English Parliamentarian forces, became infuriated by the Covenanters action and invaded Scotland from Berwick in late July. Over the ensuing weeks and knowing the Scottish troops were not battle-hardened, General Leslie avoided a direct confrontation with Cromwell, a man he knew quite well. Five years earlier, they had fought together. Then, Leslie led a cavalry charge for a wounded Cromwell at the Battle of Marston Moor in West York, which ensured an English victory. As September approached, the English forces, demoralized by their failed attempt to seize Edinburgh and weakened from pursuing the evasive Scottish forces, drew back to their supply depot at Dunbar, Scotland. However, Leslie, sensing their retreat, reached Dunbar ahead of Cromwell and held the high ground on Doon Hill.

John turned back toward the North Sea to face an endless gale. He tried to braid his hair, but it was useless. As he endured a lashing from snapping tresses, his mood soured. *Me have failed me father so.* He continued to dwell on his failure until the sun broke through the clouds and reflected off his pike. As the clouds pulled back, the endless wave of pikes, held erect by numb hands, created a rolling wave of brilliance that lit up Doon Hill. John's mood brightened. He hoped the shock of radiance would blind the enemy below and terrify them into

---

5   *The Covenanters were a Scottish Presbyterian movement that played an important role leading up to the battle. They were determined to dictate the future course for both England and Scotland, and Charles II signed a covenant with them on June 30, 1650 upon arriving in Scotland.*

surrendering. But the clouds rolled back quickly, and a squall ensued. John wrapped his arms while struggling to hold his pike. He quivered until the rumble from a large blue flag with a white cross distracted him. 'COVENANT for Religion Croune and Countrie' rippled in the breeze, important words to the Covenanters, but still meaningless to John.

"Here laddies, eat hearty," said the syrupy voice belonging to Angus MacTavish, the sergeant in charge of food provisions.

John eased his shoulders back and laid his pike on the ground. The meager warmth, which huddling had created, vanished, and he shivered again. After several stiff-legged steps, his leg muscles regained life. He reached the swarm around MacTavish and jostled with others to ensure he would get fed this day since there had never been enough food. Most believed MacTavish and his minions ate more than their fair share, and MacTavish sold additional rations before ever serving the troops.

A cold blob of gruel was slung into John's cup as he was handed a slab of bread. MacTavish sat, smiling with his hands resting on his belly. He had a basket full of bread at his side, which John sensed he would sell later. *May God strike that bastard dead*, thought John as he exited the ill-formed queue.

"Sit among us, laddie," said a beckoning Malcolm Dinsmour. John was surprised as Malcolm was a highlander, who kept minimal contact with the recently recruited lowlanders. He and his cronies were the few veterans in the Scottish Royal Forces who had survived the Scottish defeat at the Battle of Preston two years earlier. They seldom mingled with inexperienced youth, especially one as young looking as John Law. His wispy facial hair seemed out of place on his childlike face. Although he was as tall as most men, due to a recent growth spurt, he lacked muscle tone and appeared more gangly than hearty. His voice often cracked when he spoke, immediately telling those who heard him that he was not quite yet a man. John had yet to experience a battle, and whenever scuttlebutt about a possible confrontation arose, he became nervous. He found hovering around Malcolm and eavesdropping on his conversations inspiring. His stories of smiting the English always calmed his fears. As he approached, he hoped Malcolm would accept him into his group.

Malcolm sat upon a grassy mound, elevated above the others, appearing like a king on his throne. John sat next to him. "The English be weary. We fight today, eh Andrew?" said Malcolm.

Andrew lowered his cup. "It be the Sabbath. The Covenanters will nae allow General Leslie to attack."

"Be fittin' to slaughter the English on the Lord's Day," said Malcolm.

"Cromwell's baking ovens be cold," said Andrew. "The English be starving. So why fight?"

"To slay the bastards who invade me Scotland."

Andrew flashed a dismissive hand, and Malcolm leaned from his throne and glared. "Andrew Wright, be you Scottish, or be you a coward?"

Andrew gulped and said, "Scottish."

"Aye, we Scots be brave lads," said Malcolm as he nodded to John. He turned back to his cronies. "We will push the English into the sea and let them swim to their precious England." Malcolm eased back and slapped his knee. "Then me can get back to me wenches."

"Me could use a lass," said one who swirled his index finger inside his cup. He jammed his gruel-laden finger down his throat, wrapped his lips and eased his finger out. His lips popped, and he said, "Me could make any lass me wench, or die trying."

Others, now stirred with carnal thoughts, chimed in. The laughter grew with each comment. John appreciated the banter, and seated near the throne and sensing acceptance, he chimed in. "Me needs to get back to me mum."

"Your mum?" asked Andrew.

"Me father passed, and me needs to care for her."

"Don't fret laddie. A clansman probably be taking good care of her, right now," said one while looking at his smirking companions.

"Enough," said Malcolm.

"Maybe many be taking care of her," said a lascivious looking brute. He raised his kilt and moved his pelvis in and out. One convulsed with laughter and held his shaking belly. Another wiped tears away, but his laughter returned when the brute's dangling penis and scrotum swung in unison with his thrusts. John toyed with his gruel, wishing he could shrink away. He didn't belong.

The sound of a sword being unsheathed pierced the uproar and jolted John back to reality. Malcolm arose and swayed his basket-hilt sword back and forth. His well-defined forearm muscles rippled as his arm rolled. He positioned for an upward swing, an avenger powerful enough to lop off the thickest of limbs. He inched forward while glaring over the tip of his outstretched sword. He diverted the tip to make eye contact with each, and when he did, each head lowered. After every man had bowed, Malcolm sheathed his sword. He moved back to John and tugged his cheek's fuzz. "He still be a wee lad."

John was now the focus of the group, and he wondered if he had been accepted by Malcolm's cronies or only created envy among them. His cheeks reddened, and he prayed his fuzz obscured his embarrassment. But a clamor around MacTavish ensued, distracting the group, and they turned their attention to it.

The food, which MacTavish's minions had been distributing, was completely dispersed. Those still unfed jostled and barked at one another. MacTavish arose and tossed chunks of bread to disperse some of the unruly. He backed closer to his minions and waved several loaves of bread. "How much do me get for the last of it?"

John ceased nibbling and inched closer to Malcolm's throne to watch. A few men pitched coins toward MacTavish and moved to await their purchase. As MacTavish neared, he bent, with his eyes focused ahead, picked up the coins and tossed loaves to the buyers. Those still without food twitched in anticipation of possibly getting what little remained in MacTavish's hands.

Malcolm put his hand on his sword's hilt and leaned to John. "Eat quickly, laddie." Malcolm's comrades shuffled closer to him.

Those still waiting for food had their jackal eyes on MacTavish. He hurled the remaining bread into the pack, and they descended upon it like wolves devouring a picked over carcass. A rabid looking wretch stepped toward John as he gobbled his last few bites. Malcolm inched his sword from its sheath, and the wretch's eyes darted to a lone, still-nibbling pikeman. MacTavish scurried away with his lackeys as a rearguard, counting coins and slipping them into his pouch.

John heard a thud and turned toward it to see a pikeman collapsing from a blow delivered by the wretch's club. The wretch scampered away, tearing into a half-eaten slab of bread. John could have been that unsuspecting and now collapsed pikeman if not for Malcolm. He glanced up at Malcolm who still had a grip on his sword.

Once Malcolm sensed his comrades were safe, he settled back on his throne. "Me wonder what MacTavish will do with his coins?" he asked.

Andrew stared at the ground and responded. "His coins will pay for a safe passage should Cromwell prevail."

"Cromwell prevail?" asked Malcolm. He leaned to John. "What say you, laddie?"

John shook his head, and Malcolm patted it.

Malcolm turned back to Andrew and sat fully erect. "We will slay Cromwell first. Then me will slay MacTavish and use his coins for me wenches." Everyone laughed, except for Andrew who still stared at the ground, seemingly in thought.

As twilight ebbed, John arose to pace, his routine these past weeks before utter darkness ensued. Another day had passed without him being able to honor his vow to his father. How many more nights would he have to endure? In daylight, his sense of his father's disappointment was not ever-present. But as sunset encroached, John's failure dominated his thoughts, and his melancholy grew more vivid. Pacing, like most actions, kept the images faint. But he couldn't pace all night. Eventually he would need to lie under a black void, an ideal backdrop for his demons to taunt him, and relive his failure. Perhaps this night would be less bleak as Malcolm had a solution. If the Scottish Royal forces could push the English into the sea, John could return home to his mother and honor his vow.

Chapter Three

2 September 1650

John's torso sprung up from the ground like a catapult. Sitting, he stared into darkness toward sounds of movement. He saw nothing, and his racing heart eased. This night, his worries of an imminent attack had been intensified from misinterpreting unfamiliar sounds. A prolonged gust now drowned out most sounds, and John reclined. When the gust subsided, John cocked his ear as his heart raced in anticipation. He was still adapting to being alone, absent a mother's embrace or a father's rational explanation for the unknown. Several horses whinnied, and when one snorted, John scrambled to his feet.

"Rest laddie," said a voice.

Adrenaline spiked through John. "Malcolm?" he asked.

"Aye," said the silhouette of a resting warrior who was clenching a sword to his chest.

John's heart throttled back as he moved to Malcolm. He squatted and said, "Horses coming up the brae."

"It be our horses. Rest, we fight tomorrow." Malcolm sat up to be eye-to-eye with John. "Do some killing. You be ready?"

John bobbed his head as he gulped.

Malcolm's sword glistened as he rolled his wrist. "Been sharpened this lass," he said, and he flicked a finger on the blade. He gripped John's shirt and pulled him close. "You stay nigh." A stench followed after Malcolm's words, and John reeled back from it. Malcolm tugged him back. "You'll be safe with Malcolm." He released John. "Then you can be with your mum." As he reclined, he added, "And me to me wenches."

John went back to his pike accompanied by Malcolm's words, "Sweet lassie, come to your Malcolm." John's tarnished spearhead on his thirteen foot pike was difficult to detect from the ground that it lay upon. It didn't matter, he was too weary to grind it to create a gleam like Malcolm had done with his sword. He lay on the sodden ground, rolled to his side, cuddled his pike and reflected on the day when the Clan Commander, Jamus MacLawson, arrived at the family hut.

"Me needs your Johnnie," said Jamus to John's mother, Mary.

"He be too wee to be among your motley lot," she replied.

Jamus put his hand on Mary's shoulder. "Me got me quota to fill."

Mary gave John a resigning nod as a tear trickled. The anguish in her face was as vivid this night as it had been then.

To shake the image of his mother from his mind, John turned his thoughts to Jamus. He was clad in his tartan kilt with a fur trimmed sporran[6] hanging in front and a crested sgian dubh[7] sheathed in his knee high sock. When this inspiring warrior squeezed John's shoulder that fateful day and said, "You'll be a hearty warrior," John believed him.

John sat up, arched his stiffening back and thought how the past several weeks had proven Jamus wrong. He was a frightened lamb in a den of wolves, unlike Malcolm, who was a true warrior. He rubbed his back and reclined. Jamus reappeared, patting his mother's shoulder and saying, "Your Johnnie will be back by summer's end." John believed Jamus, but his doubts had increased since then.

After Jamus left, John remembered holding his mother, stroking her hair and occasionally brushing her tears away. "Don't fret," he said as he stroked her hair, "Me will return in time for the harvest." He knew now his mother found his words hollow, but she had accepted them anyway. John realized his words were incapable of soothing her like his father could.

The image of his father appeared. He was lying on the dirt floor, covered with a sheepskin, soaked with perspiration and shivering. "You'll soon have all that me has," he said. "You be a young lad, but when me goes, your youth goes, too. Care for the land, and it will care for you. Take a lass as pure as your mum. Have many sons. They will help care for your land, and when God calls for you, your sons will care for your aged bonny lass." His father coughed and struggled to arise, but couldn't. "Me time be nigh, and me has told you much."

---

6 *A pouch that performs the same function as pockets on the pocket-less kilt, which is worn on a leather strap or chain, conventionally positioned in front of the groin of the wearer.*

7 *A small, single-edged knife, originally used for eating and preparing fruit, meat, and cutting bread and cheese, which is tucked into the top of the kilt hose with only the upper portion of the hilt visible.*

The tears, which John struggled to hold back while in front of his father, now fell. John replayed in his mind his last minutes with his father. "Father, if me has questions," he asked.

"Others will need to answer them."

"But me need answers from you."

"It can nae be. If nae the elders, then God. He always hears." His father lay quiet for a seeming eternity until his eye's regained life. He sat up, and with an arm feebler than John had ever felt before, he drew him close. Unlike his arms, his father's eyes were still overpowering. "Always care for me bonny lass, your mum." John bobbed his head as his father drew him closer. "Always," he whispered.

His father's dying words had given John a purpose. He toiled daily, determined that his mother would have food and shelter. John and his mother adapted to their changed relationship and survived their first winter. John relished the thought of those bygone days. But his appreciation left when his thoughts turned to their nights together. His mother's nightly sobs were now distinct in Doon Hill's rustle. Whenever he heard them, he asked God for answers to ease her pain and end the ringing in his head. God never answered. Perhaps God was as powerless as John to soothe her. Perhaps only his father was able to end her sorrowful weeping.

*****

As the sun crept over the North Sea, Malcolm strutted along the hillside. "Be moving down the brae soon," he said.

Andrew frowned and continued pitching pebbles.

"Where be that fat bastard MacTavish?" asked Malcolm. "A glorious morn to do battle, me feels it."

Andrew arose and pointed east. "The Coxsburnpath, the road south to Berwick, be held fast by us Scots." He swung his arm from the south up the brae and around back to the Firth of Forth. "We control Doon Hill. Cromwell be encircled and outnumbered." He turned back to Malcolm, "His baking ovens be cold, and his men be starving."

Malcolm stepped toward Andrew and unsheathed his sword. "Starving be nae goot."

"Me can smell the stench of Cromwell's dying men whene'er the winds blow from the sea," said Andrew. "Me say we should wait."

"Me needs blood on me sword," said Malcolm as he held his sword erect.

The silent confrontation remained until John piped in. "Drive Cromwell into the sea, and me can get home." Andrew spun around, annoyed that Malcolm's protégé had become so bold.

Malcolm nodded an approval, pumped his sword skyward and bellowed, "Alba gu bráth."[8]

John, unsettled by Andrew's scowl, left. As he moved along the hillside looking for MacTavish, his stomach growled and his mouth salivated. After a while, he realized there would be no food this morning. He had heard The Covenanters believed men fight better with empty bellies, which furthered his belief

---

[8] *A Scottish/Gaelic phrase used to express allegiance to Scotland. Idiomatically it translates into English as "Scotland forever"*

of an imminent attack. He sat in the cool mist and stared below, trying to ignore his hunger and his fears.

In the afternoon the men began to stir, and a hungry John ceased worrying and arose, too. The cavalry was ordered to lead the forces off of Doon Hill, closer to the town where Cromwell's forces were positioned. As John descended, he was accompanied by the rumble of the Scottish throng, and his worries lessened. He scanned the hillside and sensed he was but one among thousands. He concluded, naively, the horrors of battle were for the others.

Once the Scottish army had reached flat land, a majority of the infantrymen were ordered to move west. There, they bunched themselves between the Brox Burn and the slopes of Doon Hill to form the Scottish left flank. A smaller force, including the pike men that John was among, was ordered to stretch their line east. Some cavalrymen and a regiment of foot soldiers joined the Scottish force, massed on the Coxsburnpath.

John moved east and held his position. As he looked west, he saw the Scottish forces at the base of the hill fanned out as far as he could see. He knew even more were hidden by the hillside, which lay further beyond. When he turned east, he spotted Andrew and several of Malcolm's cronies. John moved to Andrew, and with a new found sense of self-confidence, he said, "A widened circle means a larger noose to snare Cromwell."

Andrew spun around, annoyed to hear Malcolm's protégé offering simple, erroneous battle tactics. "We left the brae in daylight, laddie," said Andrew. "Now the English know where we be."

Undeterred by Andrew's haughtiness, John pointed to the Coxsburnpath. "Let Cromwell try to get back to England now."

"Cromwell be nae a fool. He won't go south. But he may attack our right flank directly."

John gulped. "The right flank be us. Why would he attack us?"

"Laddie, we have stretched our battle lines too far. He can easily drive through us and turn our flank." Andrew pointed toward Brox Burn. "And our left flank be too far to help." He swung his arm as he continued to speak. "The brae be at our backs, and the Brox Burn be in front. We got nowhere to move should Cromwell attack." He looked to the cavalry, which had spilled onto the beach aside the south road. "Horses need room to maneuver. They be useless now." Andrew ceased expounding and glowered. "Ever see penned in swine awaiting their slaughter?"

"But we be warmer off the brae," said John.

"You be warm now, but you'll be dead cold tomorrow."

John forced a stone face to mask his fear and to feign indifference. Andrew sneered and wandered away. John remained uneasy until he spotted Malcolm in the distance, brandishing his sword in mock battle.

As the sun descended below Doon Hill, John wondered what the next day might bring. Horses with scarlet-clad riders moved across the brae to distant tents and commandeered farmhouses. The Scottish officers would again sleep in comfort. Once they disappeared, the discipline they had been providing began to ebb. Many men now either sat or lay on the ground. Only a few kept a vigilant watch.

John moved toward a cornfield to lie down with some men. He thrashed among the few standing corn stalks for comfort and squirmed into the sodden ground. He laid some fallen stalks over him to shelter him from the mist. He felt hidden and safe for the night. He didn't need to cuddle his pike this night. He curled to a fetal position and let fatigue ooze through his body to create a peaceful slumber.

Chapter Four

3 September 1650

"The Lord of Hosts."

John's eyes flew open with the bellow from approaching soldiers at about 4:00 a.m. and in a dark, misty fog. He had heard movement during the night, but Malcolm's mentoring had made him a warrior. He had ignored the sounds, just as Malcolm would have. But there was no mistaking this bellow. It was an English battle cry. He threw off the cornstalks and struggled to arise out of the mud that had jelled around him.

"The Lord of Hosts" was bellowed again.

Silhouettes of cavalrymen, followed by Roundhead soldiers, splashed out of Brox Burn between the Scottish cavalry on the south road and the infantry to the west. The Scottish force around John was at the center of the English attack. They had been caught unprepared and now scrambled to face the onslaught. Thundering hooves trampled some, and clanging iron felled others. The Scottish force was being pushed up Doon Hill. John searched for his pike among the darkened jumble of mud and stalks. He dropped to all fours and thrashed where he had slept. A crescendo of agonizing screams came from his retreating comrades. His heart pounded and head swirled as he rummaged. When a retreating comrade stumbled and flipped across John's back, he scrambled on all fours until he had room to arise and sprint away. He covered his ears to lessen the reverberating screams, clanging iron, musket fire and occasional rumble of cannons. Only one cry seemed constant.

"The Lord of Hosts."

John continued his panic-ridden scamper until he felt safely away. He removed his hands from his ears and placed them on his thighs, hunched over and panted. The Scots now seemed to be holding the Roundheads in check with ferocious hand-to-hand combat. John turned toward Doon Hill and thought about running further away. Once beyond it, his joyous, promised journey home could begin. The sun would soon be emerging from the North Sea. He needed to act while dim light still prevailed.

He sprinted up the brae, but stopped to see a distant swing of a rider's sword cut through the hamstrings of a fleeing pikeman, who struggled like a newborn foal to arise as he gripped his dangling flesh and begged his assailant to end his life. The cavalryman laughed and rode away looking for more fleeing Scots. The hillside was covered with sword wielding English cavalry.

"Alba gu bráth," was bellowed in perfect Gaelic dialect. A swarm of Scots rushed past John to join their countrymen still engaged in hand-to-hand combat. The battle cry and images of Malcolm brandishing his sword and Jamus MacLawson clad in his tartans appeared. John was reinvigorated and joined the counter surge. But his excitement ebbed when he realized he needed a weapon. He spotted a glistening, partially unsheathed sword of a fallen warrior and ran to it.

The warrior was clad in the familiar saffron cloak, which was belted to form a pleated kilt. He was lying face down with his skull partially crushed by hooves. John rolled him over to unsheathe his basket hilt sword. As he did, the open-eyed warrior stared back. John's stomach knotted, and he collapsed onto the ground. "Me God, it be Malcolm Dinsmore." John pulled his knees to his chest. He lowered his head and swayed it back and forth. His mighty warrior, his mentor, his fleeting surrogate father had never used his sword. John remained paralyzed until rage freed him. He looked heavenward and gave a defiant head shake.

John arose, gripped Malcolm's sword and rolled his wrist. The gleam was fascinating, and John didn't notice the back pedaling Scots or those who broke rank and ran. Amid the roar of battle, a fallen Roundhead's murmur grew distinct. As John neared him, his murmuring became taunting whispers from a haughty Englishman, the sole cause of John's despair. He raised Malcolm's sword, and with an impulsive surge, he slashed through the Roundhead. The murmuring ended, but John's misery didn't. He hacked until weary and paused to gather enough strength for a final blow. As he raised the sword, blood trickled onto his hand, and he smeared it onto his tired, sinewy forearm. Its sticky warmth made his spine tingled. He smeared it on his face, and his tingling exploded though his entire being, eclipsing his despair. He was electrified when he roared, "Me Scotland will nae die. Alba gu bráth."

But the roar quelled his bravado, and the carnage about him extinguished it. He had slain a lone, helpless Englishman. He cocked his arm to heave the sword, but paused. He ran to Malcolm and fitted the sword back into his hand. He moved Malcolm's arm so his sword now lay across his chest. Malcolm's opened eyes seemed appreciative. Lacking the bluster of before, he said, "Alba gu bráth, me friend."

Roundheads had now driven through the Scottish line. John was cut off from the left flank. The English were all around him and moving closer. *"Ever see penned in swine awaiting their slaughter?"* As Andrew's word echoed in his head, John now knew he had trusted the wrong man. Andrew Wright had been more perceptive than Malcolm Dinsmore.

A few Scots tried to break through the ever tightening circle, but were immediately slashed down. John remained confined as the English shoved their swords at the Scots on the perimeter. Some Scots shrieked and fell when English swords penetrated their sides. John fought through the clustering Scots to get further away from the edge. The poking into a ball of humanity continued until the English grew either arm weary or just bored with their sport. The terror-filled Scots remained transfixed on the sneering, English faces, wondering when they might resume their amusement. The English began to giggle, and it rumbled into laughter. They broke their stares and eased back while still laughing.

Officers trickled across the field to take charge of the captives and restore order to the unruly Englishmen. The Roundheads' exuberance quelled, and some paused to ponder the horror strewn about them. The Scottish relaxed their huddle now that threats of pike thrusts had diminished.

John sensed the attack was over for now, and he moved from the center of the clustered Scots. The sun had burned the mist off of Doon Hill. The gloomy past few days had been replaced with radiance. Doon Hill seemed like it has been for ages, unaware of the carnage below, basking in the sun while salty dew created an awe-inspiring, prism-like glow. John had marched up Doon Hill and back down it. Now, desperate Scots ran for their lives back up it. He thought of the irony and insanity of it all. Even his naïve mind realized the Scots had been given an incredible advantage, and they wasted it. John seethed as he thought, *The English will e'er be bastards. Me will nae forget.*

John turned away from Doon Hill as Andrew came near. "Seen Malcolm?" he asked.

John pointed to the distance. "Dead."

Andrew shook his head. "Well, he wanted this fight. Me be sure he slayed many before he died."

"Aye, thousands," said John. Andrew's eyes widened until doubt weighed on his eyelids. John broke his eye contact and noticed Andrew's shoulder. "Me God, you be wounded."

"Nae be much," said Andrew as he pressed on his shoulder. "You be blood spattered too. You will be heading to yah mum, real soon."

Had John heard the always insightful Andrew correctly? Had God finally heard John's pleading? His mother's agonized image finally smiled. He would be home in time for the harvest, swinging a scythe under a brilliant autumn sky.

"The English only want the hearty, nae the wounded," said Andrew. He pressed harder on his shoulder to try to clot the now spurting blood. "Of course, we have to make it home. How bad be your wounds?"

"Me nae have any," said John.

Andrew coughed and spat some blood. "Aw, too bad laddie. Guess you'll nae be seeing yah mum after all." He laughed until he choked on a gurgle of blood. He spat the bloody phlegm close to John's feet and resumed chuckling.

John's delight of reuniting with his mother had been snuffed out as quickly as it came. Were these false hopes merely God's cruel trick to keep him from facing reality?

Chapter Five

London, England
Mid-September 1650

After the destruction of the Scottish Royal army at Dunbar, Cromwell marched unopposed back to Edinburgh and captured Scotland's capital. John Law was among the 5,000 prisoners that were force-marched south to Durham, England, arriving eight days after the battle on September 11th. There, John would await his fate. Meanwhile, further south in London, two business associates were meeting, which would affect John's destiny.

Outside the heavy, chocolate-colored door to John Becx's well-appointed office in London's financial district, Richard Leader paced while clutching his documents. Richard had been in charge of the Braintree Ironworks operation in the Colonies, as agent for the Ironworks' financial investors. By 1647, the Braintree operation was failing, and Richard found another location on behalf of the investors, north of Braintree on the Saugus River. He had been instrumental in getting the Saugus site built and operational, yet the investors lost faith in him. John Becx, a resident of London and a wealthy industrialist, was the lead investor for the twenty-four who financed the Ironworks. Richard had left the Colonies in the summer to meet with Becx in England.

One of Becx's aides opened the door, and Richard hurried into the office. Becx sat between heavy wooden supports for his over-sized desk. The legs of the diminutive Becx dangled from the leather-padded chair just above the floor. He ceased swinging them back and forth and said, "Richard, I provided the financing for the Ironworks, and my decision is final. John Gifford and William Awbrey are replacing you."

Richard raised a hand to stop Becx from saying more. "I come not to ask thee to reconsider," he said.

"Wise on your part," said Becx as he slid off his chair to pace. "I respect your engineering talents. You built a magnificent ironworks, yet we still lost money." He ceased pacing and turned to Richard. "What happened?"

Richard squirmed. "Magnificent truly, but we lacked sufficient labor."

"How can that be?" asked Becx. "Governor John Winthrop was keen on our venture. Said it was important to his common weal. His son oversaw everything until you replaced him." Becx's eyes widened. "Aha, was it spite?"

"Perhaps, it was spite." Becx frowned, and Richard quickly continued. "No matter, the Governor is deceased, and John the younger is in Connecticut. The Winthrops will no longer interfere."

"Splendid, the situation is improved. Gifford and Awbrey will turn a profit."

"Doubtful, the problem is bigger than the Winthrops. It's that damn colony."

Becx raised his head, seemingly wanting to learn more.

"The men are clergy, or artisans, or farmers, and the rest are their goodwives[9] and children. The Ironworks never had enough labor."

"Then we should have imported some laborers," said Becx.

"Impossible. The Governor determined who would leave England for his colony. He oversaw every ship that arrived and sent back the ones not to his liking." Becx glared his skepticism and Richard added, "Well not every ship. Thou art a Dutchman, ye understand."

Becx smiled briefly and said, "But you still hired laborers."

"We trained a few yeomen. But we needed colliers, furnace men, and…"

"You should have trained more yeomen," interrupted Becx.

"There are not enough men to train. Even so, it is a dear wage we pay. And force them to deliver a fair day's work, why the constable, clergy, the whole town are upon thee."

Becx sighed. "I've read the court proceedings and paid the fines."

"They are all kin. It's never a fair court."

"Less dear labor," said Becx as he paced while pondering. "We need to reduce our costs." He stopped and turned to Richard. "How about the natives?"

Richard sneered. "With sincerest respects."

"Just a thought," said Becx as he rubbed his chin. "Still a few ships with cheap labor could solve our problem."

---

9 *Goodwives was a polite form of address often used where "Mrs." would be used today.*

"Governor Endicott[10] would never allow it."

"Nonsense. A few ships will not spoil that new world experiment."

"But if he does object, what becomes of these undesirables?" asked Richard.

"The Governor can determine their fate." Becx pondered further and a smile crossed his face. He gave a concluding head nod and turned back to Richard. "Now, what's your purpose today?"

"A saw mill in the colonies," said Richard as he laid out his documents. "Thou will make a fortune."

"And is Governor Endicott keen on this venture?"

"The mill will be north of the Massachusetts colony, on the Piscataqua River."[11]

"I like that," said Becx as his smile broadened.

"There is plenty of timber hither," said Richard as he pointed to a spot on his map, "with a river to the sea. It's ideal."

"And labor?"

"It will be dear, but worth it." Richard picked up his other documents. "I have computed the labor costs in these journals."

---

10 Endicott was the 1st, 10th, 13th, 15th, and 17th Governor of the Massachusetts Bay Colony, and was succeeded, at times various times, from 1629 -1649 by Governor Winthrop. Endicott was Governor in the periods 1649-1650 and 1655-1664.

11 The Piscataqua is a 12-mile long tidal estuary, the last 6 miles of which forms what is now Portsmouth, New Hampshire's inner harbor, before it empties into the sea.

Becx grabbed the documents from Richard. "I admire your engineering skills, but you are not a financial man. I must study them further. Adieu Richard Leader."

As Richard turned to leave, Becx said, "You know Richard, if the Governor protests too much about undesirables in his Massachusetts, we could send them north."

"Be assured," said Richard as he paused at the door, "he will protest."

Chapter Six

Durham Cathedral, Durham, England
Autumn 1650

As John lay on the Durham Cathedral floor, a speck beneath the towering Norman-styled arches, he pondered. Andrew Wright had been dead-on correct again. The English only took the healthy, and now John knew why. The sickliest of the more than 5,000 prisoners had perished on the eight day, 120 mile 'death march' from Dunbar, Scotland to Durham, England. Andrew Wright was still in Scotland, perhaps with his clan, and John was further from his mother. Maybe John had been less fortunate than he thought. Maybe the truly blessed ones were the 2,000 prisoners who littered a southern road into England.

John lowered his melancholy eyelids, and when they reopened, he contemplated the designs on the arches. His usual worship place was Spartan by comparison. Even the church, which his father insisted John attend the year before he died, couldn't compare to this magnificent mammoth structure. The walk to that Scottish church was cold and lengthy, and John complained constantly. But his father was resolute; John needed to witness what his father had witnessed as lad. As John reminisced, he appreciated his father's insistence.

That church was candlelit, insufficient to heat its stone structure, but sufficient to warm John's heart. The cleric's robe swooshed as he moved about the altar. An organ shattered the stillness, and the congregation sang. The shivers, which John had then, returned. He inched close to his mother since her sweet warble was more appealing than his father's off-key monotone. Her mouth and lips changed with each syllable, and when she smiled at him while singing, his body prickled. The walk home was neither cold nor lengthy, but silent, except for crunching feet on the meadow's rime and his mother's hum of a previously sung hymn.

Durham Cathedral's stench grew overwhelming, and John ceased daydreaming. Vomit and urine splotches, excrement in nooks, doses of rotting bodies and traces of disease from those waiting to die created a noxious concoction. Even Durham Cathedral's towering arches were insufficient to allow the stench to dissipate. John wiggled his nose and rolled to his side. One stained glass window still remained intact. Jesus, with inviting open palms hanging at his side, stared back. John had prayed to that window, but God hadn't hear him. He glared at Jesus and thought about praying again, but he rolled away and became captive to the nave's ribbed arches that formed part of the Cathedral's vault.

As twilight came, the predictable feeding clamor ensued and distracted John. He arose and noticed a desperate, thin, and seemingly familiar wretch, pleading with a guard. Coins fell into a guard's open palm, bread was handed over, and the wretch backed away. John's memory was finally triggered. *It be MacTavish. But he nae be a fat bastard.*

He wondered if God had rendered justice after all. MacTavish, the swine, ate his fill at Dunbar, and the English probably mistook him as hearty. Now, he grovels for swill and is forced to live in this hell with the rest of us. John smiled as his eyes rose up the arches and through the ceiling. He nodded a 'thank you' to God. But God didn't acknowledge it. Only Andrew's earlier words echoed down from the arches. *"MacTavish's coins will pay for safe passage after Cromwell prevails."*

John whirled to the stained glass window of Jesus, but he couldn't maintain eye contact with him. He thought further as MacTavish moved out of the nave toward the choir section, before disappearing into the darkened recesses of the aisle on the south side. As John waited for his food, Malcolm's previous boast throbbed in his temples. *"Me will slay MacTavish and take his coins."* The words continued to resonate while John ate.

When John finished eating, he moved toward the choir section. When he caught a glimpse of Jesus, he moved back to the nave. He sprawled onto the stone floor, allowing the Cathedral's drone to be his lullaby as he tried to sleep. Unlike his mother's soothing tones, this lullaby was a jumble of scuffles, raised voices, thumps and howls, which dimmed to murmurs. But this night, a persistent thought accompanied the lullaby. *Slay MacTavish and take his coins for safe passage home.*

John couldn't sleep, and he arose and drifted toward the darkness again, unsure of what he would do. A broken, jagged-edge spindle from the altar rail lay on the floor of the choir section. It seemed to beckon, and John grabbed it and held it like a dagger. He moved to the darkened recesses near the small arches that formed the aisle of the choir section's south side. Using the aisle's outer wall for bearings, he stepped further away from the nave while searching for MacTavish. When he saw a silhouette of a man just ahead, his heart raced as his vision blurred. *MacTavish? Propped against that column?*

MacTavish's ashen cheeks were noticeable in the darkness and seemingly summoning John. He raised the altar spindle and took deliberate steps. As he drew closer, John noticed MacTavish's eyes were opened, and he held his last step in mid-air. His thigh began to quiver. *Me God, does he see me?* John lowered his leg slowly. MacTavish hadn't noticed.

He inhaled while contemplating his next step, still unsure of what to do. But MacTavish's ashen cheeks and open eyes morphed into mocking. John lunged and drove the spindle into his MacTavish's chest. He put his hand on MacTavish to push himself away. He was as cold as the walls that John had used for his bearings. Red finger imprints were on his neck, and his emptied money pouch was at his side. The jackals had already come.

John struggled off MacTavish, but he still seemed to taunt more than before. John kicked him, but the mocking remained. John stopped kicking and yanked the spindle from MacTavish's chest. He raised it for another stab, but paused and screamed. His shriek echoed among the arches, and when John kicked again, MacTavish teetered and thumped onto the floor.

The constant drone in Cathedral ceased, perhaps to allow the captives to wonder what had just occurred. But the drone returned as quickly as it had ceased. Their reality of hunger, disease, and death eclipsed wonder. A distant Jesus was still watching, and John threw the spindle, which hit a column and bounced along the floor. He stepped out of the southern aisle into the choir section. He looked skyward through the massive vault, shook his fist and screamed out. "This bastard leaves your hell and nae me? Why did you choose me to suffer?"

God didn't answer, and John bellowed again, "Why?" He only heard his question reverberating among the small arches. His bowels rumbled, and pain shot through them. He crunched over and hastened along the smaller arches of the south aisle. A devilish light flickered among them, and Doon Hill's horrors changed with each flash to create a terrorizing reel of images. His bowels gurgled again. *Has me been inflicted with what felled so many? Is that me passage home?*

Once outside, the invigorating night air eased John's rage and steadied his thoughts. Jesus's image returned to his mind, and John responded to them. "He be dead. Me nae killed him." But Jesus stayed, and John squeezed his eyes and said, "He be dead, me say." Jesus's image grew faint as John twitched. "Aye, he be dead." John was at peace, for now, with what he had just done.

John lowered his breeches, and his buttocks chilled. He squatted, and without even a grunt, his bowels emptied and cramps subsided. Maybe his plight wasn't hopeless. Maybe his unanswered questions to an unhearing God had removed one possibility. Death was not an answer. His stench contaminated the air. A bleak reality returned. John gripped his breeches and hopped toward a sod clump. In a cloister, dwarfed by a magnificent edifice erected to the glory of God, John wiped his bottom and looked heavenward, still waiting for God to answer.

Chapter Seven

The Cathedral's stench now had a tinge of smoke added to the concoction. For warmth, the Scots started fires with urine soaked hay and fueled it with splintered pews, altar rails and books. They shattered the stained glass windows to improve the ventilation. The window with Jesus now had holes in each of his palms, and his once peaceful visage was a blur of pulverized glass. Even though John had convinced Jesus that MacTavish was dead when he drove the spindle into him, Jesus needed to be reminded often. But now, with his image less distinct, John felt less compelled to explain his actions to Jesus.

Deaths had increased from a trickle to an unmanageable torrent. A mass grave was needed, and John was taken with others to dig it. Even though his scrawny muscles had atrophied, he was one of the few captives that had yet to be severely infected with the flux.[12] Being outside cleared his lungs, brightened his thoughts, and being physically exhausted at day's end, created undisturbed sleep.

On a chilly autumn day, John took a breather from his digging. He leaned upon his spade as sweat dripped down his back. The massive grave, partially filled with bodies, ran

---

12 A medical term used at the time for dysentery.

due north for several hundred feet in a straight line from the Cathedral. He wondered if soon the grave would stretch far enough to be in Scotland. His sweat chilled, and he shuddered and resumed digging until English guards brought the evening rations. The spades clanked, and the grave diggers scrambled to the guards, except for John who ambled. Even though he had heard most of the food rations destined for the Scots had been sold by guards to local merchants, he realized the guards would always feed the Scottish grave diggers; otherwise they would have to dig the grave. He sat alone on the cold ground, in the fading sunlight as his muscles tightened.

The guards began prodding some diggers, and John arose to trudge toward the Cathedral's door. In the distance, several well clad men and guards were talking. A diminutive man, holding an unrolled parchment, seemed to be instructing the others. Intrigued, John paused until a jab in his back moved him along. As he neared the Cathedral's opened door, smoke from the several fires inside drifted out. He paused to study the elaborate carvings on the door and wondered when it might be reduced to firewood.

A guard shoved him inside, and he wandered until he found an open spot of floor to lie upon. Days of digging had finally taken a toll on John's back, and lying on a cold stone floor made it worse. During the night, he awoke often, and in pain. To ease his soreness, he rolled to one side and curled to stretch his taut back muscles. Eventually, stretching became pointless, and John lay awake pondering the vault.

The smoky cloud now hovered below the highest story of arches that were atop of the columns that formed the north and south aisles. But the cloud appeared to be lowering. John wondered if smoke would soon engulf him. He coughed, rolled and spat, and rolled back to stare. Early morning light seeped through the highest openings and illuminated the haze to reveal the ribbed vault. He remembered his one trip to the church that his father had insisted he visit. Then, his mother had told him as she pointed to the vault, a church is always shaped like an upside-down ship. His mother's words now came down from the smoke-filled ceiling. *"Johnnie, you'll always be safe in God's great ship, just like Noah."*

God, here me lay, peering into this ship's bottom, thought John. *Noah, sail me safely home to me mum.* He rolled to his side, and surprisingly his pain had eased. He dozed and dreamed. Noah's great ship had carried him to his mother. He was at peace until a guard's pole thumped his aching back.

"Up, join the rest of your bloody Scots."

Awakened, yet sleepy, John arose and slowly joined the others who were up and milling. More men than in previous days were standing. John hoped they were all volunteers for grave digging – his back could use a rest.

He gimped outside, sucked in the fresh air and coughed. He started with the others toward the grave, but they were quickly diverted to join two gentlemen from the previous night. Once all the captives had arrived, a guard shoved a simple looking oaf toward the two gentlemen. The captives drew closer together, and they watched, wondering what was to come.

"Remove ye top," said one of the gentlemen who held a walking stick. He circled the shirtless giant, inspecting as he did, yet maintained a self-imposed barrier, lest he get too near. "Bend over and spread them," he said.

The confused oaf looked over his shoulder.

"Ye arse, spread it."

The oaf flipped his tattered kilt over his back, grabbed his buttocks and pulled. The gentleman stooped, poked with his stick and peered. He flicked his stick between the oaf's groins to dislodge some dried feces.

"Now the front."

The oaf thought for a moment, stood erect and raised his kilt to his chest. The gentleman used his stick to lift the galoot's penis and to push his scrotum from one side to the other.

"He'll do."

The Scot was led to the assistant who stood several feet away, holding parchment and a quill. "Name?" he asked.

"Robert MacEntire."

"Mac what? Spell it."

Robert MacEntire looked to John, who wanted to help him, but all he could do was shake his head. Robert's smile said 'thank you', and John smiled back. The assistant showed his scrawl to the gentleman. He shrugged and said, "Seems close enough to me."

The inspection continued. Some men were so weak, they were dismissed without inspection. Others, with deep scars on their backs, were rejected, as were those with creatures entangled in their genital hairs. John was shoved forward.

"What's wrong with this gangly one?" asked the gentleman.

"Nothing, his limp's a fake," said a guard.

"Top."

"No wounds on this coward," said another guard. A few grizzled Scots grumbled, and John stared at the ground.

"Breeches."

John lowered his pants and stood with them around his ankles. He was a naked teenager in front of a mass of men and self-conscious about it. The cold air brought renewed energy, and his blood pounded. Sometimes in the mornings, his penis would unexplainably become erect, and he hoped that would not be case this morning. When the gentleman slid his stick up John's inner loin, the sensation tingled his genitals. He closed his eyes in an attempt to control the growing surge he was feeling. John wanted to flee, but his breeches were ankle high and held him in place. He dared not to look down at the sensation he felt might be growing.

"He'll do," said the gentleman as he removed his stick from John's loins.

John raised his breeches and scurried to the assistant.

"Name?" asked the assistant.

John muttered, and the assistant scribbled. What he scrawled, John never knew.

John joined the captives who had been previously selected, avoiding eye contact with anyone. He was still mortified and wanted to be invisible. He stood next to Robert MacEntire, hoping his towering frame would shield him from the others.

"How many do we have?" asked the gentleman.

The assistant used his fingers as a counting aid as he scanned his scribbling on the parchment. "Less than two hundred," he said.

"We promised Mister Becx more." The gentleman turned to glare at a guard and said, "If thou spared the lash and had not brought whores for some of them, we would have ample numbers."

"We control these dogs as we fancy," said the guard.

The gentleman broke his stare and turned to the group with John. "Scottish men, through Lord Cromwell's divine mercy, thou will soon no longer be prisoners."

John's early morning dream returned. "Me be sailing to Scotland and me mum," he said.

"You'll never see your bloody mum, you fool," said a sneering guard.

John's dream was shattered as quickly as it had returned. He shook his head, rubbed his hands, and had an urge to pace. But he couldn't, so he shifted from side to side. Nothing comforted him until an ape-like arm fell on his shoulders, and a bulky forearm pulled him closer. "Easy laddie," said Robert.

"Once in ye colonies, ye will be indentured servants," said the gentleman.

John looked to Robert and asked, "How far be the colonies?"

"Tis far."

"And me indenture?"

Robert shrugged.

John's emotions exploded. He was devastated by his plight, saddened for his mother, incensed at the English and angry with a deaf God. His life, his back, everything was out of kilter, except for his shoulders, which were still pressed close to Robert.

Robert squeezed him again and said, "Stay nigh, and you'll be safe."

"Me needs to get to Scotland," whispered John.

Robert raised an index finger to his lips. "Perhaps along the way."

Chapter Eight

On the road from Durham

Perhaps John had pestered Robert MacEntire too often about escaping. They still walked near to one another, but now in silence. Robert, weary from John's badgering, lagged behind. John heard a moan, followed by a thud, so familiar a sound, he was initially unfazed. But curiosity overcame him, and as he turned back, Robert was on his knees and swaying. John pushed through the muddle of walking zombies and placed each of his forearms under Robert's armpits to steady the giant.

"Easy laddie," said John.

Robert smiled at the irony. He had spoken those words frequently, and now his little friend was imitating him. John struggled to keep an insipid-smiling, vacant-eyed Robert from collapsing. But a butt end sent John one way, and Robert teetered and fell. He clutched his tattered kilt and curled his knees. John scrambled up, but another butt end dropped him next to Robert.

"Me'll care for you," said John. "God please, get up Robert."

"It be all right. Me will be with me MacEntires soon."

Several guards pulled John away from Robert. As two guards kept John erect, another one rammed his midsection with the butt end of his pike, and John doubled over. A guard jammed his palm under John's chin, and his head snapped back while his attacker readied for another thrust.

"Enough. We can't beat them too severely. They're Becx's property," said the lead guard.

"Just one more." John's stomach was thumped again, and the guards released their gripped. John staggered while clutching his stomach and gasping for air.

"We are far enough away from Durham. Becx's men can no longer watch us. Break out the chains."

The rattling of the chains stirred the prisoners, and most submitted without incident. The few who tried to resist were beaten by the guards until they submitted. Some sneered at John, the cause of their added troubles.

A manacle clanked around John's wrist, and he was led by it to another, and they were manacled together. His chain mate was several years older, with deep creases in his forehead and eyes that seemed to droop as much as the skin beneath his eyes did, perhaps from witnessing too much horror or from a genuine concern for his brethren. He offered an inviting hand, and innate warmth broke through his somber face. "Andrew Adams," he said.

"Will you help me escape to Scotland?" asked John.

"Scotland?" Andrew laughed and raised his manacled hand. "You be daft."

"Then you nae be of use to me." John looked over his shoulder as several guards used their pikes to roll Robert into a watery, roadside gully.

"Too bad about your friend," said Andrew.

John turned back and said, "Me nae have friends." Robert splashed into the gully. John looked back again.

"Too bad, anyway."

"Maybe he be the fortunate one," said John.

"Maybe, but nae you die while chained to me." Andrew rattled their common chain. "Me nae be dragging you throughout England."

John glimpsed back over his shoulder often at the gully where Robert lay until the scene disappeared from view. Robert MacEntire, another fleeting surrogate father passing through John's life, would lie off an unknown road for eternity. The scene was forever etched into John's soul.

"Alba gu bráth," said Andrew.

John glanced at Andrew. He was focused straight ahead, and John did similarly. The two trudged in silence, unsure of where they were going.

London, England
11 November 1650

A bollard, laced with securing lines from the ship's stern, was next to John as he stood on the dock waiting to board. UNITY had been chiseled into the escutcheon on the ship's stern and painted a golden color. A few red rosettes adorned either side of the name. Dwarfed by the poop deck, John shuffled to the boarding plank. A crewman's head dotted each of the crow's nests. Other crewmen stood on yardarms, clinging to the spar and the ship's rigging.

John followed Andrew up the steeply pitched ramp onto the main deck. The Captain stood on the poop deck with arms behind his back, watching the loading of human cargo. Two uniformed crewmen stood at the bottom of the companionway. More authority stood atop the forecabin. John's hopeless situation had grown to an inner anger, and he scanned the horizon to ease it. More prisoners boarded, and John shuffled away from the bulwark. His chain was tugged, and he followed after Andrew to a deck hole and was led down the narrow stairs by the clanking chain.

The lower deck was dimly lit, cold and musky, a stark contrast to what John had just left. Feet clomped above, and men shouted commands, many of which made no sense. Flags flapped, similar in sound to those on Doon Hill, ropes whirred, and the floor rocked.

"We casted off," said Andrew.

John nodded, pretending he knew what the words meant. His head swung toward each sound as it occurred.

"John, we're going to the colonies."

John understood those words. He squeezed his eyes and stared at the ship's side, avoiding Andrew's concerned expression.

"Scotland be gone forever, except in me mind," said Andrew. "Me got pleasant thoughts, got sad ones, too." He lowered his head and said, "Too many sad ones." When he raised his head, a sense of determination and placid stoicism had spread through him. "Me will remember the pleasant ones."

The water lapped at the ship's strake in steady rhythm from the movement of water from beneath and the ship. John's mind drifted to when his life was worry-free. Pleasant thoughts of his parents came, and the gentle swoosh along the ship's side made them even more vivid. It did not take long for mumbling to break John's pleasant interlude. Conversations followed as crewmen descended the stairs in single file. They looked around while conversing in muted tones. Finally one spoke. "We've left English waters. We'll unchain thee, but take heed. We can chain thee again."

John's cuff swung down. He was finally rid of Andrew, but neither of them moved. John pondered his journey when he had been chained. He feared another friendship would evaporate before it was formed. But Andrew remained earnest, offering support to a troubled comrade. John tried to remain aloof, but he couldn't. Andrew was too comforting. John now realized how much he needed a friend.

December 1650
On the North Atlantic

"God," said John as he sat on the lower deck floor, forcing his back into the *Unity's* bulging side, "this nae be Noah's great ship."

The swelling sea eased, but soon returned with a thump harder than before. The planking creaked and bent inward as water oozed between the sideboards. Oakum dangled from a seam, and John used his frozen finger tips to press it back in sideboard's seam. He dug his heels and pressed with more force than before, no longer trying to hold steady against the ship's roll, but struggling to stop the ship from seemingly imploding.

He shivered and pulled his knees to his chest, but his chills didn't ease. His muscles ached from endless huddling in frigid conditions. The Cathedral's stench had returned, but whiffs of brine now replaced the smoke. Two dead men rolled whenever the yaw was severe. One was naked, his boots and tattered clothing now donned another. Once the seas calmed, the dead would be taken to the top deck and tossed overboard.

With a lightheaded mind from the constant ship's yaw, John harkened back to his last trip topside. The captain stood on the quarterdeck, offered a prayer, and crewmen tossed the body into the sea. A despondent captive standing next to John simply followed after, stepping into a beckoning sea. He bobbed and flailed while yelling, but his words were unintelligible. He ceased thrashing and bobbed further, eventually drifting from sight.

The *Unity's* side was thumped again, jolting John from his ever-growing wooziness. Every board creaked from the duress. The oakum dangled again. *This ship will be splinters and then it be me, bobbing on an icy sea*, thought John. Water poured down the stairs, and several splintered planks allowed some of it to drain further below.

Watching an eddy around the splintered holes was now John's distraction from his dizziness. He crouched down near one breach and peered below. The ship's bottom resembled an inverted Cathedral ceiling. When he was under Durham's massive vault, he had felt secure, never really believing the smoke would engulf him. But as rising water seemed to be covering the ship's inner ribs, John thought he would soon drown. *God, did you ever hear me or did you just misunderstand me?*

God didn't answer. John sprawled face up and flowed into delirium. With the ship's roll, water rushed into his open mouth.

He choked, bolted upright, gasped and collapsed back. He curled to a fetal position and closed his eyes as water washed over him. It seemed to grow warm and soothing. Brilliance lit his closed lids. Oddly, he was dry, warm and basking. A red headed angel with a gentle voice emerged from the glaring light. She grew more vivid as the glare eased. She caressed his cheek. "Let me comfort you, Johnnie," said the vision.

The touch, the voice, it was his mother. Maybe God had heard him?

"You have suffered much. Stay with me for eternity," his mother said.

Her words were inviting, and cradled in her arms, John moved closer to her bosom. Tranquility seemed to be washing his body. He dared not open his eyes for fear his mother would evaporate. He lay, eyes shut, being caressed.

"The heather is in full bloom. Smell it, Johnnie." A familiar fragrance enhanced John's peace until his mother eased him from her bosom. John's sense of tranquility ebbed when his mother said, "The heather nae longer blooms for you."

The *Unity's* stench tickled John's nose. He thrashed, wanting to regain the bosom that suckled him as an infant. "Scotland be for your ancestors. Go and plant your seed in a new world."

"But who will care you, mum?" asked John.

As John awaited an answer, Andrew noticed a lifeless John with his head rolling with the yaw. He pulled John's head from the water and caressed his cheek. John opened an eye, but he closed it immediately.

John needed an answer, but nothing came, so he asked again. "Who will care for you, mum?" Nothing came but an unsettling commotion, so John prayed. *God, block me ears and give me silence. Me needs an answer from me mum.* But John's appeals to God went unanswered. His mother dissipated and only a solid white brightness remained on his closed eyelids. When he heard Andrew say, "Hoot mon, you can nae leave me now," John opened both eyes. He was sitting upon icy water, deep within the *Unity's* bowels.

"Me feared me lost you," said Andrew. A sense of relief came over his face.

John was still woozy, and could only nod his appreciation to Andrew. A despondent soul next to Andrew was clad in his tartan colors. In an earlier time, his attire would have been similar to Jamus MacLawson's. Now, his tartan colors were stained, tattered, unadorned and faded, another remnant of a vanishing Scotland.

The *Unity*, a mere speck of assembled timber that dared to cross the Atlantic, continued to be tossed until it neared the New World coastline. Twenty years earlier, another similar speck, the *Arbella*, dared to cross the great divide. The *Arbella* carried a leader, John Winthrop, and families from similar parishes who were united in religious purpose, supported by Cromwell and inspired to begin life anew. A Great Migration[13] followed the *Arbella,* and each ship carried a similar cargo. The wilderness was carved to their specifications, a covenant with God was crafted, and fledgling settlements grew into a Puritan theocracy. The *Unity* was a similar construct to the previous ships bound

---

13 *The term Great Migration refers to the migration into Massachusetts between 1629 and 1640 of English settlers, primarily Puritans in search of freedom to practice their religion.*

for the New World, but its cargo was far different. Leaderless and dispirited men from different Scottish clans, Cromwell's prisoners, 'Catholics' in a Puritan theocracy were aboard the *Unity*. A swarm of similar ilk would not follow these men. The *Unity's* cargo was the first foreign drop of undesirables into a heretofore, virgin sanctuary.

Chapter Nine

Charlestown, Massachusetts Bay Colony
Winter 1650 - 1651

"What cheer," said John Gifford to an approaching William Awbrey, his business associate.

Standing on the pier Awbrey gestured to the sea, and his cloak draped off his extended arm. Its graceful folds hung, offering an accentuating backdrop for his knee-high leather boots. "Storm clouds loom on ye horizon." He scrunched his shoulders and said, "And there is bite in the air."

"Ye storm clouds are too distant," said Gifford. "But thither is The *Unity*, a godsend for our problems."

"Some, but not all. I have seen thy account books."

"Ah William, always so skeptical."

"We need craftsmen, skilled ironworkers and…"

"Exactly what Becx promised, and exactly what will be arriving."

"Dost thou believe Scotland has any skilled men in their land?"

Gifford turned away from the open sea and stood with arms akimbo. "We will train them. May cost a farthing or two, but worth the outlay."

"First thou must feed them and ..."

"Cease William, thou hast soured this beautiful day enough."

Gifford left Awbrey and hurried along the dock as workers scurried to their posts. Awbrey followed, clicking his walking cane as he ambled. Securing lines were tossed to the ship to ready it for unloading. Gifford remained buoyant. His problems would be solved. When Awbrey sidled close, Gifford stepped away.

Below the top deck of the *Unity,* the docking had stirred the prisoners from their despair. John crouched and stepped around men toward a light coming through a slit. His eyeball swept across the harbor to land, a welcoming sight he hadn't seen since leaving London several weeks earlier. On one of those days while on the Atlantic, John thought he had turned fifteen years old. He continued perusing the shoreline until the prisoners were ordered to move topside.

John braced against the ship's side and stepped cautiously until his legs found strength. The sun beamed down the ladder, and invigorating salt air refreshed his lungs. As he moved further up the ladder, the sun blinded him. Disoriented, he crawled out and scurried, like a ship's rat, away from the hole. He rose on his tiptoes, enjoying his freedom from the restrictive, ever-present, low-hanging ceiling. He inhaled and strained his face toward the sun while surveying the harbor's surroundings. Unlike London, only a few buildings dotted the landscape, a new world with boundless land and endless opportunities.

A boarding plank rumbled into position, and the prisoners neared it. John was among frail, half-clothed, odorous, hollow-eyed Scots, who were struggling to remain erect. Yet, as he looked out from this despair, below were wide-eyed, rosy-cheeked, properly clothed men, his future. A man wrapped in a finely woven wool cloak stood straddling an ornately carved cane. As the two groups, prisoners and business men, assessed their stark differences, John wondered if someday he might be among the fortunate.

Gifford moved to Awbrey and said, "Becx promised only the hearty."

"Probably were hearty when they left England."

"Well, clothe and fatten them. They are of no use now." The air wafted from the top deck, and Gifford's nose twitched. "But wash them first."

As the Scots staggered down the ramp, one slipped, and his flailing arm hooked a guide line that saved him from tumbling into the harbor. The dock workers gasped, but those disembarking were too weak to respond and too inured to empathize. Once offloaded, the captives milled and occasionally flexed their legs. John turned east. Scotland was far beyond the divide, and he knew he would never see it again. Yet he wasn't depressed and didn't know why. When Gifford and Awbrey neared, he congregated with his countrymen.

Gifford said, "Welcome to ye new home. Thou art indentured for seven years, and then ye will be free." Gifford's optimism was waning, and his distrust of Becx was growing. "Have any of ye worked at an ironworks?"

The disheveled Scots muttered and looked at one another. Awbrey grew smug, irritating Gifford further. "Can ye fell trees?" asked Gifford.

Several hands arose, and one said, "Me can use me pike, real goot." The Scots laughed, and a few nodded their heads. They were becoming comfortable with their surroundings.

But the Scottish brogue baffled Gifford. "Scottish man, I did not understand thee."

Another bellowed, "He be a pikeman and has done his share of felling English bastards." The Scots roared, and their confidence continued to increase.

"Pikeman, dost thou know Goodman[14] Awbrey and I are English?"

Quiet ensued; of course the Scots knew Awbrey and Gifford were English, they had forgotten that fact for only a moment. Yet Gifford seized it to laud his birthright, not as menacingly as his countrymen had done at Doon Hill, but, nonetheless, to stress English superiority. The Scots' fragile confidence was devastated. They shrunk together, except for John who was focused on Awbrey again. His cloak had opened to reveal an embroidered jerkin, flared at the waist, with shiny buttons that tailored it perfectly from his torso to his shoulders.

"Who's a farmer?" asked Gifford. Several muttered, and a few raised their hands. "Or a shepherd?"

John's hand shot up as he looked at Awbrey. "Me be a good shepherd," said John. Awbrey tilted his head, and John

---

14 *Goodman was a polite term of address, used where Mister might be used today*

appreciated the acknowledgement, oblivious to the disapproving head shakes from his countrymen.

Gifford turned to Awbrey and smiled. "Woodsmen, shepherds, these thieving Colonists shant get a farthing from us anymore for their timber and scrawny livestock. There is thy precious ledger books' savings. Now dost thou see?"

Awbrey didn't answer the question, and Gifford turned back to the Scots. "Dost ye have questions?"

A hunched over Scot gripped his stomach and said, "Aye, gae me food for me belly."

Perplexed by the Scottish dialect, Gifford turned to Awbrey who said, "He wants to eat. Hard to believe it's the same language."

"William, it isn't," said Gifford.

Awbrey roared, and by wont, the Scots drew close, unsure what Awbrey's laughter meant. But John remained aloof, focused on Awbrey's attire and fueled with the hope of someday being a prosperous shepherd.

The Scots bunked at the warehouse while waiting to be dispersed. Many were in poor health and unable to work immediately. Over time, John and many others went to the Ironworks on the Saugus River, others boarded the *Unity* and sailed north to the Piscataqua River and a few were indentured to locals. Most were unskilled in ironwork operations, just as Awbrey had foretold. The unskilled grew crops, cut hay, felled timber and mined bog ore. The few with initiative and intelligence were trained as colliers and furnace men, but educating them was slow and expensive. Gifford's problems persisted. Becx's cheap labor was exactly the opposite, an expensive burden on a struggling operation.

Chapter Ten

*Scotchman House, Middlesex County,
Massachusetts Bay Colony
Summer 1652*

Samuel Bennett, the master carpenter who built the Ironworks, constructed a boarding house not far from it. It consisted of two rooms, centered on a chimney that had an oven. There were eleven beds, and the workers slept two to a bed. John and his *Unity* chain mate, Andrew Adams, were now bunk mates.

After a day's work and later than usual, John entered the boarding house with damp clothes and dripping shoulder length hair. The heat from the cooking oven combined with the warmth pouring through sunlit windows to create a hellhole, which intensified the stench of perspiring, unwashed workers. The laborers congregated about two large planks that served as a dining table. A few sat, but most stood as they ate and drank.

Andrew Adams handed John a bowl of pasty corn meal and a slab of brown bread, which Andrew had saved for him. As John wolfed it down, Andrew asked, "It be late. Where you be, laddie?"

"Cooling in the Saugus River. God forsaken heat, even the bloody river be a boil."

"Mind your oaths, or you'll be fined."

"Huh? We be with our lads, like we be in Scotland."

Andrew forced a laugh. "Aye, just like Scotland."

Michael MacGoon, a burly man with scraggly hair, a food encrusted beard, and a sweat-stained, ale-splattered shirt, sipped from his tankard. He sat away from John, yet his bleary eyes were riveted on him. He struggled up from his stool. "Me belly needs food." The din quieted as MacGoon swigged his ale and weaved toward John. "This laddie has food. Give it here."

John handed his empty bowl to MacGoon, who swayed while trying to focus on it. "You bastard," and MacGoon flung the bowl at John, who ducked, and it caromed off a timber post.

A hearty laugh broke the silence, and MacGoon turned to it. A few twitched as he surveyed the men about the table. He kept muttering and slammed his tankard on the table. It overflowed with foam, and MacGoon charged with arms outstretched. Andrew stepped in front of his charge, only to be hurled aside. John was driven into a post. Pain shot through his spine, and he feared his back would crack. MacGoon was inches from his face, and when he belched, John shook his head to disperse the stench.

"Where's me food, ya wee bastard?" As MacGoon reared back to drive his shoulder again, John squirmed away, and MacGoon hit the post and careened onto the floor. He rubbed his shoulder, stumbled to his feet and prepared for another charge. John grabbed a stool and cocked it back as Andrew moved between the two combatants.

"C'mon Michael, leave the lad be," said Andrew.

"Oot of me way."

"Michael, your ale," said another as he swished MacGoon's tankard.

MacGoon staggered to his tankard, gulped it dry and tossed it. It clanked along the table and fell onto the floor. He burped and swayed, trying to maintain his balance. He lowered his eyelids, re-opened them, crammed his meaty hand into his pocket and removed a few coins. He stared at his coins while swaying. "Come laddies, me have enough for the tavern."

MacGoon led his few followers toward the door. John cocked the stool again as MacGoon neared. When MacGoon paused, John's heart raced, belying his steely eyes and determined grip on his defense. MacGoon turned to his gang, reeled back at John and swatted the stool from his hand. John scrambled to gather it while MacGoon reveled in his toadies' cheers.

"Leave this dog to cuddle his milking stool," MacGoon said. "Me needs a lassie to cuddle. Who be with me?"

"But a bonny lass, this night," said a crony.

MacGoon glared at him, and he now rued his outburst. "Every lass be bonny once me lays upon her hairy mound," said MacGoon.

His audience roared, and he weaved toward the door. He stopped and staggered back to a crouching John. MacGoon bent down, eyed John and caressed his soft wispy beard. John swatted MacGoon's hand away, and he jolted back.

MacGoon turned to his minions and said, "This laddie's softness be better than any lass's mound." He turned back to John and tugged at his breeches. "What do ya say, laddie?"

John scrambled away, and MacGoon stepped closer. The silence was heavy with contempt for what might happen next. The room was paralyzed until Andrew said, "Michael, your favorite lass be at the tavern this night." MacGoon turned toward Andrew, and he added, "Aye, and with another lass, Michael."

"Two lasses to mount this night," chimed in one of MacGoon's toadies. "Let's be going."

MacGoon gave a deliberate head shake and left with his entourage.

Andrew offered a hand to John. "Seems me always be helping you up."

John twisted his torso. "Me back may be broke."

"Me'll do your chopping for you, me brother."

"Brother?" asked John as he ceased massaging his lower back and thought. John never had a brother, but now he sensed what an older brother might be like.

"You nae seem too busted up," said Andrew.

"A busted up Scot be like a lame ox."

"The English shoot lame oxen."

John glared and said, "Me knows."

Andrew broke eye contact. "That MacGoon be different when he drinks. Me pities the wench he beds tonight." He turned back to John and continued. "But his lot hurts us Scots. The English think we all be cursing and chasing their lasses."

"Damn the English. They filled this place with the likes of MacGoon. It nae be Scotland."

Andrew smiled, his friend was learning. The din from those who remained in the house returned, and John's annoyance subsided. "MacGoon be right about one thing. Me sure could use a lass," said John.

"Come on, let's get some air," said Andrew.

The two left the hellhole for the cooling twilight. They strolled until they neared John's favorite tree. He sat on a tuft next to it. Andrew sat down near John and leaned against the tree.

"When me was in the Saugus, two lasses came near," said John as Andrew leaned forward. "Be splashing aboot, and did nae notice until one giggled. Sunk down to me neck, me did."

Andrew tilted his head.

"Me clothes were still on the river bank, Andrew."

"A naked Scot and two English lasses would nae be goot," said Andrew.

"Me was bathing."

"Did they know you be naked?"

John shrugged.

"Had they known, the constable would be here by now."

John grunted, nettled at Andrew for interrupting his pleasing fantasy with facts. But John continued his story. "One lass neared. Ah, how her hips swayed. And when me said, 'Goot evening', she giggled and covered her face." John paused to savor that image. "How those cheeks glowed on that angel face. When she lowered her hands and said, 'Oh, Scottish art thou?' the devil twinkled in her eyes."

"John, you didn't."

"Nae, the other lass told her to stop tempting Satan. But me still can see her buttocks swaying as she left. But she be a fair lass, not a wench." John turned to Andrew. "She be intrigued that me be Scottish."

"She may be intrigued, but her father and kin would nae be. They be particular aboot who gets their lasses; a minister's son, a captain's son, but nae a Scottish man."

John eased back onto the tree. Stars were emerging in the fading light. One shone exceedingly bright, and held John's attention as he asked, "Then how does me get a lass?"

"Well," and Andrew leaned back and sighed, "maybe we only get wenches."

"Nae a wench, but a lass; to be me wife," said John as the star that still engrossed him grew brighter.

Andrew leaned from the tree and looked at the flickering star that had captured his friend's attention. "Me suppose," and Andrew slumped back and thought further. His friend deserved a thoughtful answer, and he didn't have one. "Me suppose, we Scots will only get wenches, but they be English ones. English wenches be purer than Scottish ones." Andrew forced a chuckle.

John broke his trance and turned to Andrew. "Do you want a wife and a family some day?"

John's innocent stare remained, and Andrew knew he had to say something. He had always been there for John with an answer. "Um," but Andrew couldn't add more, so he muttered, "someday." Andrew pondered when his someday might come.

"Aye, me too, and she will be a pure lass," said John as he eased against the tree and returned to the brightest star. They sat in silence, and John thought, *Aye father, a bonny lass as pure as me mum.*

Chapter Eleven

Wooded lands, Middlesex County, Massachusetts Bay Colony

"Your back seems fully mended," said Andrew. "You keep felling trees, and me will return later." As John turned back toward the woods, Andrew said, "Hoot mon, cover yourself. Your back be as red as berries."

John trudged into the woods and found his shirt, peppered with wood chips and sawdust. He shook it and put it on, but wood chips still clung, which aggravated his sunburn. John couldn't reach a nettlesome spot, so he leaned against a tree and rubbed his spine. His itch left, but his sunburn was now aflame. With his buttocks against the tree, he inched down and collapsed. His pungent body odor hovered, but leaning against the tree in the shade was irresistible.

Eventually, he crawled from the tree to his satchel and goat skin. He removed pieces of salted cod, two ears of corn and two slabs of brown bread. While eating the corn he thought of his last night in the cornfields below Doon Hill when he was half-starved. Much had changed in his life, some good, some horrendous, but at least now his belly was full.

He uncorked the goat skin with his teeth and sucked in the watery ale. He husked the second ear, ate, took several more sucks of ale and burped. He patted his stomach while pondering the bread and salted cod. He should eat them later, but he piled the cod onto a slab and ate anyway. The heat combined with a full belly, intoxicated head and a breeze to sap John's energy. He soon fell asleep.

After a while, a voice asked, "Art thou chopping or resting?" John rubbed his eyes and heard, "Who art thou?" John sprang up as two men approached.

"What are ye doing upon this land?" one of them asked.

"Felling trees for the Ironworks."

"Ah, as I reckoned. Well, Scottish man, last year we were chopping trees for shillings. But this year, because of you Scots, we get nary a farthing."

"Gifford's got his slaves now, Father," said the younger of the two, who seemed similar in age to John.

John glared at him and said, "The coloreds[15] be slaves, nae me."

The eye contact remained until the son sneered, lowered his eyes and sidled closer to his father. "Gifford got what he paid for, a lazy sot," said the son.

John picked up his axe and spread his legs to shoulder length. His thigh muscles bulged and rippled his breeches. When he squeezed the axe handle, his forearm flexed. He cocked the axe, and his once imperceptible muscles had matured to be as well–defined as Malcom Dinsmore's. John was no longer the

---

15 *Massachusetts was the first slave-holding colony in New England, which predated the settlement of Massachusetts Bay colony in 1629. Captured Indians deemed too dangerous, like those from the 1637 Pequot War, were transported to the West Indies in exchange for African slaves.*

gangly adolescent of Doon Hill, but a powerful man, able to hack the thickest of limbs. John looked daggers and thought, *bloody English.*

"Art thou going to chop us?" asked the Father.

"Me will, if you don't get your God damn arse oot of here."

"Mind thy devil-filled tongue, ye Scottish heathen. What is thy name?"

"John."

"Ah, the constable knows how to deal with blasphemers," said the Father. "John what?" John lowered his ax, and his chest deflated. "Pray tell, John what?"

"MacLawson," said John.

"Ye will hear from the constable, John," said the Father, adding with a sneer, "MacLawson."

"You bloody bastards," and John charged after the two. With a wild swing, John lost his stride and stumbled, but regained his balance. He regained some composure too. He wondered if he would he be dragged away, whipped, or imprisoned. He was unsure, but he knew of others who had received similar punishments for lesser crimes.

The two now ambled in the distance with loud bluster. The words 'slave', 'heathen' and 'blasphemer' were distinct amid their guffaws.

John trudged back to the tree that he had considered chopping before breaking for his meal. He chipped, alternating downward swings with upward ones. A notch was forming slowly since too many blows just produced a watery juice without chips. Exasperated that woodchips were not flying, he swung while leaving his feet. The tree sucked in his axe, and sap oozed around it.

"God damn this tree. If it ain't me dull axe, it be me stuck axe." John chipped around his axe with Andrew's, wiggled his axe free and resumed chopping. "Come on you bloody tree, fall."

As John pondered the Colonists' threat again, his swings grew more forceful. When the tree creaked, by instinct, he scurried for safety. The creaking sound ceased. Now, all John heard was the blood pounding near his temples. He returned to the tree and swung easy. When the tree crackled, he bolted. Crackling turned to creaking, and the tree began to fall among the standing ones. But it veered from the path, which John had intended for it, and became suspended on nearby limbs. "God damn, felling trees in summer be loony."

"Scotsman, watch thy tongue," said a voice.

Fear shot through John. *Had the Colonists returned?*

"Misjudged again, Johnnie?"

The brogue was now distinct, and John relaxed. "Too many leaves be hiding the branches," said John to an approaching Andrew.

"Get your axe," said Andrew. "Your tree will be there tomorrow." John headed toward the suspended tree as an unexpected squall ensued.

"Get me axe, too," said Andrew. "Can nae be leaving it for these English thieves." John didn't understand Andrew's last words as the roaring wind muffled them. He waited for the roar to subside. The suspended tree started to roll off of the limbs that suspended it. "Me God," and Andrew cupped his hands around his mouth to bellow. "John, the tree."

John was knocked to the ground, and Andrew raced to his friend. "Be you hurt, laddie?"

As the squall subsided, John arose from a leafy prison. He rubbed near his cheekbone where limbs had whipped him. Blood trickled, and a welt was swelling near his temple. John stepped around a limb, pushed others to one side and hurdled over a large one. Horror crossed his mind as he suddenly felt as though he was at Doon Hill. He lay bloodied with broken limbs, alone, writhing in pain and dying a slow death, like so many of his countrymen that day. He shook his head, and his horror left. But its impression was indelible. He dabbed his face again and sensed the blood had clotted.

"Me almost lost you again," said Andrew. He grabbed John's chin and swung it to look at his welt. "Your scar will now remind you how close to death you came."

"Me been out of sorts," said John as Andrew swung John's chin to be face-to-face. "Two English called me a lazy sot. So me told them to get their God damn arse away."

"Oh Johnnie," said Andrew as he let go of John's chin.

"Me know, but me told them me be John MacLawson."

Andrew shook his head and asked, "How many Scots be here in the colonies?"

"Nae many."

"The constable can easily find you, and then you'll be a blasphemer and a liar." Andrew thought further and smiled at his friend to cheer him. "Ah, don't be fretting. The English have more important matters to worry about." He kneaded John's shoulder and said, "They know we Scots all be liars and blasphemers."

John wrung his hands. In his anger, he despised the haughty Englishman and his lackey son, but now he feared them.

Chapter Twelve

Concord, Middlesex County, Massachusetts Bay Colony

John Gifford and William Awbrey entered the Concord meetinghouse. They brushed dust from their clothing as Goodman Robert Blood and Captain Simon Willard, two Concordians who had requested the meeting, led them down the aisle. Awbrey and Gifford straddled two benches with their hosts sitting across from them.

"We appreciate thy efforts to endure such an arduous journey," said Blood.

"So far from the coast and near Indian country, are we safe?" asked Gifford.

Blood turned to Captain Simon, who spoke. "Indians reside across the river, but they bear no malice."

Blood turned back to Gifford. "Captain Willard first trekked here in 1636. There was no Bay Road then, like ye road thou just traveled. He had to hack briars and avoid the marshlands. With the grace of God he arrived at Musketaquid.[16] He still remains adventurous, resides across the river and thus

---

16 *An Algonquin word meaning 'grassy plain', which was used to describe the low lying areas between the Assabet and Sudbury rivers. A six-square mile portion of Musketaquid was purchased by the first white settlers and renamed Concord.*

encounters Indians. He may say they bear no malice, but many of Concord's good men believe to the contrary. However, it is the Captain's discovery along the river that hath given rise for this meeting."

Blood gestured to Willard who spoke. "Soil near the riverbank hath intriguing colors and unusual odors. Not ideal for farming but, per chance, ideal for mining. Iron ore, or even copper may bless ye soil."

Gifford's eyes widened as Blood added, "We want not for investors." Blood smiled at Willard and continued. "We want men possessed with great wisdom who can assay the bog and turn its ore into metal." Blood eased back onto the bench. "We have many queries."

Gifford inhaled deeply and expounded. Blood and Willard listened while Awbrey remained quiet, occasionally brushing dust from his clothing. Gifford regaled his interested audience with his knowledge of ironworks operations until the meetinghouse door opened and light filled the room. Blood and Willard arose, and Gifford followed their lead. Awbrey eventually rose, too. A man, dressed in drab olive green, stood at the door. A rectangle of finely-meshed white lace, which lay beneath his chin, was the only hint of gaiety. The door creaked as he shut it, and his boots clacked the floor as he moved down the aisle.

"Concord's esteemed Reverend Peter Bulkeley," said Blood. "To what do we owe this great honor?"

The clack continued until The Reverend stood among the four. "I prayed for Goodman John Abbot's justice," said The Reverend. "But justice hath not been rendered, and with God's providence, I now speak."

The Immigrant

He turned to the visitors, and Awbrey straightened his slouch. The Reverend's left eyebrow had a distinct arch, a wise horned owl, alert and ever skeptical to what was about him. "A Concord Ironworks holds great promise. But only Englishmen will toil for it. When we arrived at Musketaquid, we chased depravity to the wilderness. We shall not import more depravity from the east."

Gifford nodded, but Awbrey remained uneasy.

"Goodman John Abbot and his Goodwife, Rebecca, arrived with me on the *Susan and Ellen*. Their son, John the junior, was a boy at the time. They did not leave England to still suffer the rage of a Scottish heathen." The Reverend's eye latched onto Gifford and he asked, "Dost thou have a John MacLawson in thy servitude?" His eyebrow didn't flinch as he awaited an answer.

Gifford turned to Awbrey, who shrugged.

"Thou must," said The Reverend. "It was only through Lord Cromwell's benevolence that Scottish men were shipped hither."

The Reverend placed his hands behind his back and paced. "Ah Cromwell, had thy success arrived earlier, my confrontation with Archbishop Laud[17] never would have occurred. I would still be preaching in my blessed Odell.[18] If only God's providence had..." The clack echoed as The Reverend continued to pace and pondered. He spun back and said, "Evil doers seep into our New World. I leave the MacLawson matter with thee. Justice must be rendered."

---

17 In 1634, Bulkeley refused to wear a surplice or use the Sign of the Cross at a visitation for Archbishop William Laud. For this infraction he was temporality ejected from the parish.

18 Odell, in Bedfordshire, England, is where Peter Bulkeley was born and where he succeeded his father as Rector before coming to the Colonies.

Gifford bobbed his head until the owl's eye blinked. The boots echoed away, and Gifford turned to Blood and said, "Truly, I do not know a John MacLawson."

"No matter," said Blood. "When I journeyed with Goodman Abbot several weeks past, his concern was with his loss of income, not with threats from a Scottish dog."

"Our account books have an entry for a Goodman Abbot," said Awbrey. "Substantial as I reckon."

Gifford turned to Blood. "If we employ Goodman Abbot again, would Reverend Bulkeley deem it just?"

"I can't answer for The Reverend," he said. "But Goodman Abbot would find it just."

"Then Awbrey, do it forthwith."

"I would wait until the weather cools," said Blood. "Felling trees in summer is, indeed, unjust."

"Surely, even dogs rest in such heat," said Gifford.

The meeting adjourned, and Gifford and Awbrey followed their hosts out of the meetinghouse. The hosts headed to The Reverend's manse where he and others were waiting outside. Awbrey paused at the cart while Gifford climbed aboard it. The Reverend looked toward Awbrey, several times, as he conversed with Blood and Willard. After a few minutes, the group went inside the manse.

Awbrey climbed into the cart and sat next to Gifford. "I suspect the meeting of the investors is now commencing inside the manse," said Awbrey as he snapped the reins.

"I believe I impressed Goodman Blood and Captain Willard with my knowledge."

"They have their investors," said Awbrey, "and thou hast given them thy knowledge. They have no need for us any longer."

"But we would be partners," said Gifford.

Awbrey sensed Gifford's naiveté, and trying to explain the obvious any further seemed pointless. Awbrey remained silent, focusing on the road as he held the reins. After a few minutes, Gifford spoke. "Art thou sure John MacLawson is not one of ours?"

"MacLawson is probably John Law," said Awbrey. "The names sound similar, particularly when muttered in a Scottish tongue."

"Then we must give John Law to the constable."

"If we do, there would be fines. And The Ironworks doth not need another black stain."

"Alas another black stain," said Gifford as he frowned. "That wretch MacGoon gave us good one not long ago, fornicating in public." Gifford grimaced. He pondered a while and asked, "What is less dear to the Ironworks, paying Goodman Abbot a steep wage, or paying John Law's court fines?"

Awbrey didn't answer.

Gifford sighed. "Yet another dilemma these Scots create for the Ironworks." He turned to Awbrey and said, "I believe Becx spoke with a deceptive tongue. Perhaps, I trusted him too much."

The cart hit a rock and jostled the two. Awbrey concentrated on the road ahead and didn't respond to Gifford's newly found insight.

Chapter Thirteen

Middlesex County, Massachusetts Bay Colony

John and Andrew left the Scotchman's House for another day of toil. Andrew was invigorated and stepped lively. "Breathe that cool air, laddie. Be a good morning for felling trees."

"Me be breathing smoke," replied John. "Be working a charcoal pit today."

"Going to be a collier, are you?"

"Me be a shepherd, seems Awbrey forgot."

"So why you be making fuel for the blast furnaces?"

"Nae be sure, maybe because of them colonists."

"The ones who harassed you?"

John's brow creased with concern as he nodded.

"Ah Johnnie, me doubt it is because of them. Being a collier is a good trade, so listen and learn."

John left his friend for his new assignment. Smoke laced the crisp air, which grew more noticeable as he neared. He sauntered to a man, standing with arms akimbo and admiring a nine foot, cone-shaped stack of smoking wood. John could feel the heat that the cone was releasing.

"You be in charge?" asked John.

The man dropped his arms and turned around. He was hefty, similar to Robert MacEntire, but with vigilant eyes and in command of the structure that was behind him. A distinct black smudge cut across his grimy, sweat-speckled forehead. His freckled cheeks glowed, and his shirt was as soot splattered as his breeches, except for his thighs, which were more encrusted and threadbare than soot laden. His crimson cheeks lifted up as he wiped his hand on his thighs and offered it. "James Moor, welcome to me charcoaling operation."

A meaty grip engulfed John's hand. James stood with head held high and made direct eye contact. John slouched and offered fleeting glances. John scuffed the ground and said, "Me be a shepherd, so me know nothing about charcoaling."

James laughed and put his hand on John's shoulder. "Well laddie, you'll learn."

They began to walk about the cone's twenty-five foot perimeter. James talked, pointing at times, as he walked. "We just lit this wee lass, so it will be several days before her charring be complete. We started with a center stake, a few weeks ago, and then we built around the stake her feet, legs, waist and head. Her feet and legs be thick logs that we set in place and stacked ground to sky." James paused with hands on hips. "She may have thick legs, but this lass still be wee and so alluring. Me leaned her legs to taper and to give her a narrow waist."

The stack did taper, perhaps like a woman, but it lacked any allure for John. He waited, not wanting to interrupt James's enchantment. James sighed and continued his tour. "We piled wood strips across the top her legs and filled any crevices with wee pieces. But she still be nae tight. Me lassie needs to be tight, so me packed her with sod, leaves and tar." James pointed and said, "Like in that bucket."

John swung to where James pointed.

"Me mounted her last night, pulled the center stake out of her head and lit her. Now she be aglow."

John cheeks warmed, seemingly as much as James's appeared to be. John was engrossed, enjoying the warmth and feeling like a collier.

"Any questions?" asked James.

"Um, she sure be big."

James laughed and said, "Nae, she be a wee one. We only need you and me to keep watch for now. But when she be fully charred in a week or so, we will need more men to strip out the charcoal for maws of the blast furnaces."

John walked the perimeter, feigning that he knew what he was doing. James sat on an upright stump, admiring his cone. He rolled another stump near to him. "Come, sit," he said as he patted the stump. "We need to watch the cone. She should glow pink, nae red. Red means me lassie be too hot. Charring is best when she glows a steady soft pink."

John's eyes danced around the cone, but he was unsure where pink left off and red began. James broke the silence. "Too much air makes her red, and we'll have troubles."

"What do we do?"

"Poke with me pole, find the hole where the air be rushing in and fill it."

"With what?"

"If she be small, with this," said James as he raised a bucket with a lumpy mix of tar, ash and leaves. John stuck his finger in the bucket. The mixture was similar in texture and color to James's tar-stained palms and encrusted breeches. John wiped his gooey finger on his thigh. His breeches were beginning to resemble James's.

"If her hole be large," said James, "we rearrange the pile, stick logs in her hole." John's eyes widened. "It be tricky. She could explode if we nae be careful. You get me. Me nae does want to lose you too soon." James slapped his knee and laughed.

John's attention had been so rapt James's levity escaped him. He forced a laugh, and James slapped his knee again and arose. Since gusts least affect the cone's leeward side, James assigned that position to John before leaving for the windward side.

As John sat on the stump, he concentrated on the cone, looking for signs of irregular burning and perfecting when pink became a salmon, or a cherry or a red hue. But concentrating was boring and soon became hypnotic. When a pink area grew darker with a prolong gust, he considered calling out. But the wind subsided, and pink returned.

As tedium ensued, John's thoughts wandered. Not working with Andrew still annoyed him. He wondered again if his rage at the two colonists was the cause. Pondering about the colonists became worrisome, and John turned his thoughts to his new assignment. Even though he was predisposed to dislike James Moor, he didn't. James's good nature was infectious. But as John thought further, he couldn't recall him from the *Unity*.

A gust came, as did a red glow that didn't fade when the winds subsided. John waited, hoping for pink. Only a naïve teenager would call out prematurely. His heart raced as a blood red spot grew. It wasn't a spot, but the entire cone. John bellowed, and James appeared quickly, gasping and looking to where John was pointing.

"Me thinks you've got one," said James. John backed away, allowing James to probe like a surgeon. The entire cone wasn't blood red. There was only a barely noticeable red dot. John sensed he had panicked like the naïve teenager. What would James think?

"Hoot mon, she be a big'un," said James. As James worked at filling the hole, John studied his movements. Maybe he wasn't as naïve as he previously thought? When James bellowed for the goop bucket, John scurried while worrying he had waited too long before calling out. He prayed for pink to return.

"She be plugged now," said James. "Nice work, laddie."

John hadn't done anything, but he appreciated the words. Oddly, even though James was clearly in-charge, John didn't feel like an inferior. James was easy going and approachable. "Me thought me knew the *Unity* faces," John said. "But me nae know yours."

"Me was on the *John and Sara*,[19] laddie." James beckoned John to sit next to him. With an eerie glow as a backdrop, James said, "Me was at Worcester. After Dunbar, we went into England, chasing them bastards."

"Goot, me hates the English," said John as he slammed a fist into his palm.

---

19 *In 1652, this ship carried 272 prisoners captured at the Battle of Worcester to Boston, some of whom served as indentured servants at the Ironworks.*

James laughed and said, "Every Scottish laddie hates the English, so much so there nae be clear thinking." He grew serious as he continued. "We waited at Worcester to avenge our defeat at Dunbar. But Cromwell circled us and waited too. He wanted to slaughter us on the same day as Dunbar, only a year later. When he attacked, it was another disaster. Charles II fled for France. His nightmare had ended, ours began."

"Charles II?"

"The king we be fighting for," said James. He chuckled. "Have you forgotten?"

"Me was fighting because the Clan Commander took me."

"Aye, as it was with me."

"But with Charles II gone," said John, "Scotland can be Scotland again."

"Nae laddie," said James as he grew somber. "The defeats at Dunbar and Worcester have taken all the hearty lads. Cromwell let the sick go, poor bastards died before they e'er saw Scotland, sold the hearty to bondage and executed the rest."

"Executed?" asked John. He had heard about executions, but hadn't witnessed any.

"Cromwell captured too many. In me group, they took every tenth lad, ran them through, chopped their heads off."

"You be there?" asked a wide-eyed John.

"Aye, me be the ninth lad, me chum be next to me." James bit his lip and lowered his head. When he raised it, his ever present twinkle had given way to horror. His crimson cheeks were ghostly, drained of their color. "Oh laddie, the screams, me still hears the fear in them screams." His face was paralyzed by horror until he slapped his knee and said. "Maybe we be the poor bastards, eh Johnnie?"

The eerie light, James's emotional commentary and a heat-emitting cone had drained the energy from John. He didn't respond. James couldn't stop lamenting.

"Nary a lad be in Scotland to tend crops and sire lassies. Scotland be full of bonny lasses, working the fields, and auld lasses grieving."

John regained some energy. "Tell me aboot the auld lasses."

"Me nae know aboot them."

"You had auld lasses in your clan," said John as he leaned closer to James.

"The tribal chief took care of them."

John shrunk back as images returned of men pumping their pelvises with lecherous faces as they had their way with his mother. But he leaned again and asked, "But if the tribal chief was married?"

"Nae matter, the auld lasses helped his wife. One chief had several auld lasses." John's disgusting Doon Hill images faded away as James said, "We Scottish lads always care for our lasses, especially the auld ones." James relaxed and said, "The chief's wife liked having the auld lasses aboot. You know how auld lasses prattle. Maybe someday the chief dies, and his wife be looking for a home."

John was listening to every word.

"But Johnnie," said James, "the chief only lay with his wife." James poked at John, who blushed. James chuckled and added, "Aye, the auld lasses may be grieving, but they be fine."

"Did your clan lose many at Dunbar?" asked John.

"Aye, and we said, 'nae again', and then Worcester came a year later."

"How did you know who died?"

"If they nae come home, they be dead."

John felt naïve again, but was undeterred by it. "But some were prisoners."

"Prisoners died too, or prayed that they did."

John stared into James's eyes and asked, "James, does your mum know you be in the Colonies?"

"Me pray me mum knows," said James, and his eyes lost their twinkle again.

"Does God hear you?"

James had asked himself the same question, and still had no answer for it. "Don't pray," he said, "just talks to me mum, at night, when me be alone staring at this lassie's glow. If me looks long enough, me see me mum."

John eased back and looked away.

"Me nae be crazy with drink," said James. "But me see her, and she comforts me."

The two sat quietly, mesmerized by a glowing cone. When James's introspection left, he arose and said, "Me lassie be all right now. But you keep watch."

John tilted his head.

"You be hearing me?" asked James.

John sat erect and said, "Me does." He arose and patrolled the perimeter to reassure James of his vigilance. After James disappeared, John returned to his stump, sat and pondered the glow. As tedium set in, his mother appeared, spinning wool in the MacElwees' home. Shamus MacElwee was an elder, who had comforted his mother after his father's passing. Now, it was obvious to John that Shamus would care for his mother. John's question as he lay on the floor of *Unity* near death, 'and who will care for you, mum?' had an answer.

His thoughts danced with the flickering glow as his mother spun the finest wool in Scotland. Her spinning wheel's hum was soothing, and she responded to each of John's thoughts in harmony with what John thought she would say. Their delightful chat could have lasted an eternity, but an ember popped, shattering the enchantment.

John rubbed his eyes, arose from the stump and stretched. The sun was shining, and the flickering pink images had lost their allure. "Such a ghoulish light with its trickery, it nae be real." John headed toward James's snoring. But he needed a last look at the cone that now resembled a bonny lass, much like his mum. He turned from the cone and shook his head. *It can nae be real.*

Chapter Fourteen

John's friendship with James Moor blossomed as did his apprenticeship. Perhaps when he would be free from servitude, he could be a respected craftsman. But after several weeks under James's tutelage, he returned to felling trees, this time, alone and at a different location. He now worked with James only on rare occasions. So his collier dream vanished, and with infrequent visits, so did his camaraderie with James.

Andrew Adams, his long-time and closest friend, had left the Scotchman House to work exclusively for Sam Bennett. Other acquaintances had trickled away too. Only MacGoon and a few grovelers remained at the House, company John feared and avoided. Rumors swirled whenever someone permanently left the House. Some seemed incredible, but grew quite real with several tankards, only to be utter nonsense in the morning. Many of the indentured had simply been bartered to locals.

As MacGoon amused a few lackeys, John lay in his bunk, reflecting on a familiar pattern to his life. He had the continuous security only a father can give, which vanished when he died. Reflecting now, Jamus, the Clan Commander, had filled a fatherly role. But at that time, John was grieving and obsessed with caring for his mother to notice. Andrew Wright, Malcolm Dinsmour and Robert MacEntire were fleeting comfort. Andrew Adams provided a lasting influence and James Moor a strong one, but now John seldom interacted with either of them.

MacGoon's toadies roared, disturbing John from his reflecting. He yanked a nettlesome piece of straw from his bedding, picked his teeth with it and reflected anew. How he envied the young lads who had a constant blanket of security around them. His blanket had been a loosely-knit, patchwork of older males who provided security at times, but little else. When he had sons, he would give them what he dearly missed.

John was nineteen, and thus an adolescent need for fatherly role models was becoming less important. He needed to strike out, most likely all alone, gain some land, wed a pure lass and start a family. John clearly saw a future, yet also saw decreasing opportunities to achieve it.

Summer 1654
Concord Meetinghouse, Middlesex,
Massachusetts Bay Colony

"We must not tarry another day," said Robert Blood as he surveyed the group gathered in the shade not far from the meetinghouse. "Concord needs more land." His countenance dared anyone to challenge him. One did.

"Our initial grant remains sufficient. Thou need not act in haste."

"Our initial land was wet meadows and pine forests," said Blood. "A veritable, barren wasteland compared to what our seacoast brethren received."

The Deacon chimed in. "And the Lord hath blest our goodwives with fertile wombs. Our inland plantation grows, and our sons need land of their own."

A disheveled Roger Draper stepped forth. His frayed waistcoat bulged at his stomach and his white linen collar was peppered with moth holes. "Ye general court granted Concord a second parcel years ago. But soon after, Reverend Jones[20] and others left. Concord grew sparse, and we tarried." He turned to Blood, "Ye courts will regard us as filled with avarice for land if we petition again."

"That second grant was long ago, Goodman Draper," said Blood. "It is quite remarkable thy fogged mind recalls."

Roger's blurry eyes glared. "I signed that petition, my good man," he said.

A tension lingered until Goodman Smythe said, "Goodman Draper doth pose questions needing answers. What are thy intentions, Goodman Blood?"

"Ye cow common is a barren, stubble filled patch," said Blood as he gestured toward it. "The great meadow's red-top and lute grass is much damnified. We need virgin meadows to fatten our livestock. And later, the land would go to our sons."

---

20 *The first Concord church in 1636 had Reverend John Jones as "the Minister" and Reverend Peter Bulkeley as "the Teacher". By 1644, Reverend Jones and seventeen families left Concord for what is now known as Fairfield, Connecticut, thus easing the financial burden for the small Concord settlement of supporting two Reverends.*

"Grazing across the river?" asked Goodman Fiske. "Why ye Indians would return our flock as mutton in barter for hard water."

"Surely thou would not trade hard water with the Indians?" asked the Deacon.

"Surely not," said Fiske. "Ye laws forbid it."

"As doth the Lord's," said the Deacon as he bowed his head.

"Ye fears have validity, Goodman Fiske," said Blood. "We could employ a public herder to protect our livestock."

"Who would reside away from the safety of Concord?" asked Fiske.

"I do," said Major Willard.

Blood smiled an apology and said, "Public herding is a lowly task, not one for our newly commissioned Major."

"Then Perhaps an indentured, like thy Duncan," said Fiske.

"My Duncan fancies himself a man servant, not a herder."

"Another Scottish man, perhaps?" asked Fiske.

"Reverend Bulkeley would forbid it," said Blood.

Major Willard glanced at The Reverend, who was now heading to the meetinghouse. "Thou misjudge our Reverend," he said. "His quarrel was with Archbishop Laud, not with every Scottish man that ever lived." The Reverend paused at the meetinghouse door and stared at the gathering.

"We must not tarry," said Blood. "The Reverend grows impatient."

The group scurried toward the meetinghouse, but Blood ambled, thinking aloud with Willard. "A Scottish man, allowed to squat upon common land and to herd for the common weal." He rubbed his chin. "And he would be alone, out of sight of The Reverend." Blood smiled his pleasure, but his forehead soon creased. "But when time arrives to parcel land to our children, then what?"

"The Scottish man could journey west with the Indians," replied Willard.

"And if ye bogs yield iron ore?" asked Blood.

"We will invest in it, and remove the squatter elsewhere."

Chapter Fifteen

Summer 1655

Awbrey had summoned John to Charlestown. He sensed his time at the Scotchman House was about to end. Even though the House now consisted of the unsavory, they were still Scots. Ethnic bonds may fray, but they seldom break. But if John's remaining indenture was sold to locals, he would soon be a sole, Scottish man adrift in an English sea, a prospect that worried him.

Awbrey, the richly dressed Englishman, was inspiring and intimidating. Would he remember John was a shepherd? And if he did, what would it mean? Would he recall that momentary bond when John first arrived that impressed John? And if so, would he feel similar? John tried to remain upbeat, but, too often, reality slammed him down. He was an indentured Scot, controlled by the whims of Englishmen.

The night before John had bathed in the Saugus, bringing clothes to wash, which he later dried near the oven. While bathing he thought of the lasses who had spied upon him. Erotic thoughts came and lingered, a pleasing distraction from his foremost concern. He raked his hair with his fingers and positioned his head before sleeping to maintain his coif. He cleaned his boots and trimmed his beard. His peach fuzz of a naïve youth had been left to the breezes of Doon Hill.

It was a new day, and John stepped outside the House. He inhaled and realized his laborer's stench had been left in the Saugus River. He grew more comfortable when he heard a squeaky cart. Andrew Adams neared on a tip cart hitched to a horse.

"Me God mon," said Andrew, "it be Awbrey you be meeting, not the good Lord."

John's confidence sagged. Perhaps he had overdressed and primped too much. But his swagger quickly returned. "Awbrey be bartering me to a prosperous Englishman with bonny lasses."

"You nae be talking that way," said Andrew. "It could be the lash."

Another jolt to John's fragile confidence, adapting to being among the English would be difficult. The two hopped onto the cart, Andrew clucked, and the journey began. The air was brisk during the early morning ride. As the sun rose higher, John ceased huddling and enjoyed the warmth.

Several miles into the journey, Andrew asked, "How many be in the House?"

"Me and three others."

"MacGoon still there?"

"Nae."

"I pity the poor colonist who bartered for him."

"He just be gone," said John. "In jail, or maybe he be dead."

"Or maybe," said Andrew with a wry smile, "he grinded himself to death with his wenches."

"Me does remember him groaning when he tried to piss." John chuckled, "Drunken bastard may have crawled away, filled with piss and exploded." Andrew roared, which delighted John. "The rest of his lot be there," said John.

"Not the best to be with Johnnie."

"They still be Scots. The English have their scoundrels too."

"Their scoundrels still be in England. Only the pious be here. The English scoundrels could nae stomach the pious, so they threw them here. And the worst scoundrels went with Cromwell." Andrew turned and asked, "Bloody wretches, eh Johnnie?"

Doon Hill came to John's mind. His fears then were similar now. He thought aloud. "Ever wonder what our life would be, if there nae be Dunbar?"

"Used to, but nae more." He touched John's shoulder and said, "If me nae be at Dunbar, then me nae be carting me friend to Charlestown."

Andrew's touch and his words momentarily drew John from his worry. As Andrew continued to banter, John returned to his concern. When Andrew joked about the close encounter with the tree, John touched his scar. John's insipid smile remained as Andrew expounded with silly details about the incident until another fear was triggered in John's mind. What if Awbrey had bartered him to those who he had threatened? Or if not them, Colonists like them?

The cart stopped at a small dock away from the main wharf. John was shaken from his worry and looked quizzically. "We have arrived," said Andrew.

John was still unaware of where he was. "Did we pass through Charlestown?"

"Me avoided most of the town. Nae need to be answering questions aboot me horse and cart."

John pointed at a hill that arose from the harbor side. "Did we cross that brae?"

"Too steep for me cart."

Across the harbor, ships were tied at the wharves. The sun had dissipated the fog, but dew remained on their masts. They glistened, similar to the masts that bobbed in the Firth off of Dunbar. John was as awestruck then as now, and he thought, *Aye, it be a mighty empire we fought. Nae wonder the English prevailed.*

The hill on Charlestown's peninsula sent chills through John's back muscles to the nape of his neck. The hill wasn't a windswept brae, it was nothing like Doon Hill, yet, for some unknown reason, it was. He stepped toward it and saw the future. He sensed soldiers storming the hill, and fear-filled men atop the hill, hiding behind breastworks. John was afraid, and an incomprehensible eeriness captivated him. Perhaps his soul knew a descendant, Reuben Law, years later would be behind the breastworks, atop of what would then be known as Bunker Hill. Perhaps his soul knew a musket ball would tear through Reuben's braided queue as he and militiamen abandoned the hill; perhaps or perhaps not.

"Laddie, what is it?" asked Andrew.

John pointed and said, "There be Doon Hill," and he swung around, "and there be Cromwell's warships."

Andrew shook his head. "Me need to return Bennett's cart." He jockeyed the cart into position to leave and stretched onto it. "Be leery of Awbrey," he said, "he be a slippery alewife." Andrew received a nod from a somber, well-groomed man, seemingly lost and out of place near a small dock, awaiting his fate. "Aye Johnnie, you be fine," said Andrew. He clucked, and the cart creaked around the hill. After it disappeared, John continued staring at Andrew's route away from him until the creaking left.

He headed toward the main warehouse on the large wharf. Soon, he was walking on the same wharf he had stood upon when he first arrived in the Colonies. His aspirations then were rekindled.

Inside the warehouse, Awbrey was talking with another man, and John paused to straighten his coat. Awbrey swung around and was startled to see John. "Who art thou?" he asked.

"John Law. You summoned me."

"Thou should have waited outside." Awbrey turned back to the man, said a few more words, and the man departed. Awbrey's boot heels reverberated as he approached. John rubbed his hands and shifted from side-to-side, trying to control his urge to pace. The intimidating echo ceased, and Awbrey eyeballed John. Awbrey's jerkin was soiled, missing buttons, and the embroidery was frayed. He was unshaven and appeared harried. John was more finely clothed and seemingly more relaxed, so different than their first encounter.

"Art thou John Law," asked Awbrey, "or art thou John Mac Lawson?"

A tidal wave slammed John. Awbrey knew more than John imagined. He grew light headed as his blood now pulsated around his temple scar. He swallowed, focused on Awbrey's button dangling and said, "Me be John Law." John clenched his teeth and kept eye contact, but his temple continued to throb.

"As thou say," said Awbrey as he scuffed the floor. "It has been four years past since thou arrived on the *John and Sara*. Thou art a herdsman, as I recall?"

"Me came on the *Unity*," said John.

"But a herdsman," said Awbrey. John nodded and awaited Awbrey's acknowledgement of his confusion about the two ships. Awbrey rubbed his chin and said, "Concord hath received land for grazing, and…"

"Goodman Awbrey," interrupted John, "the *Unity*; me indenture be five years."

"My faculties are amply blessed," said Awbrey as he raised his head and narrowed his eyes, "capable of hearing ye the first time." John curled his shoulders and rubbed his palms. "As I was saying, Concord hath land across the river from its town center. Thou will be far from the townsfolk."

John smiled at the thought of not being in a sea of Englishmen.

"Or the bloody English," said Awbrey, "as ye Scots are fond of saying."

John flashed an incredulous look and said, "Me nae e'er say…"

Awbrey raised his hand to interrupt John's deceit. "It will be ye and the Indians," he said.

"Indians?" asked John. This time, his disbelief was genuine.

"They are Praying Indians," said Awbrey with a face that expressed concern for John's safety. "I've met them often." John raised his eyebrow, and Awbrey continued. "Thou will be a herdsman, just as ye were in Scotland." Awbrey swung his arms up and out as he said, "There is no better Scottish man in these colonies for such an esteemed station." His dramatics ended, and he riveted his eyes on John, "It is what ye always desired."

"Who will be me master?" asked John.

"The selectmen have not been forthcoming. Duncan will tend to thee."

"Duncan who?"

"Duncan Mac…," said Awbrey as he grimaced. "Duncan, the only Scot in Concord."

"Whose livestock will me be tending?"

"Ye Concord Selectmen have paid me a fair sum for thy indenture," said Awbrey as he drew his head back. "Duncan will tend to thy needs. It's all ye need to know. But John," and Awbrey's seeming concern for John's well-being returned, "once ye are a free man, thou will own all the land." He expanded his arms wide again and said, "Meadows and brooks, musquash, hinds, alewife, a veritable bounty of food."

"And me family?"

"Family?" Awbrey's brow furled. "Of course, so settle on a fertile parcel, plant thy seeds, and reap thy just rewards."

'Plant your seeds' were his mother's words too. Perhaps she and Awbrey had a similar vision for him.

"The Indians have cleared the land," said Awbrey. "Pleasing to hear, is it not?" John rubbed his callused palm. "Thou shall not fell a tree ever again. Thou will be John the shepherd."

A Scottish man with a title sounded impressive to John until Andrew's words echoed. *"Be leery of Awbrey, he be a slippery alewife"*. "Does Duncan know me indenture expires in two years?" asked John.

"Most assuredly, Duncan is of your ilk," said Awbrey. "He will treat you justly. Thou hast many questions, but all will be fine." Awbrey held his hands out and rolled them to offer inviting palms. "I give thee my solemn promise."

Andrew's cautioning had now been replaced by reverberating boots of two men strolling in unison toward the door. As John headed out, Awbrey asked, "If thou dost know the whereabouts of John MacLawson, let The Reverend know. He demands justice for this despicable John MacLawson."

As John looked at a smug and smiling Awbrey, he said, "Me nae know him."

"As thou hast said." Awbrey's smile remained. John turned away and exhaled, letting his stone face crumble. "Just the same John Law," said Awbrey as John pieced together his face and turned back. "Thou might avoid The Reverend. His manse is the grandest on Concord Common with diamond-shaped window panes, standing near ye grist mill."

As John left Awbrey and the warehouse behind him, his temple scar throbbed, an unnerving reminder of his fictitious John MacLawson. Now, he had an immediate fear, The Reverend Bulkeley. How long would his distress over encountering this revered Englishman torment him?

Chapter Sixteen

Concord, Middlesex County, Massachusetts Bay Colony

While on the Bay Road leading to Concord Center, John paused to study a shelter built into the ridge across from him. It didn't appear too complicated to erect once a suitable ridge was found. He now wished he had sharpened his axe, which lay in his cart, before departing. But his concern then was to conceal it from Sam Bennett. He moved up and down the road to gain further perspectives, visualizing the framing as he did, until a door opened and a man stepped out.

"Art thou in need?"

John thought briefly about asking if he could come inside and inspect the framing from within, but didn't.

"Thou with the cart, tarry no more."

John continued west, only glancing at the shelters. When two men came down the road toward him, he moved toward the side. He was a stranger pushing a cart and had already caused stirs in other towns along his route. John avoided eye contact with the approaching men, hoping to pass without incident.

"How now, dost thou arrive to barter goods?"

John shook his head.

"What doth bring thee to Concord?"

"To meet with Duncan."

"Aha, another Scot. Duncan resides at Goodman Blood's house, five houses past ye meetinghouse." John continued along, pleased by the pleasantness, until he heard. "Another Scot, what will become of our Concord?"

As he neared Concord Center, the houses were rectangular, with centered chimneys that had several flues, were clap-boarded and free standing. Some had an appended room, and a few were two-storied. A lone, gambrel-roof seemed out of place among the many gable roofs, and it appealed to John. Someday, he would own such a house.

A grist mill was at the edge of a pond, and a house, thatched with meadow blue joint, stood prominently nearby. As sunlight reflected off its diamond-shaped window panes, anxiety returned to John. Fortunately, no one was about the manse, and John hoped he could pass without encountering The Reverend.

Several men congregated near the commons a few hundred feet away from John, enjoying one another's company. By instinct, John veered away from them and stayed on the road, close to the ridge. A notice tacked to a publishing post near the wayside fluttered and distracted John. He turned his attention from the fluttering to the pillory stage and stocks, secured with padlocks. He scrunched his shoulders and wondered if a padlock would ever open for him. He hastened around the bend.

Once further away, he turned back. The grist mill, the manse and the meetinghouse with gravestones sprinkling its western slope, reflective of a peaceful village, were safely distant. The friendly banter on the Common was muted, broken only with occasional laughs. Sounds reminiscent to when his father amused his friends. A boy with a switch moved a cow off the Common. Concord Center was like many villages, and John had passed through virtually unnoticed. He was relieved, yet knew he didn't belong.

John counted the houses and, after five of them, arrived at Goodman Blood's. He knocked on door, stepped back and wrung his hands until the door creaked. A man, wearing a black doublet with a broad, white linen collar atop his shoulders, appeared. His loose fitting breeches ballooned at the knees. Garters held his stockings in place just below his knees and above his plain, black shoes. He was not as adorned as Awbrey, yet still appeared wealthy. He was far more intimidating than Awbrey had ever been.

"Me be John Law and ..."

"Duncan is in the shed around back. He will tend to thee." The door closed as quickly as it had opened.

John pushed his cart to the back of the house, relieved he would be dealing with his own ilk. The shed was larger than some of the humble houses, which had dotted the Bay Road. John went inside the shed looking for Duncan, but became intrigued with the interior. He studied the posts, beams and cross supports. "Aye, just as me suspects. This nae be too troublesome." He tugged at a few posts, hung from a cross beam and dropped down. "They be solid. Got to hone me axe."

John headed toward a sharpening wheel, which was cradled in a stand with a foot treadle, several yards from the shed.

"What art thou doing?"

The English sounding words didn't mask the Scottish burr. It must be Duncan. His clothes were loose fitting and of a coarser fabric than Goodman Blood's, yet he offered an air of importance far greater than his attire implied.

"What did thou pilfer?" asked Duncan

"Nae a bloody thing."

Duncan drew back, and with a limp wrist he gestured toward grain sacks. "Goodman Blood will pay for ye diet," he said. "Thou can return for other provisions when needed."

"And me sheep?"

"My master's sheep will come. Others will arrive too. If they desire tending, then thou may barter for thy service."

As John lifted a grain sack, it slipped from his grasp. He struggled with it while looking to Duncan for help. "I do my master's bidding, not thine," said Duncan. He headed back to the house and entered through the back door.

What be worse, an Englishman, or a Scottish man who dishonors his father's blood? thought John as he loaded his cart. Once his cart was loaded, he headed to the sharpening wheel. He pumped the foot treadle and eased his axe blade onto the wheel. The grinding was noticeable. He needed to work quickly.

The rear door opened. "What art thou doing with my master's wheel?"

John feigned he hadn't heard Duncan and continued to grind.

Duncan stepped out of the house and Goodman Blood soon appeared at the door. "Duncan, allow the man to hone his axe." He flicked his hand and said, "Carry on John Law." Duncan grimaced and returned to the house.

Aye, me misjudged this Englishman.

John wheeled his cart further away from Concord Center and arrived at an intersection. To the west was a bridge, and to the east, a trodden path. He needed to cross over the bridge, but an eerie feeling crept over him. He dithered and walked east to a vast open meadow, sections of which suffered from the ravages of grazing. He came back, and his eeriness returned. But he couldn't dither forever, and he continued west.

The cart wheels rumbled over the bridge's wooden planks, creating a noise far greater than John had expected. He stopped, but the rumbling, although distant, continued. Eventually it ceased, and John thought, *Aye, an echo.* His nerves calmed as eddies gurgled around a piling. Their swirls were fascinating. He could have spent an eternity watching, but he didn't. As he stepped, the rumbling returned, louder than before. When he scampered, it intensified. Others were seemingly running with him. Once across the bridge, the rumbling ceased. The bridge still creaked and swayed, recovering from John's hastened pace. But John's fears about Concord's North Bridge didn't recover. *She be haunted by ghouls, me thinks.*

The heavily rutted road became a trampled footpath, which grew less trampled and eventually disappeared into a meadow. Unlike the earlier meadow, this was unspoiled land. Awbrey's words came back. *"Thou will own all the land, meadows, brooks, woodlands."*

"Me mistrusted thee too," said John. He shook his head and chuckled. "Me God, me be talking just like Duncan,"

John's cart swooshed through the meadow as he paralleled the river. When he steered close to it, he got mired in the sodden lowlands. He veered to higher ground and remained on it. Weary, he paused and breathed deeply. The meadow's fragrances were similar to ones from his youth. Across the river at the meadow's margin were woodlands, just as Awbrey had promised. The undergrowth was minimal, accentuating the towering trees.

He picked up his cart and froze. He eased it back down, but remained transfixed on three deer at the woodlands' edge. A big doe raised her nose and sniffed frequently as two smaller ones grazed nearby. She cocked her head and rolled her ears to hone in where John was standing. She broke eye contact, sniffed and bobbed her head. She flicked her white tail, and the other two deer ceased grazing. They looked toward John and cupped their ears. The big doe took a few hesitant steps. When John unfroze and stood erect, she wheezed, and three white tails bounded into the woodlands.

John continued his journey, and as he neared a reedy inlet, ducks rose out of them. Their whooshing wings and quacking startled him. They circled high, descended and glided into the river away from John. Their splashing and quacking continued until all of them had splashed down. An annoyed heron waded away from the flock, yet still kept a watchful eye for movement in the shallow water.

He continued west, counter to the river's flow, like a salmon homeward bound to spawn. A ridge, similar to the one on the Bay Road, sheltered the north side. Far beyond that crest, the few Concord residents who journeyed west would travel. "Aye, it will hide me from them bastards."

The river that sliced though the meadow now flowed close to and in front of the ridge. Further west, it bubbled over rocks and disappeared into the woodlands. "And a moat will protect me too."

The treetops that hugged both sides of the river provided a darkened contrast to the meadow's glare. Shadows of flickering leaves softened the stark differences. The gurgle was a beckoning siren, and John answered it. He sat upon a boulder, listening to a serenade. Mist permeated the air. The aroma of wild grapes drifted in. A wood duck winged by, landed in a tree and hopped about. Limbs, laden with chestnuts, sagged with the weight of their bounty.

John could have sat for an eternity; but in the shade and alongside the bubbling water, his body cooled, and eventually his buttocks ached. He shivered, climbed off the boulder, looked skyward and with an emphatic nod said, "This be me New Scotland. Me will plant me seed here."

Chapter Seventeen

In the summer of 1655, a twenty year old Scottish immigrant began a new life alone. On his first night lying under a darkened sky, Doon Hill's apprehensions returned. It wasn't the English advancing up the hill, but something, most likely Indians, lurking in the hardwoods. His fears left with the morning sun, only to return when it set. But as the gurgles, hoots, and howls grew familiar, John grew more comfortable with his new home.

By day, he hewed hardwoods into posts and rails, weaved smaller limbs between them, leaned pine boughs and piled sod to fill in the gaps. The Bay Road's shelters and James Moor's imparted knowledge were his mental blueprints. His shelter was not a cone, but three sided with the fourth side being, substantially, the ridge, which he used for the chimney's backing. He extended a wooden flue up through a slightly pitched roof.

As autumn advanced, the sun's warmth ebbed, and morning frosts lingered. John had to stop admiring his firepit and use it. He struck flint to create sparks into wadded parchment, blew upon a reddish hole, added dry moss, blew, added dried reeds and a flame grew. Smoke wafted and funneled out of the shelter. "Aha, me did it, James," and John stoked his fire further.

The smoke continued rising, but John wanted more. A flame grew, lighting his shelter with man-made light for the first time. He no longer would sleep in utter darkness if he so desired. He added more wood, a burning limb popped, and the smoke that the pop had created rose to perfection. He danced around, pointing, "Take a look, James," he said. "Me lass be as sturdy as yours. Can you see her James?"

The dancing stopped, and he pondered how proud James Moor would be with him. But another pop from the firepit shattered his thoughts and quelled his youthful exuberance, just like James Moor would have done. James's admonition came. *"Laddie, treat a wooden chimney with clay or limestone wash. You nae want a fire in it."*

Water doused his first fire, and its hominess disappeared as sodden limbs hissed. He had another task before winter set in, which through bartering with Duncan as Goodman Blood's agent, he accomplished. His firepit with a properly treated chimney kept him warm throughout the winter. But Awbrey had misled him about not felling trees once his shelter was built. He had to cut many for firewood. John finished the winter with only a few twigs in his woodpile, another task to complete, but not before addressing a more immediate concern. His diet from Goodman Blood lacked variety and was barely enough for him to survive. He did supplement it with meat from hunting. But too often he had too little time to do so. So he negotiated a reduced diet in exchange for other provisions and planted a garden.

As John tilled the soil that first spring, the peculiar feelings of his first nights in his New Scotland returned. He stopped tilling and looked toward his fears, but he saw nothing. That night, as he lay alone in his shelter, he heard noises. With heart pounding, he arose to look over a moonlit meadow, but again he saw nothing.

The next morning his angst returned, and when it became overwhelming, he spun to face his fears. An Indian had drifted near as quietly as goose down. He was taller than John with long, straight, raven hair. His wide-set black eyes latched onto John's pale blue ones. John's adrenaline spiked, spurring his weariness away. His smooth copper skin was a stark contrast to John's blotchy paste. His mouth was drawn straight, a grave face revealing nothing. He was broad shouldered with brawny arms and a trim waist. Hides covered his mid-section, yet revealed powerful haunches, much like his father's prized ram. Even though this heathen wasn't dressed like the Englishman, he was more intimidating than one. When his haunches tightened, John gripped his hoe to defend against a charge. But the Indian raised a hand, thumped his curled fingers on his breastplate and said, "Nagoglancit."

John eased his grip, thumped similarly and said, "Aye, me be John Law."

"English?" asked Nagoglancit as his stone face cracked.

"Scottish."

Nagoglancit perused John, and more questions seemed to fissure his face. He gestured for John's hoe, and John handed it to him. He walked past John, and John followed as idle chatter from the Scotchman House came into his mind. *"Them Indians will steal everything."* He wondered if he had been too trusting.

Nagoglancit stopped and chopped into the meadow. "Squaw Sachem says plant here." He grabbed a handful of moist, dark soil and grinded it among his fingers and thumb. He tossed it down and pointed to where John had been tilling He gestured for John to do similarly. John grinded a handful of dry soil, and dust flew from his grip. Nagoglancit pointed to where the water flowed below the riverbank. He raised his hands, and then lowered them while flicking his fingers and said, "White rains come."

He pointed to where John had been digging and made a sweeping motion toward Concord Center. John recalled seeing the river swelling as the snow melted with the spring thaw and washing over the meadow. He smiled as he realized the rich soil where he had been digging had been swept away. John nodded. Nagoglancit did, too, and returned John's hoe to him. "You chop, John Law," and Nagoglancit headed over the rise toward the northwest.

Nagoglancit returned periodically that first summer with no warning. He surveyed what John had accomplished, explained more about the land through animation and broken English and escorted John into the woodlands and beyond. On their first trip, a beaver's slap broke the quiet. Streams had been dammed to create a flooded area with mounds and dead hardwoods scattered through it. When Nagoglancit placed his hands aside his head and shuddered, John sensed his ears would not be frost bitten this coming winter once they were covered with a beaver pelt. Nagoglancit held his curled palm close to his mouth and snapped his teeth. John wondered how fire-roasted beaver might taste.

On another trip to a weir past the beaver pond, John tried spear fishing. The following night Nagoglancit arrived with a flaming flambeau and fishing nets. They returned to the weir, and Nagoglancit netted while John held the flame. Netting was far easier than spearing. Bartering for fishing nets became another priority for John.

Later, on yet another trip, apple blossom scents drifted in a breeze as the two emerged from the woodlands. Nagoglancit thumped his breastplate, held up three fingers and made an arch with his other hand, which John interpreted as three moons passing. Nagoglancit placed his hand, with thumb and index finger spread apart, to his mouth and made an exaggerated bite. His usual grave face smiled. A farmhouse was at the end of the orchard, and John smiled. "Need to harvest at night, eh Nagoglancit?" His friend thumped his chest, but John doubted he understood his tongue-in-cheek question.

Nagoglancit kept returning at unexpected times. One day in late summer while John was trimming tree limbs to make an enclosure for the town sheep, Nagoglancit silently approached. He watched John hew, before emerging from the woodland. When John finally heard him and looked, by habit, he thumped his chest, and Nagoglancit did the same.

"Can nae gather food today," said John. "Need stakes for me pen."

John picked up a straight limb and simulated pounding it into the ground. He turned his palm down and wiggled his fingers to mimic livestock legs. He was unsure if Nagoglancit understood, so he said, "Hold me sheep nigh, or they be missing by the morn." John chuckled as he asked, "Me wonders who might steal them, eh Nagoglancit?"

His friend remained expressionless and went to the pile of straight branches. He dragged a few toward the river.

"Hoot mon, me needs those," said John.

Nagoglancit raised his hand, and John ceased protesting and trailed after him. Nagoglancit laid the branches across the exposed rocks where the stream narrowed. Because it was summer, the stream was still shallow enough to ford. But Nagoglancit continued to build a crude bridge, and once done, he stepped into the water and inspected his work. He nodded to John and flicked his fingers, saying, "White rains come." He raised his hand up from the water to a height just below the bridge and nodded. He stepped onto the bank, moved across the newly constructed bridge and beckoned to John.

Nagoglancit moved along a narrow footpath on the other side of the river with ease. In John's haste to keep up, he tripped on a concealed root and fell. He brushed his knees and continued following Nagoglancit, who now moved slower than before. Nagoglancit finally stopped, and John scanned the treetops as sunlight filtered through them. He was encased in a stand of straight hardwoods with ideal diameters for posts and rails. Nagoglancit's mission was accomplished. He thumped his chest and turned to leave.

"Nagoglancit," asked John as he held his hands up, "how does me get back?"

Nagoglancit pointed to a gash in a tree. John followed Nagoglancit's finger to other trees to discern a route out of the hardwoods. "You chop, John Law." Nagoglancit left, gliding like a powerful stag through his domain with nary a sound.

As the summer of 1656 ended, John had learned much about his land. He appreciated what his Indian friend had taught him. Often, while sitting by his fire pit alone and bored, he wondered why Nagoglancit had befriended him and how he could repay him.

Chapter Eighteen

West Concord, Middlesex County,
Massachusetts Bay Colony
Autumn 1657

John clutched his arms about him while sheep nibbled at the remains of his garden. The wind gusted and drove dampness further into him. John had enough, and he headed inside. He hated chopping wood and was reluctant to light a fire too earlier in autumn. But the New World autumns were fiercer than Scotland's, so he did. He remained inside until bleats interrupted the quiet of afternoon.

He stretched his cramped body, went outside and shivered. Duncan moved parallel to the river with sheep following behind. He spotted John and waved. John kept his arms about his body, not acknowledging Duncan at all.

"John Shepherd," Duncan said as he neared, "I bring more of my master's sheep."

"John Law be me name."

"And Duncan Butler is mine."

"Butler be more of an English name than Scottish."

"Truly, and I am Goodman Blood's trusted butler."

John's smirk eased into an insipid smile.

"But thou art still an indentured shepherd, and will be for another year."

Since Awbrey had never acknowledged that John was on the *Unity* and not the *John and Sara*, John had a lingering feared about his years of servitude. But John maintained his emotional mask, damned if he would let Duncan know that he was bothered.

"Tidings from thy master," said Duncan as he reached into his satchel and unrolled a parchment. "Can thou read?"

John snapped the parchment from Duncan. His head moved along and down the document. Some words he did not recognize or understand, but 'indenture' and '15 December 1658' he did. His eyes drifted to the scrolled signatures of William Awbrey and Robert Blood. He dropped his hands to his side, and Andrew Adams's words echoed. *"You can nae trust Awbrey."*

"Where art thou going?" asked Duncan.

"To me fire."

"Burn ye document, and Goodman Blood will flog thee for sure," said Duncan.

"Thou can shiver. But me need me warmth," said John.

Duncan scurried to catch up with John, and once inside, he rubbed his hands over the firepit. John perused the document again. The date was still 15 December 1658. His fears were now a reality.

"Don't be imprudent, John Shepard," said Duncan as John crumpled the document while staring at the fire. John was oblivious to Duncan's plea, wondering if Awbrey had forgotten or simply added another year of servitude for his personal gain. "Give me ye document," said Duncan. "Thou will be a free man in a year." John ceased crumpling. It didn't matter what the reason was, he was indentured for one more year than he had thought.

"Thy indenture is for three years," said Duncan. "Mine was five."

"Five," said John. "Me spent five years at the Ironworks before arriving here. Me indenture be eight in total."

"But thou art a shepherd, not trained in the fineries of being a man's servant."

John's involuntary crinkling resumed. "John," pleaded Duncan, "ye document." John hurled it at Duncan, and he scrambled to gather it. "Thou hast rumpled it badly. Help me straighten it." John knelt and helped Duncan. Once the document was rolled and re-tied, Duncan put the document into his satchel and patted it.

Duncan stepped outside and shooed his master's sheep toward the other sheep. "Master desires his sheep to graze on common lands." said Duncan. "They fatigue his land dearly." Bleating erupted as the newly arrived sheep jockeyed for territory with the others.

Duncan broadened his view and said, "A beautiful parcel of land." He swung from one pleasing view to another. "I say, simply splendid."

John's pride swelled as he thought, *Aye, it be me New Scotland.*

"Thou hast improved Goodman Blood's land. He will be pleased."

"Goodman Blood's land?" asked John with considerable irritation.

"Why of course," said Duncan as he continued to peruse the meadows. "Perhaps not all, but the choice parcels. That cropland thither," he said as he pointed to the spot that Nagoglancit had previously instructed John to use for his garden. "It is ideal for Robert Blood the junior."

"Ideal for John Law the junior," said John.

"But thou art not married," said Duncan as he turned around. "What Englishman would allow his daughter to breed with a Scottish shepherd?" He sneered and drew his wrap close, "Truly, thou did not believe the land was thine." That was exactly what John believed, but he would never let Blood's errand boy know it. "Thou art but a squatter, not an entitled landowner."

John wrung his hands, wishing they could be about Duncan's neck. His stomach roiled and his eyes swelled as anger filled them.

"I must cross to safety before darkness arrives. Fare thee well John Shepherd." John picked up a club-sized limb from his woodpile and smacked it into his palm. A departing Duncan pointed at the pen and yelled back, "Hold master's sheep nigh, or heathens will pilfer them."

John hastened after Duncan, intending to club him, but stopped. Duncan's swagger confirmed to John he was a pompous, misinformed, man servant. Why risk losing New Scotland because of an impulsive whack to Duncan's head? Andrew Adams words returned. *"You nae can trust Awbrey",* and John's arms drooped. He heaved the limb toward the wood pile and ran his fingers through his hair.

After several hours of chopping, John had rationalized Andrew's foreboding away. Yet for many nights, he was wracked with worry. Was he just deluding himself about New Scotland?

Chapter Nineteen

Smoke belched from John's chimney as he came over the rise. He was certain only embers remained in his firepit when he left. He sprinted down the hill and flew into his shelter.

Nagoglancit and two others stood, warming their hands over a blaze. John was relieved his shelter was not on fire, but perturbed that three uninvited intruders were wasting his wood. Nagoglancit thumped his chest, John did likewise, and his annoyance eased.

"Squaw Sachem," said Nagoglancit as he pointed. John was surprised to see an aged woman with a grave face staring at him.

Nagoglancit gestured again, "And John Tahattawan." This Indian was dressed like an Englishman with hair cut shorter than John's. Yet he was as somber as the squaw.

"Squaw Sachem say we must leave," said Nagoglancit.

Sadness flickered into the Squaw's eyes as she dropped her blanket and stepped forward. She pushed her arms westward and said, "Glooskap leave." She looked east, and either anger or fear came into her eyes. She moved her arms toward herself. "Malsum[21] come."

John looked at Nagoglancit, hoping for an explanation for the Squaw's sudden emotions. But it was John Tahattawan who spoke. "Squaw Sachem believes Malsum hath sent livestock to trample our crops, to drive Glooskap and the Nashobah away."

"Me nae have seen them," said John.

"Glooskap and Malsum are Earth Mother's sons. Glooskap is good, like English God. Malsum is evil, like Satan." Tahattawan looked at Nagoglancit and said, "Unlike me, many Nashobah still reject the teaching John Eliot.[22] Someday all Nashobah will believe in thy Lord." Nagoglancit shied from Tahattawan's glare. Squaw Sachem was unmoved by it.

Squaw Sachem nodded to Nagoglancit. He thumped his chest and said, "John Law, watch our land."

John furled his brow and turn to Tahattawan. "Nagoglancit says thou hast cared for Nashobah land," said Tahattawan. "Squaw Sachem wants thee to continue until Nashobah return."

"When?" asked John.

---

21 *According to Indian legend the great Earth Mother had two sons, Glooskap and Malsum. Glooskap was good, wise and creative; Malsum was evil, selfish and destructive.*

22 *John Eliot (c.1604 –1690) was a Puritan missionary to the American Indians. At one point, there were 14 towns of so-called "Praying Indians", the best documented being at Natick, Massachusetts. Other praying Indian towns (currently known as) included: Littleton (Nashoba), Lowell (Wamesit, initially incorporated as part of Chelmsford), Grafton (Hassanamessit), Marlborough (Okommakamesit), a portion of Hopkinton that is now in the Town of Ashland (Makunkokoag), Canton (Punkapoag), and Mendon-Uxbridge (Wacentug).*

"Squaw Sachem says Malsum will leave if English are here."

"But me be Scottish."

"All blue eyes are English to Squaw Sachem."

"But this land be me New Scotland. Me settled it; nae Glooskap, nae Malsum."

"Squaw Sachem let Concord English use Glooskap's land. What English say is land lease."

"Me nae heard of a lease."

"Squaw Sachem say lease," and Tahattawan nodded to the Squaw.

"Lease," said the Squaw. She turned to Nagoglancit and nodded, "Lease," and to John with a nod, "Lease." Her nod was emphatic each time she repeated a word that John doubted she understood. Any further discussion, even with an Indian more fluent than Nagoglancit, would raise more questions than anyone could answer. Besides, John doubted the Concord selectmen would allow the Nashobah back onto any land after they had settled upon it.

John thumped his chest and said, "Me will care for Nashobah land." John now had some answers to why Nagoglancit had educated him about the land. Nagoglancit's black eyes remained riveted on pale blue ones. Nagoglancit didn't understand John's words, but his eyes seemed to say 'I trust you, John Law'. John's eyes shifted away from Nagoglancit's. John would care for the land, but for him and his future family, not for the Nashobah.

Nagoglancit thumped his chest, and the three exited. John backed closer to the fire while rationalizing away his guilt.

Maybe this Malsum would continue to trample crops, and the Nashobah would never return. At first, he doubted a lease ever existed. But as he thought further, *The English say one thing and write another,* doubts lingered. Maybe someday the English would snooker him, too. Maybe they already had.

Chapter Twenty

Concord, Middlesex County, Massachusetts Bay Colony
Autumn 1658

Sheep bleated in an apparent concern about two strangers moving with other sheep near the river.

"Invaders of me estate," said John as he chuckled. He had seen nearly no one since the Nashobah's departure a few months earlier. Perhaps loneliness was making him a quarrelsome recluse. He hacked at some corn stalks, but was more intrigued with the man leading the sheep followed by another person in an oversized, hooded cloak, which, with limbs hidden, appeared to glide atop the meadow. They strode up the hill toward him, and the lead man introduced himself as Adam Draper.

"We bring sheep to graze on ye common land," said Adam. He was similar in age and build to John, yet not as muscular. As Adam eyeballed John, his air of importance seemed to increase. The person in the cloak shuffled past the two men to the hillcrest.

Adam continued his conversation. "Our land was plentiful once, but Father sold it to Major Willard's kin. Dost thou know him?" he asked.

John shook his head and turned to the person in the cloak, who was gazing toward the northeast.

"Art thou sure?" asked Adam as his brow wrinkled. "The Major's land holdings west of the river are plentiful."

John grunted while still focusing on the person in the cloak. *Who was this mysterious person hidden in a cloak?* he wondered. He concluded it was Adam's timid, younger brother.

"Thou can view our former home from that rise," said Adam. As they moved up the rise, the younger brother shuffled away. Adam pointed. "Thither smoke, we owned ten acres to the east." He swept his arm away from Concord Center and said, "And twenty acres near the hog pens, west of Quinnursnuck Hill."

"Quinnursnuck?" asked John.

"Indian word for rocks found nigh," said Adam. "Rocks ye heathens shape into arrow heads." Adam stood motionless and staring off.

John was drawn to the younger brother who was now among the Draper sheep. An arm flapped out from the cloak to urge the sheep to move along. John turned back to a reminiscing Adam. "Why did you sell?"

"Had no choice," and Adam broke his stare. "Major Willard wanted his kin near, and Father was…" Adam looked toward the cloaked person, "no matter now." Adam meandered and said, "Tis fertile land ye toil."

"Aye, it be me New Scotland."

Adam started to say something, but stopped. He ceased meandering and turned to John. "Our sheep need not be tended."

"Me can pen them at night. Keep them safe."

"No need. The Indians are gone," said Adam. "The good men wanting this land have seen to that." John cocked his head, and Adam continued. "They covet ye fertile New Scotland. So when darkness arrives, they drive their livestock to trample Indian cropland."

"The Nashobah believes Malsum brings the livestock."

"Malsum?" asked Adam as he cocked his head.

"He be their Satan."

"Thou knowest not Major Willard, but know Malsum. Are ye Indians thy friends?"

John shook his head 'no', but spotted the bridge that Nagoglancit had built. "Perhaps one," he said.

"Malsum," snorted Adam. "If only ye heathens knew God's true providence." They both turned to the brother, who was stroking a sheep with a caress that said 'I care for you deeply'. "Per chance, thou could watch Mehitable closely," said Adam.

"Mehitable?"

"Thither," said Adam as he pointed. "Our most favored sheep." He called to his brother. "Come meet John the shepherd."

He gestured Mehitable away and moved toward the two men. The hood was lowered, and to John's surprise, a tightly bonneted head was revealed. A few curls dangled near a fair face and flushed cheeks. The bulky cloak no longer hid a woman's sashay. When her eyes met John's, she shifted hers to the ground. She stopped next to Adam, still demurring.

"My sister Lydia," said Adam. Lydia looked directly at her brother as he said, "I've told John the shepherd about Mehitable."

Life flickered into Lydia's somber face, and Adam turned back to John. He broadened his shoulders and said, "Sadly, our fortune is now meager. But will thou still tend to Mehitable with diligence?"

Lydia fumbled with her cloak and pulled out a biscuit. "For thee," she said. As she held it out, her opened cloak revealed more. Her hand, arched with a grace, beckoned John. And with a lone biscuit resting on her inviting palm, carnal thoughts suddenly danced in John's head. But he quelled them as quickly as they had come.

"Me thank you, Lydia Draper," said John. Lydia giggled, lowered her arm and shied away. Her cheeks flushed further.

"Lydia heard thou were Scottish," said Adam.

"Ah, me brogue, tis different me guess." John thought of another lass who was also intrigued with his brogue when he was bathing in the Saugus years ago.

"Thy words are peculiar," said a still giggling Lydia.

John bit into the biscuit. "Corn cake, me loves corn cake."

Lydia was finally able to look directly at John. "I've more," she said as she reached inside her cloak. Her hanging curls bounced as she fumbled with the pocket tied about her waist.

"One be fine," said John.

Lydia continued to untie her pocket while the three moved toward John's shelter. John and Adam went inside. Lydia stayed outside until Adam said, "Thou may come inside with me. I shant tell Goody[23] Draper that thee did."

---

23 An abbreviated title for Goodwife often used in the Colonial period.

The shelter was dank and colder than the outside temperature. John wished he had a cozy fire burning. Lydia pulled three corn cakes from her now untied pocket. John swept clothing and several apples from a rickety table, and she placed the corn cakes on it. She proceeded to remove several parsnips from her other pocket. John was baffled and looked to Adam.

"For Mehitable," said Adam. He looked to his sister with concern. "Doth Goody Draper know thou brought parsnips?"

Lydia frowned, turned to John and slowly fanned the parsnips. "To draw Mehitable nigh when she is most disagreeable." John was so intrigued with the sway of the parsnip tops his head bobbed in concert with Lydia's slow fanning.

Lydia turned to her brother. "Our flock needs tending. Mehitable needs to be watched with diligence. We must pay John Shepherd justly."

She gestured to the table and asked, "Is this just, John Shepherd?" John continued bobbing his dead, and Lydia answered. "If it is not, I will bring more."

John grabbed the parsnips from Lydia and the fanning ceased. "Nae to worry, me will care for Mehitable."

Adam ushered his sister back into the dazzling sunlight. He paused to enjoy the panorama as Lydia went northeast, back up the rise to Mehitable, who was standing away from the other sheep with sad eyes. "Thy land, truly magnificent," said Adam.

John's pride swelled as Adam turned toward the Lydia and Mehitable. The ewe still had Lydia's attention, and John wanted her to appreciate his New Scotland as much as Adam did. "Lydia," he said, "does me estate remind you of your former home?"

She arose from her crouch and turned from Mehitable. Her somber face had returned. "Some things are best left in the past, John Shepard."

Adam immediately ceased admiring the view and turned back to Lydia. "Mehitable is in good care," he said. "We must tarry no longer."

The two strode with an abruptness that unnerved John. "Lydia Draper," said John. She turned back, and her shimmery curls bounced. John had her attention, but nothing to say. He spoke anyway. "Me name is John Law, not John Shepard." He rued his impulsive utterance as soon as he said it.

Lydia's cheeks flushed. She drew her cloak close and raised her hood over her head as her eyes drifted toward the ground. Staring at the ground, she said, "Why of course it is. Forgive me."

The Drapers left as they had arrived, a woman in a hooded cloak shuffling behind her brother. John returned to his corn stalks, but his eyes were on Lydia. When he sensed her turning back, he turned away and hacked the stalks. He wondered if she turning for him or for Mehitable? He stayed bent over, but with eyes on Lydia. He chopped intermittently. Once she was sufficiently distant, he stood erect with his hatchet at his side. Two dots moved through sparkling, autumn-hued grasslands and finally disappeared.

Lydia's image appeared often, especially at night, when John's loneliness became unbearable. She was a pure English lass with an innocent demeanor, yet her sashay, demurring eyes, bouncing curls and intrigue with John's manner of speech belied complete innocence. Her caress and nuzzling of Mehitable appeared genuine and born out of an innate mother's love. He sensed a contrasting darkness that was hidden deep within, which was tempting. Depending on John's mood, he thought further about each of Lydia's facets. They blossomed, and she became a vision he needed to make a reality.

Chapter Twenty-one

A snow dusting from the night before, a stubborn morning chill lingering in the body and slate colored skies casting a cold, pervasive hue cried out it was December in the Colonies. But this December would be special. John pounded on the Goodman Blood's back door. A muttering Duncan could be heard shuffling down the hall. "Who doth not possess the good comportment to use the front door?" The door opened, and Duncan asked, "What art thou doing across the river?"

"Me indenture ends this month."

"On the 15th, today's the 8th."

"But me needs me winter provisions."

"Several days before thou art a free man?" asked Duncan as he shook his head. He began to close the door, but John wedged his foot in it to keep it ajar.

"Who is calling?" asked a voice from inside.

"Nobody," said Duncan, "just John Law."

John pushed past Duncan and went into the main room. "Me have come for me provisions," he said. Goodman Blood looked to Duncan for an answer.

"I told John the shepherd when I gave him his leaf fall provisions they were his last."

"That nae be true."

"Master, his indenture ends in a few days."

Blood stroked his chin and said to John, "As a free man thou must fend for thyself."

"Me knows, but Duncan said me could…"

"John Law knows not thy truth," interrupted Duncan. "He's a conniver."

John took a step toward Duncan, but Blood raised his hand. "Cease ye Scottish squabbles in my house." Blood eyed the two, sighed and said to John, "Thou hast served me well. I am grateful and intend to be just."

He turned to Duncan and said, "Gather this man's winter provisions." Duncan grimaced and headed out. "But Duncan, take stock of what thou dost gather."

Blood turned back and riveted his stare into John's forehead. "This Scottish man can repay me next year." Blood took several steps, seemingly in thought and turned back to John. "Thou shall repay me first, with a measure for my generosity. Thy lease payment shant be paid until my debts are satisfied."

"Lease?" asked John.

"Payable to Concord," said Blood. "Free men pay rent."

"But me owns me land."

"Concord owns all of New Grant."

"Nae all of it. Major Willard owns his land."

"Major Willard hath protected us for years." Blood straighten his posture. "His land is a mere pittance for the safety Concord hath enjoyed."

"And there be others," said John. "Some of your kin."

Blood arched his head back and narrowed his eyes. "My kinfolk earned their land, too."

"Then how does me own me land?" asked John.

"Who told thee thou could own land?"

"William Awbrey."

Blood's face was deadpanned. "I have never heard of a Goodman William Awbrey."

"He signed me indenture over to you."

Blood's eyes shifted to Duncan, who had drifted back into the room to eavesdrop. Glaring at Duncan, Blood asked, "Thou saw a document?" Duncan cowered, and Blood shifted to John. "Thou can read?"

"A wee bit."

"Ah yes, Awbrey," and Blood took a few steps. "But that was so long ago." He turned back to John. "That scoundrel has fled just ahead of the creditors." John's stomach roiled, but he remained as expressionless as Nagoglancit. "Thou art fortunate that Awbrey sold thee to me," said Blood. "Sold thee to Concord, I mean." Blood paused to regain his composure. "If not, thou would still be indentured to the owners of the Ironworks. The Ironworks hath failed. Be grateful I have not turned thee over to their creditors."

"Nae," said John as he stared at Blood. "Me indenture ends in a few days."

"The creditors lost a fortune. Shall I give thee to them as recompense? They may seek retribution, just or not, and not allow thy indenture to end."

John lowered his eyes. He was powerless, and at the mercy of an Englishman, yet again. "So how much will me lease payment be?" he asked.

"Ye selectmen will determine it. I will speak for thee."

"Me'll speak for me self."

"Trust me," snorted Blood. "I will speak on thy behalf."

'Trust me' were words John had heard before. *This Blood be just another lying Englishman.*

"Ye rent will be fair and proper, I can assure ye." John's disappointment finally broke through his stone face. Blood's determined countenance relaxed. His face now expressed concern for John's well-being. "John Law, it is far more opportune to squat upon New Grant land and pay a just rent than to toil an eternity for disgruntled creditors."

Blood shifted to Duncan. "Don't tarry. Gather John Law's provisions." As Duncan scurried, Blood added, "And Duncan, help ye fellow Scottish man load his cart." Duncan shuffled down the hall muttering, but John remained. "Thou tarry too?" asked Blood.

"Me be looking for the Draper home."

"And how is poor Roger?"

"Me nae know. It be Lydia's ewe that concerns me."

"Mehitable?" Blood looked at the mantle and into the fire. Sadness came to his face, and he turned to ask, "And how is Roger's dear child?" John pondered Blood's question and changed demeanor and didn't respond. Blood poked at his logs. "Duncan will direct thee to Goodman Draper's house." He hung his poker on its hook. "God bye to you, John Law."

'God bye to you' such odd English words, thought John.

Outside, Duncan was struggling with a grain sack. John approached and asked, "Where be the Draper house?"

Duncan straightened up. "And what dost thou need with Goodman Draper?"

"Trust me," said John, "it be of grave importance to ye Master."

"Truly," said Duncan. "Follow the road around the mill pond to a wee house, the one in great disrepair." John drew his wrap tighter and hastened away. "Ye provisions?" asked Duncan.

"Put them in me cart," said John. Duncan muttered something, which John ignored. "Of immediate concern to ye master," said John over his shoulder while jogging toward town.

John slowed his pace to admire the stately homes. But as he neared the manse, he quickened it. Ice glazed the edges of the mill pond, and John drew his cloak close and hunched his shoulders. A man, puttering along with a cane for support, paused to watch John approach.

"What cheer?" he asked.

John nodded, but didn't break stride, leaving the man to wonder about the unfriendly stranger.

At the humblest of homes, John opened a gate, which hung askew by a lone hinge on a stone slab. He paused at the door, wrung his hands, adjusted his wrap so that it hung at equal length, and knocked. A drawstring raised the latch, and it clicked. John was relieved to see Adam.

"John Shepard, this is unexpected," said Adam.

"It be Mehitable," said John. Lydia scurried to Adam's side. "She be ornery, and shuns the flock."

"Hast thou offered parsnips?" asked Lydia.

"Aye, but Mehitable still shuns me."

Adam turned to Lydia. "It must mean the ram was successful." Lydia raised a hand to conceal her blushing cheek.

"Invite the caller in and shut the door," said a feminine voice from inside. As John stepped inside, a bonneted woman placed her sampler on a table and arose. Her brow had furrows seemingly etched by life's travails. Yet when she said, "Mary, Goodwife of Roger Draper," she seemed proud and less beaten down. And when she gestured to a woman similar in age to Lydia and said, "And my daughter, Deborah Hadlock," her faced glowed.

John, confused by the different surnames, wrinkled his brow.

"I was Goodman Nathaniel Hadlock relict,"[24] said Mary. "May God grant him eternal peace." Mary bowed her head. "But later, the widower, Goodman Draper, and I were wed."

"Who hast come calling?" asked an angular man, who hobbled into the room. His doublet was weaved from fine wool,

---

24 *The common term used for what we would now call a widow.*

but, like the house, in need of repair. Wrinkles etched his face too, and his squinty eyes were blood shot and lacked focus.

"John the shepherd," responded Adam. "Lydia and I can tend to him, Father."

Mary moved to Roger and said, "Thou should return to ye back chamber."

Roger brushed his hand at Mary and stepped deeper into the room. "Well Goodman John Shepherd," he said, "I arrived on the *Eleanor*, right after Governor Winthrop arrived on the *Arbella*."

"It was some time after the *Arbella*," said Mary.

"How would thou know?" asked Roger. "Thou were not with me." He turned back to John. "And when did ye arrive?"

"Long after thee," said Lydia.

Roger smiled and headed away. But he turned back to ask, "And thy ship?"

"The *Unity*," said John.

"I don't remember her." Roger stood wondering, before disappearing into the back room. Mary exhaled and picked up her sampler.

Lydia turned to Adam and said, "Thou knowest how disagreeable Mehitable can get. We must go now."

"I've got chores to finish."

"Then I will go alone."

Mary dropped the sampler into her lap and ceased sewing. "Not alone. Not across the river."

"But John Law can protect me," replied Lydia.

"I forbid it," and Mary arose and looked toward Deborah, who nodded her agreement. Lydia stepped closer to Adam.

"Me'll care for Mehitable until you can come," said John.

"So be it," said Lydia with an emphatic nod of her head. "But I'll bring more corn cake for thy trouble," and she smiled.

"Corn cake?" asked Mary. She looked to Adam for an answer, but he didn't respond.

"Now me know why Mehitable be so ornery," said John, "me'll know what to do." He straightened his posture and turned to Mary. "Me tended many ewes in Scotland after the ram had his way with them." He said while chuckling, "Me father's prize ram was an eager sort, mounting every ewe on the brae."

Mary and Deborah gasped, and Lydia quickly said, "But Mehitable is different."

Mary regained her composure to say, "This Scottish man seems capable of tending Mehitable." She honed in on John. "Daylight is waning. Thou should not tarry. We thank thee for thy time."

Noticing Lydia's disappointment, Adam chimed in. "I promise to complete my chores tomorrow, and we will go for Mehitable the day following."

"Can I go with Adam?" asked Lydia.

"Perhaps if…" and Mary paused as Roger shuffled back into the room.

"My mind is as sharp as a well-honed axe," said Roger. "Thought I was growing daft, but then it came." Roger's eyes now lacked their bleariness, and he focused them on John. "The *Unity* was that slave ship. Why thou art a Scottish man." Mary fumbled with the top of her dress. "Huh," said Roger as he shuffled back to his room. "A Scottish Catholic in my house."

A silence lingered until John broke it. "God bye to you," he said. The words still seemed odd to John, but perhaps they were proper words for the English.

As John left, Mary stooped to pick up her sampler. Roger called from the back chamber. "Lydia," said Mary, "tend to thy father's burdens." Once Lydia had left, Mary asked, "Corn cakes, Adam?"

"Barter for Mehitable's care."

"To that Scottish man; how many?"

"One, possibly two."

"Why that's thievery. He is but an ignorant shepherd. He didn't even know about Mehitable."

"He knew," said Adam. "I surmise Lydia hath caught his fancy."

"Adam, how dare thee," and Mary dropped her sampler into her lap. "A Scottish shepherd, surely your sister is deserving of a greater station."

Lydia returned and said, "Father's cider is too watery."

Mary sighed. "Then he hath ladled a recent batch. It hath not sung enough."

"I think Goodman Draper finished the older batch," said Deborah. Mary swung her head in disgust as Lydia returned to her father.

"Greater station Goody Draper?" asked Adam.

Mary continued stitching as Adam awaited a response. She finally stopped and said, "Thou best get to thy chores. I'm sure your sister will have a yearning to see Mehitable."

As John headed toward town, he pulled his wrap tighter. He had sensed Lydia's warmth, but it was insufficient to overcome the iciness of the others. His excuse for coming was lame, even if Lydia believed him. Perhaps his description of the ram could have been more delicate? Several alternatives ran through his mind, but he concluded his thinking with *Ah these English, so concerned with their words.* He thought about Goodman Draper. *What did he mean by his 'huh'? He nae be concerned with his words.*

John continued to wonder about his visit until he spotted a cloaked man hobbling from the manse. Their paces would have them arriving concurrently. John slowed, hoping to avoid a meeting. But the hobbling man adjusted his pace too. As they approached one another, the man, who John sensed was The Reverend, asked, "How do you fare?"

John nodded without breaking his pace.

"Thou art the shepherd of New Grant."

John stopped and turned back slowly.

"And a Scottish man," said The Reverend. His eyes were as penetrating as an owl's. John froze, and The Reverend hobbled close. "And thy servitude was at ye Ironworks." John's heart was a jackhammer. He fought to gather his Nagoglancit expression, not knowing if he had been successful. "And were thou a woodsman?"

"Nae," and John's temple scar, which hadn't throbbed for some time, now pounded. The Reverend raised an eyebrow. "Me be a collier," said John.

"Thou seem too young to be a collier." The Reverend's eyebrow arched higher.

"James Moor be the collier. Me be his apprentice."

"And where be this James Moor?"

"Me nae know."

"Were there other colliers?"

John nodded and gulped, wondering where the conversation was going. He regretted he had been so circumspect. Trying to deceive a wise old owl was foolish. He could feel the talons readying for the kill.

"And their names?" asked The Reverend.

John shrugged and gestured hopelessness.

"And where be they now?"

John wrung his hands, shifted his feet and did not respond.

"A pity, Concord is in need of a collier." The Reverend's eyes ceased their skepticism. John's heartbeat throttled back as he sensed the talons releasing him. He turned to leave. "And on what ship did thou arrive?"

The claw grip returned. John wasn't free yet, and his stomach roiled as he said, "The *Unity*."

"Was there a woodsman MacLawson with thee?"

John had dreaded that question whenever he neared the manse. He thought he would be prepared when it came. But the question pierced through him, and he forgot his rehearsed responses. He couldn't speak, but thought he might have nodded his head.

"And where art this MacLawson?"

"Um," John reined in his fears, "taken north to the Piscataqua perhaps." The Reverend's eyes remained skeptical. "Aye, MacLawson be an ornery Scot. Perhaps he be in jail, or maybe he be dead."

The Reverend nodded an agreement.

His skepticism seemed to be ebbing, and John wanted to stem it completely. "William Awbrey might know about MacLawson."

"Awbrey is gone, perhaps to England," said The Reverend. John feigned surprised, and The Reverend grew distant. He stepped away and thought aloud, "Ah, my merry England." Sadness etched into The Reverend's face. He ceased wandering and stared at John. "God doth have burdens for all of us, doth he not?"

John had feared meeting this revered man of God, this nobleman from a different world who could deliver the wrath of a Puritan God upon him. But vengeance wasn't delivered. Instead an insight about life was offered: 'God doth have burdens for us'. John sneered as he thought about his many burdens, which were far heavier than this man of privilege would ever understand. But The Reverend had said 'for all of us'. What possibly could be his burdens? John couldn't fathom an answer, yet oddly he sensed a connection with him.

The Reverend lowered his head and hobbled across the road. He paused to catch his breath. His skeptical, arched eye returned, and so did John's unease. Maybe John's MacLawson burden wasn't over. Maybe The Reverend's vengeance was not wrath, but an eternal threat of it that John needed to bear as long as The Reverend lived. 'God doth have burdens for us' continued to flicker in his mind. John knew his past and current burdens, but what about future ones? How severe might they be?

John lowered his head and resumed his travels. He had a cart to pick up, which by now was loaded with provisions to get him through the winter. He also had enchanting thoughts of Lydia to fill his dreams.

Chapter Twenty-two

Mehitable was growing ornerier with each day, seemingly ready to deliver. Lydia hadn't returned, and John tortured himself for reasons why. He had sensed a spark from Lydia, but he could have been wrong. Or maybe the family simply snuffed it out? 'A Scottish man, huh' was a phrase, which John had pondered often for meaning. Maybe his visions of Lydia were nothing but illusions.

But this day, a familiar squeaking distracted John from his repeated worry. The squeak had a constant rhythm, grew louder and finally stopped.

"Andrew Adams, what brings you to New Scotland?"

"Me be carting supplies to Nagog Pond."

"Me thought them Indians left?"

"The Praying Indians still be there. A preacher offered me a farthing to journey out, said I would be doing the Lord's work. So I took his farthing, and then sold them Indians hard water for five shillings. Aye, there be the Lord's work."

"Your cart profits you well."

"Almost lost it to Sam Bennett, though," said Andrew. "Times be bad when the Ironworks failed. Bennett, Gifford, Awbrey, they all be fighting among themselves."

"But you had papers for your cart?"

"All me had was 'trust me' and no papers," snorted Andrew. "If the Aid Society[25] hadn't helped, me nae would be carting."

"Aid society?"

"It be Scots who help us when dealing with the English." Andrew looked around and turned back to John. "You be prospering well." He noticed John's prideful smile and added, "Aye, an estate fit for a Clan Chieftain. Show me it, me Lord."

John smiled and swept his hand to follow the river. "Me moat protects me from the English."

"Aye, goot," and Andrew laughed.

They took intermittent steps as John expounded about the meadows, ever flowing brook, woodlands and what lay beyond. It was more detail than Andrew wanted, but he listened, relishing in his friend's delight. Andrew pointed in the direction of Nagog Pond and asked, "Those woodlands be yours, too?"

"Aye, and them Indians me suppose."

"Tis a wee bit curious, eh? The English take from the Indians, and whoever settles on it, owns it."

"If they be English," said John as his enthusiasm ebbed.

---

25 *In 1657, twenty-eight Scottish men signed the "Laws Rules and Order of the Poor Boxes Society" in Boston to form the Scottish Charitable Society. The Society was founded in part to assist a specific group of destitute Scots, captured at the battles of Dunbar and Worcester, who were shipped to the Colonies.*

"Johnnie, if you be having troubles, maybe the Society can help."

John shook his head. "Me land be mine. Me nae need any Aid Society."

"Still a stubborn laddie, are we," said Andrew. John's scowl remained. "It be alright, me understands." The estate tour resumed, and Andrew searched for uplifting conversation. After a few minutes, he said, "The English will change, now that their Lord Protector be dead."

"Aye, t'was glorious when me heard Cromwell died." But John's smile quickly left. "But his son be just like him."

As John stopped the tour near his shelter, Andrew said, "Johnnie, the English fear the Monarchy will return." His eyes became diabolical. "Me have seen their fear when they talk of Charles. It be a bonny good sight.

John was baffled by Andrew's logic.

"Charles," said Andrew, "the King we fought for."

"Me fought for me Clan Commander."

"Nae laddie, we fought for King Charles. We be his defenders, so we can nae be Cromwell's prisoners."

"Me thinks you had too much drink this morn."

Andrew laughed, looked at John and laughed again. Andrew rubbed his hands and shuddered. "Take me inside, me Lord, and let me warm me hands."

"Me have some spirits to warm the rest of you. But nae more talk about we be King Charles's defenders."

"If Charles be king someday, these English will change their ways." John still couldn't follow Andrew's logic, but it offered a glimmer of hope. Maybe a Scottish man's future in an English world could improve.

Chapter Twenty-three

John had overslept and awoke shivering. His firepit was flickering embers among ashes. The water bucket, next to his emptied cider cup, had iced over. He smacked the back of his hands into it, cupped his hands and gulped. He repeated his routine several times and splashed a final cupping on his face. He brushed the water that was on his face into his hair and blew on his hands while rubbing them. Once sensation came, he left for more wood.

The hoarfrost was melting, and the meadow sparkled. He jutted his face to the sun and inhaled deeply. He said 'good morning' to Mehitable, his odd surrogate for Lydia, and thought about conversing more. But his daily routine of talking to Mehitable was no longer uplifting, and he went back to his shelter with his wood.

He added twigs to the embers, blew and the flickering grew to a steady flame. His stomach growled, but his samp bowl was a hardened paste, sprinkled with ice crystals. He opted to ignore his stomach for now. Eventually, the fire was sufficient to warm water, and he trickled it down his samp scoop, washing bits of corn into his bowl. He stirred and tasted the familiar, watery mix. He looked around for some dried berries to mix into the samp until he realized he had eaten them last night. The firepit flame danced, and he thought about talking to his mother. But those conversations, like the ones with Mehitable, had grown gloomy too. After finishing his samp, he drew his woolen covering tight and dozed.

"John Law, we've come for our sheep," said a voice from outside. John rubbed his eyes and whipped off his covering. He brushed his hair back and shook his head to remove the cobwebs. He stepped out, and Adam gimped along the hillside with Lydia following him.

"How's Mehitable?" Adam asked.

"Ornery," said John, and he pointed. "There, away from the others."

"Oh," said Lydia as she clasped her hands under her chin, "she is ready." She dashed to Mehitable, but the ewe sidled away until soft utterances and a parsnip coaxed her back.

"I fell while repairing the roof," said Adam. "Still quite lame."

"Aye, me see."

"And Goody Draper's son refused to journey into this wilderness to gather our sheep. But Lydia persisted, told Goody Draper 'she would come alone'."

John raised an eye, and a splash of brightness came into his gloominess.

"New Grant is further than I remembered," said Adam as he looked for his sheep. He limped to his sister and said, "It is mid-day. We must not tarry."

John helped the Drapers to gather all their sheep. Eventually, the bleating ceased, and Lydia sidled up to John. "Corn cake for thy troubles," she said as she handed John a biscuit. She noticed corn kernels clinging to his whiskers and asked, "Hast thou fatigued of corn?"

"Nae, me seldom eats corn."

"Huh," said Lydia as she reached into her pocket. "I have an added treat; preserves."

"That's the last of them," said Adam.

Lydia turned to Adam. "John Law did more than he bartered for. If thou hadn't tarried so long, then…"

"Lydia, I could scarcely walk."

"As thou sayest," and Lydia turned back to John. "A smidgeon of preserves is but a pittance for such kindness." Lydia removed a wooden strip from her pocket, and John knifed a glob of preserves onto his biscuit. He savored the sweetness, oblivious to Adam's dismay. He brushed a sticky drop from his whiskers and corn kernels fell. He wondered if Lydia had noticed, but her attention was diverted to Adam, who began to move the sheep home.

"Use me bridge," said John. "It be shorter, and easier for your leg."

"Through the woodlands?" asked Adam.

"There be a path."

Adam flashed a dismissive hand. "I'll follow the river to the North Bridge."

"It be too far. Me'll show you the way." John turned to Lydia and said, "To repay you for the sweets." Lydia lowered her eyes, and John wondered if he had he said something inappropriate.

The two led the sheep back to Concord, pausing often for Adam to keep pace. John was anxious about his previous utterance that may have been inappropriate, and he searched for suitable conversation. "Mehitable seems contented, now that she be with you," said John. "She missed you."

"And I missed her dearly. My heart desired to come to thy New Scotland sooner. But Adam, well thou knowest."

"You were away so long. Me became worried." Lydia smiled, and it tingled John's being. "Me told Mehitable 'not to worry, you'd be here soon'." Lydia stopped walking. "I talked with her each day."

Admiration swept across Lydia's face. "Why John Law, thou art truly a caring man," she said. "Had I known, I would have brought more treats than just a corn cake and preserves."

"Seeing you and Mehitable together be treats enough." Lydia blushed, and John could have savored the moment for an eternity. But Adam hobbled up, massaging his leg.

"The South Bridge," said John as he pointed. "You be home soon."

"This is a more direct footpath," said Lydia. "Far easier for thy leg, is it not Adam?" Adam was in too much pain to answer. Lydia turned to John. "Both Adam and I are indebted to thee."

John grew uneasy and took a few steps away from Lydia. He didn't want Adam to think he and Lydia had become too friendly. "And me footpath lets me avoid the North Bridge and the town center," said John.

"But ye town center hath such good cheer," said Lydia.

"Aye, good cheer, and me misses it dearly," said John. "But the North Bridge be haunted."

"It is what lay beyond the Bridge that causes ye haunt," said Lydia. "Those haunting sounds of pagans powwowing strike terror into God fearing men and innocent children."

The thick clouds, which had loomed on the western horizon, were now over New Grant. The sun's brilliance was gone, the winds increased, and what had begun as a glorious day, grew ominous. "How didst thou learn of this passageway?" asked Lydia.

"Nagoglancit."

Her smile left as she asked, "An Indian?" *A curious question for such a name*, thought John. *Of course he was an Indian.* "But he hath removed, and only the Praying Indians remain?" asked Lydia.

John nodded.

Lydia drew her wrap closer, and they both headed to the South Bridge. The easy conversation was over, and John wondered why. He considered several ways to resume the easy banter, but Lydia was striding with an impenetrable purpose. He didn't say a word until they reached the bridge. "We should wait for your brother."

"Adam knows his way from hither. I'll take Mehitable and the others."

The wind gusted, and a chill pierced through John as waited for Adam. "Lydia went ahead," said John as Adam neared.

"Be best. A storm may be coming," said a bent over Adam. He stood erect. "We are safe from New Grant." He continued while breathing heavily, "Goody Draper will understand." He took a step and stopped. "Let's tarry a bit more."

John waited as Adam inhaled more deeply than before. "Do you know an Indian named Nagoglancit?" asked John.

Adam furled his eyebrow and shook his head.

"Does Lydia?"

Adam's eyes widened, and he said, "We best not tarry." The wind swirled, and the bridge swayed as water sloshed against its supports and lapped the river bank. "Thou should return to New Grant, John Law." Adam stepped on his arched foot, and his leg buckled. John came alongside, draped Adam's arm over his shoulder, and they headed to the Draper home three-legged style.

John talked at first, but he soon realized Adam was in pain and uninterested in conversation. They continued in silence, pausing often, before arriving at the Draper house. The gate swung on both hinges as they passed through it. John latched it securely and helped Adam to the door. From behind the house, the barn door banged. "Me'll shut it," said John. "You be all right?" he asked.

Adam grimaced and said, "I thank thee, John Law."

John didn't know how to respond, but he appreciated the words. He went around back, grabbed the banging door and pulled it shut from within the barn. Soft cooing now replaced

The Immigrant

the howling wind. Lydia was on her knees, stroking her ewe. "How is my poor, suffering brother?" she asked.

"We made it."

"He was in such pain, yet I kept persisting we come." Lydia reflected more. "If not for thee, his journey may have been too arduous. Thou art a good man, John Law." John was at a loss for words again. His being tingled like it had earlier when they were on the meadow. Lydia ceased stroking Mehitable and arose. "She needs her rest too."

John unlatched the door, and the wind nearly snapped it out his hands. They stepped outside, and John forced the door shut and re-latched it. Buffeted by the wind, they struggled to the house and went inside.

"Mercy, such wind," said Mary Draper. "Praise the Lord: ye are safe from that wretched wilderness, New Grant."

Adam sat on a chair next to the fire with his lame leg on a stool. A pot hung above the fire, steaming pleasant aromas. John salivated, moved closer to the flame and rubbed his hands. Lydia glanced at Mary, at John and back to Mary. Mary remained expressionless, but looked at Deborah, who shrugged. "Will thou sup with us?" asked Mary.

John's eyes darted to Lydia, who had an enticing smile. The other women were expressionless. A long-legged man, perhaps several years older than John, hurried into the room. His posture was stiff, his head tilted back, and his face seemed mildly shocked.

"Of course John Law will stay," said Adam. "It's the fitting and proper thing for us Drapers to do." He stared at the lanky man, "And for ye Hadlocks to do, Nathaniel, my good stepbrother."

"Lydia, set another place for our guest," said Mary.

"No need," said Nathaniel. "I fancy not to sup."

"Thy presence would be most desired," said Mary. But Nathaniel marched back to his room, ignoring his mother's request. Adam forced himself up, put on a heavy mitten and brought the pot to the table.

"Thy father is ailing," said Mary. "And without Nathaniel, will thou offer thanks to the Lord?" Adam and the women turned their palms up and looked heavenward. He said an extended grace, thanking the Lord for their safe return and for John's kindness. He concluded the grace with 'truly Lord, let it be so'. Adam removed the lid, and the aroma swept across the table.

John salivated and said, "Me's not had meat for so long."

"Alas, it's a mere re-heat," said Mary. "It may be nothing but pottage now."

John scooped the few chunks of meat from his bowl first that Adam had given to him. Once it and the vegetables were devoured, he tilted his bowl and sucked until an ear grating slurp told him it was dry. The other four bowls were still half full, and John wondered if he had acted improperly.

"More boiled dinner, John?" asked Mary.

John's eyes darted about for an answer. There wasn't one. "Me thanks ye," said John as he offered his bowl. Another surge of unease came to John as he thought, *did me just say 'ye'? Me God, me sound like an Englishman.*

"Ye savor thy supper with such vigor," said Mary.

"Aye, and you be a good cooker," said John.

"Lydia did most of it. She is the 'good cooker'," said Mary. Mary looked at Lydia and smiled her smug amusement of John's words. Lydia didn't smile back.

With a full belly and warm body, fatigue oozed through John. He longed to sit near the fire with a covering over him and doze. He relished the Draper's hominess, wishing it could last, but knowing it couldn't. "Me need to be going," said John as he arose. When he opened the door, cold air rushed in, along with snowflakes. Snow was piled at the door jambs, and the blanketed ground swirled with the wind.

"Alas, thou must not journey on this dreadful night," said Mary as she arose with concern. "Perhaps the barn, we have plenty of fresh hay since our flock has been at New Grant." She shook her head. "How foolish of me, thou knowest where our flock hath resided."

John looked at Mary and glanced at Lydia. The draft from the still open door was chilling. "Then to the barn it be," he said.

"We shall bring thee woolens for thy warmth," said Mary as the door shut. She sighed and asked Adam, "The barn is fitting and proper, isn't it?"

"Darkness hath settled upon Concord," said Adam. "Our neighbors will tarry by their hearths and not venture out. No one will know that John Law slept in ye barn."

Mary paced, talking aloud, "Such a quandary isn't it? But this good man cannot journey on such a night." Lydia re-entered the room with an armful of woolen coverings. She placed them down and swung her cloak over her shoulders. "Mercy no," said Mary. "I'll take them. Stay with thy brother."

Inside the barn, John wrapped the woolens over him that Mary had brought earlier and piled hay to form a bed. He longed for a warm house and Lydia. Yet, unlike his monotonous, gloomy days of the recent past, this day ended with joy and optimism. He cuddled a nearby sheep and dozed.

A door creaked, and radiance blinded an awakening John. "Thou hast made friends during ye night," said Lydia. John rubbed his eyes. Mehitable stood alone in the corner, looking at Lydia and her brother. "Mehitable has driven all the sheep to thee," said Lydia with a smile.

Adam stepped closer. "Lydia made flummery for breakfast."

"With plenty of dried fruit and oats," said Lydia. "Thou must have fatigued of corn by now."

"Goody Draper says 'thou must breakfast with us before starting ye journey'," said Adam. "The snow depth shant cause thy journey any problems."

John arose as the two left. He brushed off the hay and gathered the woolens. Adam returned and peered around the barn door. "Don't tell Goody Draper thou will journey on the main roads," he said. "Let her believe thy journey will be on ye secret passageway."

John smiled as he considered what Adam had just said. He could understand why Goody Draper would not want the neighbors to know a Scottish stranger slept in her barn. Yet Adam seemed to care less about it, and John appreciated it. As he picked up the woolens, he thought maybe Adam someday would be a fine brother-in-law. John was more cheerful than he had been in weeks. He headed out of the barn for flummery with Lydia.

Chapter Twenty-four

March 1659

John missed his talks with Mehitable, and with the warming weather, he decided to go see her. The meadow was a white sea with only swirling drifts providing darkened contrasts. Across the bridge, snow laden evergreens and bare limbed hardwoods arose from an impenetrable white fortress. John's short cut was snowed in. Using fence rails, the river and smoke from distant houses for bearings, John trudged toward Concord Center. As he tired, reality settled in. Mehitable was a lame excuse to see Lydia. Would the Drapers think similarly?

When he reached the occasionally traveled path, the once virgin snow had been trodden and walking was easier. Behind John were his meadow tracks, which would mark his return route since the lone smoke curl on the western horizon from his dying fire would soon be gone. He shuddered as he thought of returning to a freezing shelter. When he reached the North Bridge, his usual uneasiness about it came, and he jogged across it. Smoke streams lined the horizon. Hopefully, the townsfolk were all nestled inside.

But as John neared the Center, people were gathered near the Manse, and a group of men was near the meetinghouse. *Was it the Sabbath?* John's unease returned. A head peered from the gathering of men, stared and turned back. Several women stood near the roadside, and when one headed toward John, he became anxious again.

She glanced at his snow covered boots and dampened breeches. "Thou hast journeyed far," she said. "Hast thou arrived to pay thy respects?" This woman's somber expression was similar to those she had just left. "The good men gather thither," she said as she pointed toward the meetinghouse. "So sad, our shepherd will no longer lead his flock." John had heard The Reverend had been ailing, but didn't know he died. "Now he is at eternal rest in the bosom of God," she said. She sniffed and brushed away some tears.

A wry smile crossed John's face as he thought, *and me John MacLawson burden be at eternal rest, too.* He feigned grief and said, "God hath burdens for each of us."

The woman shuffled back to her group and said, "Ye stranger be such a righteous man." She asked of Goody Davis, who was among the group, "Dost thou know him?"

"Yes, and a righteous man he is not," she said as she crossed her arms. "He is that Scottish man from New Grant, John the Shepherd."

John thought further about the woman's sad face and now rued his flippant thought. He decided to pay his respects. As he moved toward the meetinghouse, a few men stared, and one stood with arms crossed. John paused, and when the sun glistened off the pillory stage, he retreated. He quickened his pace until he passed the mill pond. He didn't belong with the group at the meetinghouse.

As he ambled further from the crowd of mourners, he rehearsed possible excuses for his visit. A few seemed plausible, but once smoke from the Draper chimney was visible, they lost credibility too. He considered retreating, but a thought flickered. *"God hath burdens for each of us"*, and he rapped on the Draper's door.

"Good morn, to what do we owe this visit?" asked Mary Draper.

John banged his boots on the door jamb and said, "Me was in town to pay me respects to Reverend Bulkeley." Mary's face saddened, and Adam's expressed an apparent disbelief. Lydia took a few eager steps, slowed and stood near Adam. She twitched her fingers as John said, "And me decided to visit Mehitable while I was in Concord Center."

"Nathaniel is paying his respects, too," said Mary. "Didst thou see him?" John shook his head, but was relieved to know Nathaniel was away.

"A dark day for our blessed Concord," said Roger, who was slouched in his chair and holding his mug.

"Goodman Draper hath been so distraught," said Mary.

"Our bonds were formed soon after the *Arbella* arrived," said Roger.

"Aye, me knows," said John, "the *Arbella*."

Roger squinted and looked to Mary. "The Scottish man?" He slouched again, and after a few moments his head jolted up. "From the *Unity*," he said.

"Aye," said John as he rubbed his fingers against his thumb, wondering where the discussion might go next.

Roger settled back and took a sip. "He led the faithful to this wilderness, became Concord's first Reverend and carved a plantation hither for his flock."

"But thou were still in Watertown when that occurred," said Mary.

"I was here when Reverend Jones led the disobedient south, after his split with Reverend Bulkeley," said Roger as he glared at Mary. His eyes were now alert and on John. "One of Reverend Bulkeley's son betrayed him, followed Reverend Jones to Connecticut. Would thou abandon thy father?" he asked.

John shook his head, but Roger's question evoked thoughts of his father, which now were sad memories of his inability to honor his father's dying request. He shook his head again to erase the painful reminders.

Roger looked to Adam. "Thou betrayed me. Will thou betray again?"

"No Father," said an inexpressive Adam, "if ye can act civil." Lydia rubbed Adam's arm, and he smiled an acknowledgement for her compassion. But his smile seemed to be a thin veneer, which barely covered his pain.

"Reverend Bulkeley yearned for England, but God had called him here." Roger took another swig, and his eyes grew distant again as he continued. "He brought peace to our plantation." Roger leaned forward and placed his palms around his mug. "But Concord will never be Concord again, and with Cromwell dead, neither will England."

Lydia released her hand from Adam's arm and said to John, "Mehitable birthed two lambs. She was all alone." Lydia's excitement ebbed as she said, "Guess she didn't need me after all." She turned to Mary and asked, "Can I show them to John?"

Mary glanced at Roger, who was still pre-occupied with his mug, and at Adam, who nodded. "It is still daylight," she said. "But do not tarry long, dear."

The two left, and when John opened the barn door, Mehitable sprung to her feet. Her stare said 'don't you dare enter, John Law'.

"Can thy friend, John the shepherd, see thy babies?" asked Lydia. Her voice broke Mehitable's stare, and Lydia went and stroked her. "Come in John," said Lydia. "She will let thee." Lydia picked up a lamb, nestled it close and kissed it. She held it out to John, who stroked it once. "Such joys, I hope we can keep them both," said Lydia. "But times are trying, and thou knowest Father."

"He and The Reverend be close?"

"They were, but Father fell from his good graces." Lydia cuddled the lamb and said, "He longs for an earlier time. Guess it's normal." She placed the lamb down and turned to John. "Dost thou long for earlier times?"

"Me suppose, but me would be in Scotland."

"Father longs for England." Lydia picked up the other lamb and kissed it. "Dost thou long for Scotland?"

"Me long for me mum." Lydia ceased cuddling and looked at John while massaging under the lamb's neck. She had never seen such melancholy in him before. Lydia wanted to ask more, but didn't think it would be proper.

"Scotland nae be the same," said John. "Cromwell saw to that."

"Father thinks Cromwell was our Lord Protector."

"And you, Lydia?" asked John.

"Lord Protector, well I guess. Father believes it, so it must be true."

"Nae, you misunderstood me. Do you long for earlier times?"

"We can't journey back, John." Lydia placed the lamb down and turned from John. "Time giveth thy soul distance to heal thy wounds." John took a step nearer to Lydia. He wanted more, but didn't know how to ask. Lydia retreated further from John while looking at the rafters. "If thou journey back," she said as she wrung her hands, "wounds will return." John took another step toward Lydia just as Adam came in.

"Goody Draper desires thee to return," said Adam. Lydia turned slightly and brushed her cheek. "Is Mehitable faring well?" asked Adam. Lydia nodded without facing her brother. Adam glanced at John and back to his sister. "Lydia, art thou faring well?"

Lydia brushed her cheek and said, "Most surely."

She left with Adam, leaving John to wonder about her abrupt change in demeanor. Mehitable bleated and moved toward her lambs while staring at the lone, remaining intruder. John knew he didn't belong and left.

Chapter Twenty-five

Summer 1659

"Thou hast trodden a determined path to Goodman Draper's house," said an approaching stranger. John was startled and looked back at the grassland, swaying in a summer breeze, which no longer camouflaged a worn path.

"Aye," said John, "it be a quicker route to town."

The plump, well-dressed, middle aged man stepped nearer. "And quicker to Goodman Draper's door. Thou art John Law." The man stared as he awaited John's acknowledgement. John was shaken and only tilted his head. The stranger shuffled closer. "And how is Goodman Draper?"

"He seems to be failing."

"So I heard," and the man grimaced. He locked into John's eyes and asked, "And how is dear Lydia?" John swallowed and remained expressionless while holding eye contact. "Thou dost tend sheep. Surely thou hast met Lydia." The stranger broke his imposing stare. "John Hoare, Esquire," he said. His expression relaxed, and unlike many Englishmen, his smile seemed genuine. John's innate mistrust of the English waned.

"Lydia's sheep once grazed on my land, north of the former Draper farm," said Hoare. "When I came upon her, she was mortified. She said Goodman Draper told her 'it was his land'." He thought for a moment. "Ah, that Roger," he said as he shook his head. "Such an innocent child, I paid it no matter, but that was before the Indian scare."

"Indian scare, but they be Praying Indians," said John.

"Not back then."

"Heathens, eh?"

"No. Just a few filled with drink," said Hoare. His determined expression had returned. "People do evil things when filled with drink, as Goodman Draper well knows. Unlike most," and Hoare shuffled a few steps, "I do not deem the Indians as heathens." He turned back. "Surely thou hast met some."

"Aye, Nagoglancit, Squaw Sachem."

"Ah, Nagoglancit," and Hoare's smile returned, "one of the Squaw's favorites."

"He be her son?" asked John.

"Maybe, one never knows with the Indians. The Squaw has many."

"Sons?"

"No, favorites," said a chuckling Hoare. "Squaw Sachem is like ye elder clansman."

"Can nae be. She be a lass."

"Truly, she is a lass and a sachem." Hoare's smile waned. "Wasn't right what Concord's good men did, smashing fences, driving their cattle through the Nashobah's crops."

"What good men?"

Hoare gripped the sides of his waistcoat and stood straight. "As a barrister, I require evidence before I accuse, even though a village simpleton can surmise the culprits." He leaned toward John and shaded his mouth. "Take heed of who settles on Indian land, and who usurps the choice parcels." Hoare leaned back, and John's smile said 'aye, me knows'.

John turned to continue his journey, and Hoare asked, "And fair Lydia?" John turned back. Hoare had gripped his waistcoat again. "Hast thou been alone with her?"

"Me have."

"And hast thou been a man of decency?"

Surprise rippled through John's guiltless face as he nodded several times.

"And what are thy intentions?" John scuffed the ground. "Lydia must be of marrying age. Hast thou spoken to Goodman Draper?"

"Goodman Draper ails," said John.

"Then speak with Master Adam," and Hoare stepped closer, "or Master Hadlock, or Goody Draper." John slouched as Hoare came closer yet. "If thou persist to trample a path to the Draper door, thou risk besmirching fair Lydia's reputation further." Hoare pointed his finger at John and stared over it. "Make thy intentions known, John Law." He dropped his finger, and his friendly face returned. "Pray remember me, my son," and Hoare ambled back to his house.

As John continued to the Drapers, he pondered Hoare's words. He had thought often about marrying Lydia, but reality kept him from acting upon it. What Englishman would allow his daughter to wed a Scottish man? But now, Hoare's cross-examination and the apparent stir that John's frequent visits were causing were reasons to stop vacillating.

He thought about the evening, several years earlier, with Andrew Adams as they sat propped against a tree. Maybe Andrew's response had been incorrect. Maybe a Scottish man could wed a pure English lass. But Hoare's words, 'besmirching fair Lydia's reputation further', lingered and caused doubt. Was John besmirching her, or had she already been besmirched?

Chapter Twenty-six

Autumn 1659

John no longer had to offer lame excuses for visiting Lydia since Roger Draper's health continued to fail. John visited frequently, helped Adam with his chores and offered comfort to Lydia. Goody Draper now offered John the barn for overnight stays without hesitation. Nathaniel was civil, yet still aloof. John was feeling more accepted, and Hoare's urgings 'to make thy intentions known' persisted, but John was still hesitant to do so.

It was the leaf fall season, and the Draper's wood pile was as meager as it had been in the spring. Adam had procrastinated too long, and John offered his help. "Wait laddie," said John to Adam. "The lass will nae split." John spun the upright log to put the knots away from Adam's intended blow. Adam, engrossed in thought, nodded 'thanks', swung and the log fell into two pieces. As the axe hung at Adam's side, John said, "It be hard."

"I have split many logs," said Adam. "I should have known."

"Nae, it be hard when your father ails." Some life flickered back into Adam's eyes. "Me lost me father when me be a wee lad," said John as he grabbed another log. "It be hard doing me chores; consoling me mom." John placed the log on the stump. "But chores chased me worries away, and me slept worry free. Free, until me sobbing mum woke me." In John's attempt to hearten Adam, he had rubbed some raw emotions he didn't realize were still within him. He should cease rambling, but he couldn't. Oddly, this day, it was cathartic.

"One night," John said, "me mum be sobbing." He kicked the ground and turned back toward Adam. "Her sobs became whimpers, and then she lay still. Her nightly demons had left, and she slept without a stir."

"And did thou sleep without a stir?" asked Adam.

"Me was awake, and thinking about me father's dying plea."

"To honor it?"

John's eyes welled and he nodded.

"And didst thou?"

John shook his head. "Me be here laddie, nae in Scotland."

"And thy brothers?"

"There be just me." John's agitation was about to explode. So he grabbed the axe from Adam, crashed through the log and embedded it into the stump. "God damn it," said John.

"Mercy, thou hast been busy," said Mary Draper as she and Lydia came around the corner of the house. John worried his outburst may have been overheard. "Time for dinner," said Mary. "And a much needed respite."

Mary's cheeriness eased John's immediate worry about his outburst. But he was still wrapped in a self-inflicted despair and swirling down an emotional drain. He feared he would lose further emotional control in front of Lydia. "Um, nae this day," he said.

"But I have boiled a dinner for thee," said Lydia. John's eyes welled, and he turned toward the road. "With plenty of meat," she said. John turned back and forced a smile. "Come and have a posset of hulled corn and goat's milk by the hearth. And after dinner, there is pan dowdy." John kept walking. "There are plenty of parsnips in the pottage," said Lydia. John understood the inside joke, which tore at his emotions further.

Without turning around, John said, "Got me chores to do." When he reached the gate, he turned back, hesitated and continued on his way with head focused on the ground. John brushed under his eye, trying to disguise from Lydia that he was wiping a tear away, lest she be watching. Life drained from Lydia's face as she watched John leave. She continued to watch John until he disappeared from her sight. Only then, did she re-enter the house.

At the table, Nathaniel offered grace, and the usual dinner chatter followed. Lydia toyed with her food, passing time in silence, before rising to leave.

"Not hungry, dear?" asked Mary. She awaited Lydia's response. Nothing came, and she turned back to Adam. "John Law left abruptly too."

"He talked about his father's passing and distress came to him, even though it happened when he was a wee lad."

"'Wee lad'," said Mary as she smiled. "John Law hath quaintness to his words." She thought further and asked, "But so long ago, and he still grieves?"

"Misses his 'mum'," said Adam. Mary collapsed back into her chair as Adam continued. "She was a relict with an only son. The war came, and John was still young when Cromwell captured him."

"His mother," said Mary, "alone all these year." She lowered her eyes, "Alone and wondering." She ceased pondering and asked, "Doth she know John is in the Colonies?" Mary shook her head and answered her own question. "Of course she doesn't." She stared into the fireplace and spoke in barely audible tones. "She must think John is dead or… Her suffering must be unbearable." Mary broke her trance and arose. "My poor John, he hath suffered much." She shook her head back and forth, but couldn't relieve her now apparent anger. She spun back to Adam and said, "Those goodwives speak with such cruelty about my John."

"It's not cruelty." said Nathaniel. "John Law is strange, a recluse in the wilderness."

"Goody Davis relishes her cruelty," said Mary as she kneaded her apron. "As God is my witness, I know."

Adam stopped poking the fire and said, "Nathaniel, if thou knew John Law, ye might not find him strange." He returned to his poking. "Lydia's fondness doth grow, as doth John Law's."

Nathaniel inhaled and straightened up. "That strange fondness is a matter for Goodman Draper,"

"But my father ails," said Adam.

"We know," said Nathaniel. "Thus, ye matter must fall to his only son, to you Adam."

Mary's nodding head confirmed what Adam knew, and what he was trying to avoid. "I care for Lydia like she was my own daughter," said Mary. "And like any goodwife, my desire is for her to marry a good man with a proper station. But then that unseemliness occurred." Mary looked to Deborah who had been sitting quietly and listening to the conversation.

Deborah's lip quivered, and she said, "If Lydia doth not marry below her station, I fear that she is destined to be a thornback."[26] She lowered her head. "It is God's providence for Lydia to know a recluse, one who knows not." Mary's sadness grew while listening to her daughter. Deborah sniffed, "My apologies Mother, but I must retire to my chamber."

Mary understood her daughter's unease, but another bother came into her mind. "And Goodman Draper's failings hath not improved Lydia's station either." She looked to Adam and her bother grew into resentment. "Failings that need not have become a public display."

"Goody Draper, I had to," said Adam as his head sunk.

"What thou hast rendered cannot be undone," she said. Her irritation subsided. "Nathaniel speaks truly, though. Thou must act on Goodman Draper's behalf. A house full of thornbacks would only delight the evils within Goody Davis." Mary raised her finger and asked Adam, "Is this John Law a good man?"

Adam nodded, and Mary paced while talking aloud. "A Scottish man, but he doth not appear a pauper. He resides on fertile lands, barters for goods, and..."

"Concord's good men say John Law doth not barter truly," interrupted Nathaniel.

---

26 *In Puritan times, a single woman who had not married, generally by the age of twenty-five, was deemed unnatural and was called a 'spinster', an 'antient [sic] maid' or more derogatorily, a 'thornback'*

Adam looked at Nathaniel. "A man who barters with prudence will always have detractors."

"And Mother thou art mistaken," said Nathaniel. "John Law doth not reside on fertile land, but squats, without claim, like the Indians."

Mary swung around to Adam, who shrugged and said, "He doth say he hath title."

"Pray tell from whom?" asked Nathaniel.

"A Goodman Awbrey as I recall."

Nathaniel sneered and said, "I must tend to my sister," and left.

"The land, Adam?" asked Mary.

Adam shrugged and finally said, "If not now, soon I suspect."

Mary kneaded her apron while staring at Adam. "Then thou must prod John Law to act in the fitting and proper manner."

"No one prods John Law."

"Tis the Scottish way I dread," said Mary. She sighed and asked Adam again. "Is he a good man?"

Adam thought about how John had helped him when his leg was lame, and now, when his mind was troubled. Those thoughts evoked a smile of appreciation. "Even though he is Scottish, he truly is a good man," said Adam.

"Then prod for Lydia's sake," said Mary.

*****

Back in New Scotland, John entered his cold shelter, now realizing he should have never left Lydia. His stomach had knotted along the way, his head was now woozy, and his nerves were so frayed he twitched involuntarily. He ached for the only person in the Colonies who comforted him and who he had abruptly dismissed.

Lying on half-frozen ground, he drifted to an earlier time. He was working alongside his father, and when problems arose, his father resolved them. And in the late afternoon when they came home, he had the love only a caring mother can give. His thoughts drifted deeper. His parents were rustling under a sheepskin in dim light. He lay on the ground, not far from them, with eight year old eyes squeezed shut and hands clamped on his ears. When he was a wee lad, the rustling shadows, moans and panting unnerved him. But now, he understood a loving world comes when a man and woman are united as one.

He rolled to his side. Other strong males who had trickled into his life after his father's death had tainted what a father should embody. He had to stop searching for a father figure and become a man, like his father – strong and determined, softened by a pure lass and protector of his family. He and Lydia would have sons, maybe even a daughter, and he would care for them, like his father cared for him. And when he was gone, his sons would care for Lydia.

His inspiring thoughts were thrown to a darkened recess. Would his sons fail Lydia like he had failed his mother? Melancholy peered over the edges of John's mind, but on this night he drove it back. His life needed purpose. No time for gloom; he would return to Lydia tomorrow and do what his mind commanded and his heart desired.

The following day John's resolve remained. As he passed by John Hoare's home, Hoare's urging became a constant drumbeat. But when he opened the Draper gate, Nathaniel's sour face chiseled into his resolve. And when Lydia offered icy pleasantries and went inside the house, it crumbled further.

John helped Adam split the remaining logs. They worked in silence, each one avoiding eye contact with the other. When they paused for a rest, the silence became unbearable for John. He knew if he didn't act now, his resolve would be lost for an eternity. He turned Adam's shoulder to be face-to-face with him and asked permission to wed Lydia. Adam's face collapsed in relief, and his pent up words flowed. He coached John at length on 'the fitting and proper manner' to ask to marry Lydia. Once Adam was comfortable that John understood, they went inside the house.

When the door opened, Lydia started to move toward John, but stopped. Her iciness returned. "Lydia," said John, "me has asked ye brother's permission." She fidgeted, and anticipation melted her iciness. Goody Draper fumbled with the top of her dress, and Nathaniel drew close. John gulped and said, "Me ask of thou, of thee," and John spun toward Adam, who nodded. He turned back to Lydia. "Will thou me wed?" Lydia ran to John, embraced him and kissed him vigorously.

"Lydia," said Mary, "get Satan behind thee." Lydia ceased her display of affections, but Goody Draper's dismay remained. John flushed with embarrassment.

"So be it," said Nathaniel, and he strode out of the room.

"This is truly God's providence," said Deborah. Her smile seemed genuine, and John's confidence grew.

"God's providence will find you too," said Lydia with an equally genuine smile for Deborah.

"I fear not," said Deborah. As she thought of her dim prospects for marriage, her joy left.

"What doth give rise to such ado?" asked Roger as he hobbled into the room. The three women looked at one another.

John stepped forward and said, "Goodman Draper sir, me…"

"Father," interrupted Adam, "as agreed, and as ye only son, I have acted on ye behalf. John Law, an honorable man, hath asked in a fitting and proper manner to wed thy daughter."

"And where be this honorable man?" asked Roger. Adam pointed, and Roger eyed John for a seeming eternity. John's blood pounded so hard, his temple scar ached. Finally Roger said, "The Scottish man." John's stomach roiled. The anticipation was excruciating. Roger turned to Adam. "And doth John Law be a man of substance, and not a pauper?"

"Yes Father, he doth."

"And doth he have sufficient land to care for Lydia?" Adam paused before answering as the women clustered closer.

"Aye, me does," said John.

Roger turned to John and asked, "And who gaveth thee thy land title?"

"William Awbrey."

"I know not a Goodman William Awbrey," said Roger.

"He arrived in the Colonies after you," said Adam as he stepped closer to John.

"Ah, so many," said Roger, "I can no longer remember them all. But there was a time when..." and Roger tottered toward his chamber. "Huh, a Scottish man," he said before disappearing into his room.

Chapter Twenty-seven

Winter 1660

John relaxed near a fire in the Draper home as Mary, Lydia and Deborah finished cleaning up after the evening meal. Adam had said the grace since Goodman Draper remained ailing in his room and Nathaniel was away for a few weeks, much to John's pleasure. Once the women had finished their chores, they came back into the room. John arose, reached into his shirt for a wood carving and handed it to Mary. "Why thank thee," said Mary. She moved the carving around in her hand for a few moments, and then stopped to look at John.

"Me whittled a sheep for you, like me did for me mum when me was a wee lad."

"How quaint." Mary examined the carving again, trying to imagine a sheep.

"Put it next to them cups," said John.

"My pewter cups," said Mary. "Oh surely not. Thy gift needs prominence."

"Now that me and Lydia will soon be wed, it be fitting and proper to bring me intended's mum a gift." John looked to Adam for reassurance, but he was pre-occupied.

"Lydia dear," said Mary. "Thou must prepare for thy walking out sermon."

"I've met with Reverend Bulkeley twice," said Lydia.

"Bulkeley," said John, "me thought he be dead."

"But his son carries on," said Mary. "Another Bulkeley in Concord is truly God's providence." Mary waited for John's acknowledgement, but he was in thought. *Another Bulkeley, what does this bastard know? Aye, me thought me was done with his lot.* "John, God's providence is it not?" asked Mary.

"Aye, God doth have burdens for us all."

John's response confounded Mary, and she turned back to Lydia. "And what hast thou chosen?"

"Paul's letter to the Ephesians, chapter 5, verses 22 to 28."

"Ooh, I must get Goodman Draper's Bible," said Mary.

"No need," said Lydia. "God hath placed it in my heart." She cleared her throat and spoke: "Wives, submit thyselves unto your own husbands, as unto the Lord. For the husband is the head of the wife, even as Christ is the head of the church; and he is the savior of the body. Therefore as the church is subject unto Christ, so let the wives be to their own husbands in everything."

Mary was solemn, relishing every word. Lydia turned to John and continued: "Husbands, love your wives, even as Christ also loved the church, and gave himself for it; that he might sanctify and cleanse it with the washing of water by the word, that he might present it to himself a glorious church, not having spot, or wrinkle, or any such thing; but that it should be holy and without blemish."

John thought about his night with Andrew Adam under the tree. *Me Lydia without spot, wrinkles; holy and without blemish.*

Lydia concluded: "So ought men to love their wives as their own bodies. He that loveth his wife loveth himself."

Mary clasped her hands together. "So tender, it may even shine light upon Goody Davis's darkened heart." Mary asked Adam, "Hast thou spoken with Goodman Flint?" She turned back to John. "He will serve as magistrate for thy wedding."

"Adam, hath ye posted the first of the three wedding Banns?"[27] asked Mary. Adam continued stirring the embers. Mary bit her lip while staring at Adam. "Lydia and John must know each other further." Adam poked at a log, a flame grew, and he tossed a few half-split logs onto the grate. "Goodman Draper still ails," said Mary. She cleared her throat, and Adam ceased poking.

He brushed soot from his hand and swallowed. "John, thou need not lay in our barn this night." Lydia raised her hand to her blushing cheek as Adam continued. "Thou can lay with Lydia with a bundling board between thy bodies."

"Bundling board?" asked John. Adam left, and John looked to the women for an answer. No one responded, and the room remained quiet until Adam returned.

Soon, Adam came back into the room, holding a plank that had leather straps at each end. "Ye board is between Lydia and thee and lashed to the bed posts," said Adam.

---

27 *Banns had to be published before a marriage could take place. Their publication was an announcement by the Reverend that two people wished to marry and an invitation to declare any unlawful reason why they should not marry.*

"And Goody Walker has lent me a bundling stocking," added Mary.

John had dreamt of laying aside Lydia, but not with a board between them. And what's a bundling stocking? He was aroused, but unsure if it was from lust or fear.

"Thou shall tarry the night. But ye board and stocking keeps the devil in the wilderness," said Mary.

Mary and Lydia left for Nathaniel's room, which was far from the main fireplace. Inside his room, Lydia disrobed, hunched her shoulders and covered her erect nipples.

"Tis natural dear," said Mary. "They protrude when aroused."

"And when cold," said Lydia as she shuddered. She sat on the bed and struggled to pull the tightly knit stocking up her legs. When the stocking was at Lydia's waist, Mary swung Lydia's bounded legs into bed. Her groin was now warm, and when she squeezed her inner thighs, it became moist. Mary fluffed a covering and let it drift down. Lydia grabbed it and rustled it across her breasts. Mary bent down and kissed Lydia's forehead.

As John waited with Adam, his head was whirling. He had many questions, but they seemed unfitting and improper to ask. Adam fumbled with the board's straps, never making eye contact. When Mary returned from Lydia, Adam rushed to the back chamber with the board. Mary wandered to the fire, poked at it and glanced at Goodman Draper's favorite chair. When her eyes met John's, she said, "It is ye fitting and proper thing to do."

Adam returned, and John moved slowly toward the back chamber. He paused, but Mary flipped her hands to usher him along. John had been afire, and entering the cool room with Lydia's scent, aroused him further. He squeezed his eyes to lessen the swirl in his head. He eased onto the bed and lay next to the board. He couldn't see Lydia, but her intoxicating fragrance lingered. He bounced his fingers on the opposing ones on his other hand. He tossed to his side and drew his arms close. "Me be cold," he said.

Lydia tittered. "I would give thee my bed covering to warm thee, but I am exposed above my waist." Her words had drawn the devil closer to John. His blood surged through his groin, and his erect extremity throbbed. "There is a covering for thee in the corner," she said.

John sat up, but his blood rush hadn't ebbed. He crashed back down onto the bed, not wanting to expose that he had an erection. "Me'll get it later," said John. He returned to bouncing his fingers, trying to cool his ardor. "So how does me tarry the night?"

"We talk," said Lydia, and John's throbbing wilted. The devil had been pushed back, but still lurked. Lydia continued, "My body craves thee, and a thin board separates Satan from us. He stirs my passion and tries to control my heart. But he hath not driven God from my mind. I love thee dearly, but I will not forsake my God."

"Aye, and me will keep Satan away too," said John.

The bundling had unbundled many of Lydia's deep emotions. She was at ease, and her words flowed. John offered comments, and the more he did, the more his carnal urges ebbed. He unbundled too, talking about his parents and life in Scotland. Lydia joined to form a conversation. He told her about his estate and their future, and promised to always care for Lydia. Lydia lay contented, willing to be swept away to wherever John's words took them. When John told her how deeply he loved her, she squeezed her thighs and rustled the covering across her breasts.

They slept little, and when Goody Draper came in that morning, their first bundling ended. Both were disappointed that the night had ended. They wanted more bundling nights, which would come soon.

Chapter Twenty-eight

Across from Concord Commons, two women had gathered. They were reading the parchment that had been attached to the publishing post, near the wayside.

"Aha, ye third Bann notice, posted yesterday," said Goody Davis. She ceased reading and her naturally shriveled lips puckered further, as if she had bitten into an onion. "Suppose it's the best Lydia could do."

"I prayed Lydia would not be a spinster," said Goody Walker.

"A woman who doth die an old maid is destined to lead apes in hell."

Goody Walker knitted her eyebrows. "Thou hast the devil in thee to repeat such a cruel adage."

Goody Davis straightened her back and glared over her hooked nose. "Satan hath been nigh, but he doth not reside in me."

"Nigh?" asked Goody Walker.

"Wolves howled yester eve on ye Great Meadow. Satan had to have been thither."

Goody Walker flipped a dismissive hand. "No doubt howls of delight as they devoured a hind."

"The howls were dread filled," said Goody Davis's as her eyes widened. "And this morn, cloven hoof prints."

"Perhaps a sheep or a ..."

"Or a goat," interrupted Goody Davis. "But the hooves were too large for just any goat. They were made by Satan as he roamed." She gestured toward the notice. "Satan drew nigh yester eve to read his pleasing posting of this third Bann."

Goody Walker frowned. "Thy mind has wandered into an apparition, perhaps caused from thy fitful night's sleep?"

"Nonsense," said Goody Davis as she crossed her arms. "Lydia is a mere child, with time to be particular. Yet she settles for a Scottish man."

"Goodman Draper hath given his consent."

"Doth Goodman Draper know what he sayeth?"

"Doubtful, but Goody Draper says John Law is a good man."

"Yet Scottish," said Goody Davis. She brought her hands to her mouth and gasped. "Dost thou suppose Lydia is with child?"

Goody Walker was taken aback, and she crossed her arms. "Only the devil would speak such slander."

"Simply a Godly question," said Goody Davis. She glared and raised her head. "Necessity doth compel impudent actions, doth it not?"

Goody Walker shrunk from the stare. Her grimace said 'yes'.

The posting of a third Bann was required for an orderly marriage. Without it, Goodman Draper would have been punished for acting improperly. The Reverend wove the Ephesians' verses into Lydia's walking out ceremony. By custom, John was not present at the ceremony. Afterwards, cake was eaten and sack posset was sipped, which loosened some tensions. The gifts were scarce. Even though the ceremony was unlike most, Lydia was oblivious to it. In a few days, the wedding would be held when The Magistrate would ask John and Lydia 'if they desired to be wed'. If they both responded affirmatively, they'd be married.[28]

*****

The night before the wedding, John came into the bundling room with his head even woozier than the first time he entered. He lay next to the board, closed his eyes, and his spinning eased. "Your ale be a wee bit strong," he said.

"Lots of malt. Goody Draper brews with vigor," said Lydia.

"And has she trained me Lydia?"

"Indeed. Not just ale, also hard waters, and when she hath bartered for molasses, we make rum. I made the posset you and Adam drank so heartily."

"Me head be spinning with just the thought," said John as he concentrated on controlling his whirling head.

A quiet ensued until Lydia asked, "Dost thou drink often?"

---

28 *The Puritans rejected many Anglican ideas and believed marriage was not a religious ceremony, but a civil contract. They required this covenant must be agreed or executed before a magistrate, and not a minister*

John kept his eyes shut and said, "A wee bit."

"And dost thou over imbibe?"

John opened his eyes, and his dizziness accelerated. "Nae. But tonight it be Goody Draper's strong brew, or maybe your posset."

"And when thou dost over imbibe, how is your demeanor?"

John shut his eyes. "Me become amorous." He hoped his response would veer the conversation away from a grilling of his drinking habits to romantic chit-chat. Such banter aroused him and intensified his wedding night fantasies. But nothing came over the bundling board, and John's erotic musings faded. He was beginning to sober from his slight intemperance. "Lydia, even with a wee bit too much drink, me will keep the devil away."

Lydia moved her head against the board. John was so near, yet Lydia feared her questions may have distanced him. Her lips quivered, and she was about to speak, but John broke the silence. "When me be alone with me ale, staring at me fire, me thinks of me mum."

A tear trickled onto Lydia's cheek, but she let it lay. She inhaled and asked, "Dost thou grow angry?"

"Angry?" asked John. "Me loves me mum." He chuckled and said, "Nae be like me passion for you." Lydia sniffed, and John propped his body up and looked over the board. He brushed her tear aside and asked, "What be the matter?" Lydia sniffed again, and John kissed his hand and placed it on her cheek.

Her tears now streamed, and her lips quivered until she asked, "Would thou ever mistreat me?" John clenched his jaws as horrifying images flew into his mind. He squeezed his eyes

The Immigrant

and thought, *What ravages has Lydia suffered?* "When Father hath too much drink, he mistreats Goody Draper," she said.

"Did he mistreat you?"

"His wrath was with Goody Draper. Adam had to help her." "Poor Adam," and she exhaled a sigh, "he had to testify before The Magistrate. Goody Draper and Father have never forgiven him." Lydia brushed her tears aside and stared at John. "Would thou ever abuse me?"

John swung his head back and forth. "Never, me love thee."

"Father loves Goody Draper."

John's head sunk. "Me promise," he said. He thought of other times when he had said 'me promise'. The words were hollow then, unlike now. Would Lydia accept his promise as the truth? He lay back onto the bed. His father never abused his mother. He could not fathom ever abusing Lydia.

"Thou must not say a word," said Lydia.

John nodded his head, and Lydia awaited his 'aye'. It didn't come because John Hoare's words about 'besmirching Lydia' were now in John's thoughts. He wondered if Hoare was aware of the wife abuse. Probably, he was a lawyer.

"Dost thou promise as the Lord is thy witness?" asked Lydia, still awaiting John's 'aye'.

John nodded again, but was still pre-occupied with the meaning of Hoare's words. Wife abuse would besmirch Goodman Draper, perhaps Goody Draper, but not Lydia. Was there something else to Hoare's remark?

Lydia grew anxious with the silence. She had just unloaded a painful burden onto John, and now her lip quivered with guilt. She shouldn't have been so selfish. Her burden was now John's.

"Lydia?" asked John.

"Yes my love," said Lydia as her worry eased.

"Did Goodman Draper's actions besmirch thy family?"

Shock ripped through Lydia. *'Besmirch', 'thy',* she thought. *These are not Scottish words. These are not words John Law would speak. Who in Concord hath spoken such words to John?*

"Be there any actions that besmirched the Draper name?" asked John.

Lydia fumbled her fingers as her heart pounded. *What doth John know?* She had one remaining burden to share with him, but she couldn't, not now. She would have to shoulder her last burden alone, at least for the time being. Her lips trembled. The personal horror of her remaining burden exploded before her eyes, and tears streamed. She squeezed her eyes, but the horror still flickered. Finally after gaining some composure, Lydia was able to respond. "I love thee, John Law." Lydia hoped for John's rejoinder and prayed that he would let his 'besmirched question' go unanswered.

"Aye," and with a pause, which seemed to Lydia to last an eternity, John said, "me loves thee, too."

*****

On March 5, 1660, John and Lydia were married by The Magistrate. The bundling stocking had been returned to Goody Walker, and the board had been stored away. Lydia hoped someday her daughter would need them. On their wedding night, their prohibited passions poured out. Lydia now lay on John's arm with a fervent glow she hoped would never leave. Her erotic exhaustion overcame her, and her once heavy breathing was now a gentle, contented wheeze.

John glanced toward the fire and told his mother about her future grandsons. He regaled her with the size of his estate, large enough for generations to come. His mother was as thrilled as John. She could have listened to him for an eternity. But John drifted from the flame, curled his arm, and his bicep raised Lydia's cheek to his lips. He kissed her one last time before falling into an exhausted sleep.

With her eyes shut, but fluttering, Lydia smiled. She snuggled against his lean, strong body, soaking up all his warmth and goodness. Her smile remained throughout the night.

Chapter Twenty-nine

*S*uch *an austere life Lydia has in that wilderness John Law calls his New Scotland.* That troubling thought haunted Goody Draper as she left New Grant after her first visit since the wedding. She returned though, bringing spare essentials each time; a pewter trencher, a wooden bread trough, a milk ewer and two empty demijohns. She brought knick-knacks to decorate the Spartan living conditions. Lydia made improvements too, even though John insisted his shelter was more than adequate. Eventually Mary's repeated visits grew irksome, and John toiled in the fields whenever she came. Yet after she left, he appreciated the changes. His shelter was becoming a cozy home, similar to his boyhood one.

Mary's visits were also social, which was more beneficial for Lydia than essentials and occasional trinkets. When John left his mother ten years earlier to fight Cromwell, he changed from a talkative lad to an adolescent of few words. As an innocent pikeman among motley men, he was justifiably reticent. Captivity quieted him more, and he was ever wary of the Colonists. He avoided them and seldom spoke with any of them. And his conversations with the livestock or dancing flames were monologues. But now with a constant companion, John was as talkative as when he was a lad, yet still insufficient for Lydia.

The Sabbath visits were another social outlet for Lydia. She arose early, walked with John to her family's home and went with her family to the meetinghouse. She heard gossip; John was a slave, a squatter, a wild Scot and a Catholic. But she sat with Goody Draper and Deborah, shied away from the stares, ignored the whispers, winced at the innuendoes and absorbed the family lectures about John honoring the Sabbath for the good of the Law name. She never complained to John about what she endured.

One day, Adam arrived with Mehitable in tow, which after some coaxing, Goodman Draper had offered as part of Lydia's dowry. Adam returned thereafter and helped John to alter his shelter into a two room house. Adam said that it was an added dowry, but John sensed it was repayment for his earlier help. Once the leaves turned, Lydia insisted Mehitable have her own shelter. John and Adam built a free standing one, further adding to John's estate. Now Goody Draper wondered if Lydia's dowry was too excessive for what had been received in exchange.

*****

On a chilly autumn day, John sat holding a steaming pewter cup. He leaned from his upright log and placed his forearms upon his knees. "You have the most fertile plot in all of Concord, you wise Scottish man." He smiled as he took a swig and admired his new home. The aroma of the evening's meal twitched his nose. "And Lydia does so much." He took another swig and chuckled. "And she knows to prod me when me sits on me lazy arse."

The cup warmed John's fingertips, and the steam coming from it became a momentary fascination. The cup was special to Goody Draper. But because Lydia needed cups, Goody Draper had given it to her. Now, it was John's favorite when he relaxed at day's end. He ceased reflecting and took a final swig. He tossed the cup onto the ground, arched his back and stretched his arms.

Twilight crept across the meadow, and the livestock that dotted it seemed as contented as John. "Aye, me estate now, and later for John Junior," said John as he moved his head up and down like a lowing cow. He leaned against his woodpile to relax. "And me has enough wood 'til spring." As he sat, his body cooled and his muscles stiffened. A once sweaty shirt was becoming a chilled wrap. He sucked in the cool air, and the pleasing aroma returned. His stomach growled and mouth salivated. His face had flushed from the warmed cider, yet his ear lobes and nose remained chilled. Soon he would eat, and after his meal, he would let the fire dim and snuggle close to his love.

A bleat interrupted John's daydreaming. Lydia emerged from Mehitable's shelter and waddled toward him. His smile broadened with each of Lydia's swaying steps.

"Why John Law what makes thou so gay?"

"Thou my love, I love thee."

Lydia mused over John's response as she walked up the rise. It was so unlike him. "Mehitable will be lambing soon," she said.

"Sooner than thou?"

Lydia's paused to catch her breath, and her face reddened. "God's providence will arrive later for me. My midwife, Elizabeth, believes it will be in the spring, around the time of Concord's annual meeting."

"But me wants John Junior on me knee now," said John as he patted his thigh. "To see his land and smell his mum's cooking."

"And what if thy John Junior is a Joanna?" Lydia lowered her head and continued walking. As she neared, she sensed John's gaiety had left. "But I feel God hath blessed my womb with a virile laddie." she said. "Just like his father."

John's smile returned, but too many swigs on an empty stomach and stiffening muscles had taken their toll. He staggered as he arose, but regained his balance. Lydia stretched her arms around his shoulders, and John pulled her close to him from her waist. He pressed a kiss on her forehead. Even though they were alone, Lydia's eyes darted around to re-assure it. A kick from Lydia's stomach jolted into John. She giggled, looked around again to assure they were alone and grabbed John's hand.

As she moved John's hand to follow the squirms, she said, "Feel, my love. Dost thou feel thy laddie?" She glanced down at her stomach and asked, "And John Junior, dost thou feel thy father?"

John's smile widened as they continued tracking the squirms. When the squirms stopped, they waited, hoping for them to resume. But their child was at rest, and a gust urged them inside. John pulled Lydia close for another kiss, and her eyes darted around.

"John Law, thou art consumed with such ardor this frosty eve."

Chapter Thirty

Invigorating nights had turned into stinging, cold ones. Before retiring to bed, John had watched water ooze from a hissing log that offered more steam than warmth. The spirits and hot samp he had consumed earlier were insufficient to warm him now. Only cuddling with Lydia would achieve what he needed. He still could enwrap her petit frame, even with her swollen belly. As he lay cuddling, he wondered how he ever slept those past winters without Lydia. He drifted into slumber.

When his chill returned, he tried cuddling closer, but to no avail. He bolted up and shivered. Lydia had left, and the firepit was ashes sprinkled with flickering embers. He stoked the fire, threw a heavy wrap about him and left for Mehitable's shelter where he sensed Lydia would be. The door on the shelter was ajar, and John peered in. Mehitable was standing and seemed skittish.

"Be still my precious," said Lydia.

Clumps of hay matted Mehitable's backside, and sticky discharge dangled from her rear. A warm stench, which John had smelled often, rushed toward the door. Soon, blood soaked lambs would arrive, followed by a deluge of afterbirth. John's mouth moistened at the thought. He feared that he would vomit, but he fought the feeling off and walked in.

"Oh thou hast surprised me," said Lydia. "We must lay Mehitable to her side."

Mehitable's innate mistrust of John surged, but after a struggle she was down, with John pressing to keep her down. Lydia slipped a hand into Mehitable's rear. The ewe struggled again, and John pressed harder than before. Lydia forced her other hand into Mehitable, and the ewe bleated.

"Aha, as I supposed," said Lydia. "Ye lamb's forelegs are delaying the birth." Lydia's hand movements rumpled the fleece on Mehitable's haunches. Lydia was perspiring, and stringy hair hung about her determined face. "It's God's providence that sent me this night. Mehitable needs me." Lydia was in absolute control. Mehitable remained calm until Lydia yanked outward and forelegs appeared, followed by a pasty, encrusted swirl of fleece.

Mehitable kicked loose from John and shuffled to a corner. Her stare challenged John to approach, as he and Lydia remained crouched. A lamb eased out and dropped onto the hay. A rush of afterbirth followed, creating a steaming puddle in the hay. The stench intensified, and John turned away as his stomach roiled. He turned back, and Mehitable was licking her mucous new born. John shuddered.

Lydia arose from her crouch, trembling. She put her hands to her face, smearing Mehitable's slime on her cheeks. She shook again and cried. A bewildered John put his arms around her. Her cheeks were inches from his nostrils, and he eased back from the odor. "What be it? Why be you crying?"

Lydia raised her head and wiped her eyes. She sniffed, and lost her composure. "I have such fright within my soul." Lydia sniffed again and looked at John. "Will it be God's providence for me to travail like Mehitable? Will John Junior's arms block him for us?" John didn't have answers, and fear poured into him. "Or will I die while trying to give thee thy son?' She rushed her hands to her face and awaited John's response.

John was now thunderstruck. All he could do was hold Lydia. Her trembling eased, and with each sniff it eventually ceased. Now under control, she broke their embrace and kissed John's cheek. "Thou art a good man, John Law," she said. She wiped her hands on her dress, moved back to John, and her head collapsed on his chest. She was seemingly contented, but John was not.

John hadn't done anything and still lacked answers to important questions. *What if there be troubles?* An even gloomier thought followed. *What if Lydia...*, and John couldn't ponder that thought any further. The pervasive stench was now unbearable for John. John moved outside while still embracing Lydia, leaving Mehitable alone and still licking her newborn. The air was energizing, but insufficient to overcome John's lingering, depressing thoughts.

Chapter Thirty-one

March 1661

John Junior's blood encrusted head was between Lydia's legs. An umbilical cord was matted to her inner thigh, which drooped down, serpentine like, and disappeared between her swollen labia and her son's crowning head. One last push and John's heir would be born. But Lydia lay motionless, seemingly too exhausted to thrust her son into existence. A panic-stricken John now feared Lydia was dead. He squeezed his eyes shut as he continued to tear bread pieces and drop them into his pottage. This horror vanished, but others like it would return. Would his nightmares ever end?

After Mehitable gave birth, Lydia was upbeat, driven to learn everything about childbirth. At the meetinghouse, she questioned her mother, the midwife and others. Their answers were informative, which usually gave rise to more questions that lacked answers. For those, Lydia's only solace was in knowing that the midwife, with her reassuring demeanor, would be at her side when her time arrived. But her comfort was short-lived, because at the next Sabbath, a particularly chatty woman dwelled on the horrors of labor, stillborn children and dying mothers.

Winter grew ruthless, preventing Lydia from traveling to Concord. The potential problems with childbirth grew more vivid. Cooped up, she spun wool and made clothing for John Junior, occasionally humming, or chatting with John to ease her mind. John remained self-absorbed as he repaired tools and, often, fueled an insufficient fire.

On this particular day, as John came into his home with a load of fire wood, he said, "The weather be fierce. Me doubt the midwife will journey to New Scotland." John struggled to shut the door while balancing the wood. Lydia ceased humming, and John now rued blurting his remark. Another discouraging thought came to him. He was the only white person west of Concord, and thus he might be the only one helping Lydia. Plenty of hot water and cloths were all he knew. Unlike Lydia, no one had prepared him for childbirth. Staring at the fire and talking to his mum had been useless.

After a few hours, the door flew open, followed by a jolt of cold and Goody Draper's voice. "Praise the Lord; he hath guided us safely to thee."

"Goody Draper, Deborah, ye needed not come," said Lydia.

"Adam insisted another big blow was nigh," said Mary. "And Goodman Draper was muttering about nor' east winds and herringbone skies."

"But ye snow is still quite faint," said Lydia.

"Scarce it is. But those men placed my heart into a terrible fright."

"Ye walked alone?" asked Lydia.

"Adam guided us to John Law's bridge and returned home. His departing words were 'Child birthing is for womenfolk'."

As Deborah stared at her step-sister, she thought how different she had become. She was still a naïve teenager, yet her current circumstances made her appear older. An energetic glow seemed to burn from within. Perhaps, it was God's way of exhilarating the heart, even when the body is tired. Deborah longed for a similar situation, married and awaiting a child.

"Deborah, why so soulful?" asked Mary.

"Nothing Mother," she said as she gathered her cloak close and shivered.

Mary turned to John. "Per chance some pottage to remove our chill?"

John raised his pewter cup. "A taste of ale," he said.

Mary had given that cup to Lydia for special occasions. She grimaced at the sight of it in John's hands. "Hath ye ale been malted with vigor?" asked Mary.

"A wee bit," said John as he thumped the cup down onto the table and burped.

Mary glared at John. "Then I shall not partake, especially with a child so nigh."

John raised his cup to acknowledge Mary's refusal and took another swig. He remained oblivious to her glare.

Mary turned to Lydia and said, "Deborah baked some groaning cakes,[29] and I have brought special herbs to create elixirs when we need them."

Mary and Deborah spent the rest of the day preparing Lydia for her travail. Her mood brightened, something John

---

29 *Special cakes made in anticipation of childbirth, which were often, served to the women attendants.*

had been unable to achieve. He had a new found appreciation for their visit.

During the night the winds howled, and by daybreak, the snow was ankle high. Snow fell periodically throughout the day, and as the women babbled, John had a better appreciation for Adam's words, 'child birthing is for womenfolk'. He left, often, to gather firewood.

The following morning when John opened the door, the sun drenched snow cover blinded him. His eyes had been accustomed to dim light, but eventually they adjusted to the brilliance. The snow on the meadow undulated, cresting to waist high and ebbing to bare ground. The patterns sidled like a serpent with each gust. The twinkling snow complemented the azure, white puff-dotted sky. Evergreen boughs hung low, and snow crusts clung, by chance, to gnarled hardwood branches. The women came toward the brilliance and looked out. "Such an isolated wonderland, and so pristine," said Mary. "Thou art truly blest."

John beamed, Mary finally seemed to appreciate what he owned and had given to Lydia. Deborah stood motionless, rapt by the beauty. "Aye, me New Scotland, tis a bonny lass," said John.

Deborah smiled and said, "Aye, John Law, ye bonny lass is truly God's creation."

"Would thou see to Mehitable and her lamb?" asked Lydia as she struggled up from her bed.

Mehitable's shelter, with icicles dangling from the eaves, rose out of the virgin snow cover. John was reluctant to traipse through it and disturb its loveliness. But he did, even though he knew Mehitable and her lamb would be fine. He remained outside, savoring the invigorating air and dazzling sunlight, a cheerier, calmer setting than a dreary home with chatting lasses. He split a few logs, which warmed him at first. But a chill set in, and he went back inside.

Lydia was lying down, and Mary was wiping her brow as Deborah hovered close. A bowl of steaming water was nearby. John grabbed a demijohn of fermented spirits and placed it near the bowl since he had heard alcohol dulls a lass's travail.

"God's blessing is upon us. Fetch the midwife," said Mary. John gulped as Mary turned back to Lydia. "Thou must arise. Walk and eat some groaning cake." Mary propped Lydia up and struggled to get her on her feet. She turned back to John. "The midwife, thou must not tarry."

"Where be she?"

"Mercy, John," and Mary let go of Lydia who slumped down. "Three houses past ours. Her name is Elizabeth Downs."

Lydia propped herself up and peered around her mother to look at her husband. "John Junior will soon be with us," she said. She fell back and struggled to arise. "Please John, fetch ye midwife to ease my travail."

John was still held in place, completely absorbed with Lydia and the women aiding her. It took a shriek from Lydia to break his fascination and propel him out the door. Mary's consoling words followed Lydia's shriek and trailed off into soft sounds, insufficient to erase the shriek that still reverberated in John's head.

The route to the South Bridge was buried with pristine snow, enchanting, but a trap. To the north, the dales had forbidding drifts, but the crests were barren. Using fence posts, the river, and the sun for bearings, John trudged toward the main road. Once there, he found sleigh ruts and hooves had packed the snow. His damp clothing now clung, and his wet feet became more chilled with each step on frozen ground. But adrenaline was flowing, which caused his frozen limbs to seem as a mere nuisance. Lydia's parting words, 'fetch ye midwife', repeated with the rhythm of the crunching snow beneath his feet, spurring John to get to the midwife.

He passed by the Draper residence, and after three more houses, he jogged to the door and knocked. A man opened the door.

"Aye, Elizabeth Downs be here?" asked John.

"A Scot ye be. Well Elizabeth Downs doth not reside here."

John had been distraught with worry. Had he miscounted?

"Eben, who is calling?" asked a voice from within. "Be neighborly and invite him in."

"It's a Scottish man, looking for Elizabeth Downs," said Eben.

"The next house; thou dost know where Elizabeth resides."

John Law hurried away, wondering if Eben was ignorant or just uncooperative. A petit slouching woman, with gray hair hanging from her bonnet, answered his knock. She was fully clothed and clutching several wraps that draped about her. Her angelic face was more inviting than Eben's.

"Elizabeth Downs, the midwife?"

"And who art thou?" asked Elizabeth.

"John Law. Goody Draper sent me. Me needs thee dearly."

Elizabeth shuffled through her doorway and looked outside. Anxiety left John. A critical part of his mission had been completed. "Where art thy sleigh?" she asked.

"I nae have a sleigh. Me walked."

Elizabeth stepped back under the open door. "Time has weakened my feeble legs. I have not the strength to journey through such depths of snow. Goody Draper and I have spoken often, and Lydia hath listened, deliberate of mind."

John's head resounded with 'fetch ye midwife', and his frustration grew. "Me might borrow a sleigh, perhaps from your neighbor."

"Eben, a sleigh? Why he doth not have a farthing."

"Someone in Concord must," said John. "Lydia needs a midwife."

"No one in Concord would let a sleigh to a…" and Elizabeth paused to kick snow off her door jamb. "To a stranger," she said as she gathered her wrap tighter. "Lydia is in the Lord's hands now. Have no fear. Women have been giving birth without midwives since Eve. Thou art a Scottish man, but dost thou know ye Bible?"

John didn't respond, but thought, *Lydia needs a midwife, and this lass believes me be a heathen Scot without a Bible.*

"Matthew 11, verse 28: 'come unto me all ye that travail and are heavy laden, and I will refresh thee'." The midwife stepped forward and rubbed John's shoulder. "The Lord is with thee and thy Goodwife. Trust in God's providence."

Her touch jolted John, and her words soothed. 'Thy Goodwife' was an expression reserved for the English, and never spoken to a Scottish man. His relief was momentary as Lydia's shriek pierced anew. John spun toward the road and sprinted.

"God bye to thee, John Law."

John's feet pounded the snow, numb and sensing nothing, and felt like stinging ice blocks. Only the crunching confirmed his pace. He slipped once and sprung up, hardly slowing at all. The sun had descended close to the western horizon. John shivered and blackened thoughts increased as he neared the North Bridge. The image of a blood smeared angel cradling a stillborn, pleading for it not to be so appeared in John's mind. He shook it from his head and never broke his hurried pace as the crossed over the bridge.

Once off the main road, he was engulfed in fluffy snow. He paused often to catch his breath and to locate his earlier tracks. *Lydia needs you, why are you stopping?* He became disoriented in a white sea and ran helter-skelter, trampling virgin snow and obscuring his earlier tracks. But a whiff of smoke honed him in. He followed the scent, and when he paused, only his heavy breathing interrupted a deathly quiet. His blackened thoughts returned, and he wondered if he was the only one alive.

Distant, jubilant sounds suddenly rode upon the smoky air. John bounded, falling several times, before reaching his shelter. He collapsed through the door, and the women gasped. "Thou hast a son, John Law" said Mary. "The first Englishman ever born in New Grant."

He be the first Scottish lad ever born in New Scotland, thought John as he ran to Lydia who was cradling his son. He engulfed them with his arms, squeezed them tight and inhaled. He was intoxicated with the smells of a newborn. As he exhaled, all his pent up worries flowed out too. He pulled back, stared at his son and marveled at God's blessing. He hugged them again, and kissed Lydia with a passion that would have lasted an eternity, but Goody Draper's dismaying gasp caused him to end it. He stepped back and thanked the two women for all they had done. He turned back to Lydia to absorb his new family.

Lydia cradled her healthy newborn, still uneasy with the novelty. Lines etched her moistened forehead, and her straggly hair was matted against her cheeks. John's angel had aged and reflected the worst of life's hardship. But she smiled, and an inner glow overrode her outward appearance.

"Lydia let me hold him," said Mary. "Thy travail hath fatigued thee so."

As Mary cuddled and cooed, John longed for his mum. He had an updated image of her. She was still living with the MacElwees, but like all grandmothers, she was graying, and perhaps slouching, just like the midwife did.

John basked in the fire's glow, and his adrenaline receded. Lydia now seemed more alive than him. He took a swig from the demijohn. The bowl of water no longer steamed. He extended his legs toward the fire and wiggled his stinging toes. He reflected on the events beyond his control that shattered his life ten years ago. He was so devastated, yet, over time, the fragments had been pieced together. Some were far better than he could have ever imagined.

John Junior cried, and Lydia took him from Goody Draper. A hungry sucking, amid gushing womenfolk, replaced the crying. A sound that John's soul had heard often, yet it was the first time for John. It grew rhythmic, and eventually became hypnotic. At twenty five, John believed his life was complete. The final piece had just fallen into place. The Laws were isolated in a pristine wonderland and protected from invaders by his moat. He had chosen Lydia to share in his New Scotland, and now he had an heir to his legacy. But his soul, which had witnessed a new father's rapture far more times than John, knew change would inevitably come.

Chapter Thirty-two

Meetinghouse, Concord, Massachusetts Bay Colony
April 1661

As John and Lydia doted on their newborn, the Concord annual meeting proceeded. Since this year's warrant listing was neither lengthy nor controversial, it commenced in the afternoon. Concord's good men were ordered to attend, and if they failed, they would be fined two shillings. But the annual meeting was always welcomed since friendships, which had become dormant during the winter, could be revitalized. On this sun filled afternoon, the pre-meeting chatter centered on the dreadful winter - 'just the worst ever'.

Reverend Edward Bulkeley opened the meeting with prayer, after which the clerk's records were approved. The moderator introduced each item on the warrant, pontificated upon a few and moved each to a vote. As expected, many received silent approval. The selectmen, tythingmen,[30] fence viewers,[31] and a clerk were appointed; a committee was formed to establish wood cutting rules for the common; a Goodman

---

30 *'Sunday Constables' who enforced the 'Sabbath Laws', curtailed drinking, swearing and other acts deemed to be immoral behavior. Their meetinghouse duties might include quieting the restless youth or disturbing the slumber of the aged.*

31 *Fence viewers were responsible for ensuring that fences, which delineated property lines, were properly maintained.*

Sawyer was named to repair the watch house, and Goodman Brewer was allowed to sell hard water. Money was appropriated: eight shillings to assure suspicious persons do not tarry in the town; ten shillings to stake the high ground near the causeways for travelers; three shillings for new padlocks for the stocks, and ten pounds to assure paupers have sufficient diet and clothing.

Many conversed with those sitting nearby, and when the clamor swelled, the moderator gaveled. The light was dimming, but the remaining item should have no opposition.

The moderator gaveled and said, "Thou knowest John Shepard. Concord is beholding to this free, married man, whose Goodwife Sarah Shepard is with child." He cleared his throat, and the room quieted: "In consideration of John Shepard's loss of use of his arm whilst repairing the Great River Bridge in service to ye town, we humbly grant unto him, with God's blessing, thirty acres in New Grant."

The moderator re-rolled the parchment and called for a vote. Goodman Bates arose and paraphrased the moderator's proclamation. When he paused, the moderator gaveled, leaving Bates bewildered. Goodman Clark arose as a still bewildered Bates lowered his body onto the bench.

"Goodman Bates speaks the truth," said Clark. "We are indebted to John Shepard." Bates nodded his pleasure as others muttered, and the moderator gaveled. "But where is ye land that we intend to grant?" asked Clark.

"Near that Scottish man, John Law," said the moderator. "Ye land is most fertile and will yield a plentiful bounty."

Goodman Baker, a firmly-established Concordian, arose. His hearing had failed, and his mind was fogged, but he was afforded the patience that his long-term standing in Concord demanded. "John Shepard maimed an arm?" he asked. "Why he was tilling his land just Thursday last."

The crowd groaned as the moderator said, "Not possible. Thou art confused."

"Why grant John the shepherd land?" asked Baker. "He owns New Grant already." The moderator tried to resolve Baker's confusion about the two men, John Law and John Shepard, but couldn't. The grumbling increased as Baker grew more strident. "My eyes have not forsaken me," he said. "The shepherd hath two able limbs."

Baker sat down, and before a relieved moderator could gavel, another spoke. "What about John Law, doth he own New Grant?"

"Why no," said the moderator, "he's not a free man, just a squatter."

"Esteemed moderator, thou art mistaken," said Goodman Noyes as he arose from his seat. "John Law is a free man. He hath served out his indenture to Concord."

"A free man yes, but forever a wild Scottish man," said one who remained sitting.

Noyes looked to the speaker. "John Law hath tended my flock. He is a man of restrained carriage, who conducts himself with civility."

The moderator pounded his gavel, trying to quell the spirited discussion about John Law. But gaveling was useless, and he searched for a person who might lend an air of respect to the discussion. "Deacon, could thou speak about John Law?" he asked.

The Deacon arose, and the commotion ceased. He clutched the openings to his coat and said, "I cannot speak for John Law since I have yet to witness him in ye meetinghouse." The crowd grumbled, and a few reined in their snickers. "But God's providence deems my lips to speak. He fought our recently departed and great redeemer, Lord Cromwell. He never felt the righteousness of Cromwell's sword. He lives today, only through Lord Cromwell's mercy."

The Deacon pointed at Goodman Noyes and said, "Thou say he art a free man, owns land in New Grant. If thou speak truly, then he should be with thee on ye Sabbath." The Deacon lowered his finger and asked, "Why doth he not? Is it God's providence for him to reside in the wilderness with Satan?" The Deacon absorbed the quiet adoration of the gathering and sat down.

The moderator gaveled and called for a vote. John Shepard was granted thirty acres in New Grant. John Law now had his first English neighbor, settled on the most fertile plot in what John Law regarded as his New Scotland.

Chapter Thirty-three

*Governor's Chambers, Boston, Massachusetts Bay Colony
November 1661*

"I fear ye hangings of Mary Dyer and William Leddra have returned to haunt us," said the Governor's aide.

"Those Quakers were hung in Boston Common by order of ye Great Court of ye Commonwealth," said Governor Endicott. "Why dost thee have dread-filled thoughts now?"

"Samuel Shattuck hath returned with a message," said the aide.

"A message from that banished Quaker hath no meaning in ye Commonwealth."

"Governor, the message hath been scribed on parchment and hath a seal."

The Governor moved to the window and looked out at the graying skies. He grimaced and turned back. "Allow ye Quaker into my chamber."

The door opened, and a plainly dressed man with a wide brim hat entered, holding a sealed parchment. He lowered his head to the Governor.

"How dare thee show disrespect for thy Governor?" said the aide. Shattuck cowered as the aide grabbed the crown of his hat and yanked it off of his head. The aide placed the crumbled hat on the desk, took the parchment and handed it to the Governor.

The Governor broke the seal, and his eyes shifted to the signature and seal at the bottom. He dropped his hand that held the parchment to his side and removed his hat with his other hand. "It's from His Royal Majesty, Charles II," said the Governor as he bowed his head.

He held the parchment up, squinted and moved to the window for more light. An anxious aide and a now less concerned Shattuck watched the straight-faced Governor. "We shall obey as thy Majesty commands," said the Governor. "Thou may take leave, Samuel Shattuck."

Once the door shut, the Governor tightened his grip on the parchment and turned to his aide. "Summon the magistrates and ministers forthwith."

"And what shall I say to them?"

"Tell them His Majesty commands jailed Quakers, from this day forth, will be tried on English soil."

The aide bowed his head. "Very well, as thou command."

"To the contrary, it is quite unwell. Once in England, ye Quakers will bear nothing but false witness against our Commonwealth justice, prevaricating dogs to amuse our Sovereign."

"Then let ye dogs roam and howl in the Commonwealth and not whimper at the foot of our Sovereign," said the aide. "Shall I fetch William Sutton, ye Boston jailer?"

"Pray tell, why?"

"If ye jail is absent of Quakers, then no one needs to sail to England."

The Governor put his index finger to his mouth and curled it above his lower lip. He moved back to the window and gazed. He nodded his head and turned back to his aide. "Thy words ease my trepidation. But I must measure them further. Thou may take leave."

The Governor stared at the empty chair that Governor Winthrop had sat upon for many years. As he paced, he sensed the former Governor watching him. He stopped and stared back. "Ye New World that ye established on this hill is under siege," he said. "We toil to keep it free of God's vermin. But with Charles as our Sovereign, I fear we will be overrun with vermin. What will become of our common weal?"

*****

This singular event had no direct effect on John Law. But it boded well for his future. Cromwell was dead, and a new king was on the English throne. The absolute control the Puritans had enjoyed under Lord Cromwell was weakening, which might create more tolerance for Scottish men, Quakers and any others who were not deemed God's chosen ones.

Chapter Thirty-four

New Grant, Concord, Massachusetts Bay Colony
Summer 1663

"Get off yah lazy arse, Scottish man."

"Where be your squeaky cart, Andrew?" asked John as he stopped his whittling and turned to face his longtime friend. "Aye me see; a new cart." Andrew's smile broadened. "Soon you'll be the most prosperous man in Concord." But Andrew's grin grew annoying, and John added, "Nae, soon you'll be the most prosperous Scottish bastard in Concord."

Andrew roared. "It be the Concord Ironworks that makes me prosperous," he said. "But it be a pittance compared to what others be getting."

"Well, your Concord Ironworks took more of me New Scotland this year," said John.

"It be but bog land they took."

"Bog land?" John's eyes narrowed, and he threw an arm toward the west. "Me timber nae be bog land. Someday, Lydia and me lads will be freezing."

Andrew flipped a dismissive hand. "There be plenty of woodlands."

John stepped toward his bridge and pointed. "Me brook is but a trickle. The Ironworks' dam steals me water."

"Johnnie, the waters always be a trickle in summer." Andrew patted an upright log. "Come laddie, sit."

John ambled back and sat with forearms on his knees. Andrew wheeled another log next to him and sat down. "Thomas Tower from the Saugus operations got me the carting job. He now be the Ironworks' furnace man." John continued sulking while pondering his trickling brook. "They still be looking for a collier, you know," said Andrew.

John rose off his forearms and turned toward Andrew.

"Aye, me told Thomas about you," said Andrew. "Not now laddie, but perhaps later."

"Thomas found a collier?"

Andrew shook his head and sighed. "The owners told Thomas there be too many Scots at the Ironworks now."

"And who be the owners?"

"Ah it be a mystery," said Andrew. "You know how it be in Concord."

"But for sure, they be English bastards."

John arose and moved toward the bridge. Andrew followed his friend. Small bubbles swirled around the rocks near the bridge. The summer gurgle was muted, allowing the twitter of bird to dominate the air. Andrew paused and breathed in. "Aye, such a bonny spot," he said. He pointed to John's shelter. "You've added to your estate."

"Aye, me added that room this spring."

"Corn be high," said Andrew.

"Nae as high as a before," said John. "John Shepard now has me fertile land. Land that Nagoglancit once told me to plant." John placed his hands on his hips and looked toward Shepard's house. "The Englishman gets the land, and this Scottish bastard gets to pay rent."

He dropped his hands and turned back to Andrew. "Pays me rent with me corn. This spring me samp bowl be nigh empty. But if me nae pay me rent, they take me land. Me should have nae trusted Awbrey. 'Serve out ye indenture and the land be all yours' be what the bastard told me."

"He be English," said Andrew. "What did you expect?"

Before John could respond, Lydia came out, clutching the hand of a toddling, two year old John Junior. "He hath been calling for his father. Dost thee mind?" Lydia smiled at Andrew. "How do you fare, Andrew?"

Andrew nodded. "Be fine, Goody Law."

"Fa-fa," said John Junior as he ran to his father.

John raised his son over his head and rolled him side to side, elated with his giggling. He inched him lower, and the giggling ceased. Anticipation glistened in his son's eyes. John pushed him up again, and infectious laughter reverberated throughout New Scotland. Lydia waddled back to the house, and the men returned to their perches.

Andrew shielded the side of his mouth. "Another coming, laddie?" John smiled, and Andrew jabbed his shoulder. "You be a virile animal, you Scottish ram."

"Fa-fa."

John placed his son on his knee and bounced his leg. "And you, Andrew?" he asked.

"Nae a lass yet, only wenches. But someday."

A breeze swept over the rise and rustled the corn stalks. "Be another Law by the harvest," said John. "Then me will have four mouths to feed."

John's son squirmed and swatted at John's face. "Ruff," he said.

John buried his stubble into his son's cheek. "Rough, me nae be smooth like yah mum." Infectious laughter returned to New Scotland.

Andrew slapped his knee. "Best be going," he said. "Me have goods to deliver." He arose and left a pre-occupied John.

When Andrew lifted his cart and heaved a sigh as he began to push, John expected to hear the familiar squeak. He quickly realized it wouldn't come. "Nae a squeak, you be a fortunate Scottish man."

Andrew lowered his cart, and with a determination that John had not seen for some time, he said, "Laddie, you be the fortunate Scottish man." John pondered Andrew's parting words until 'fa-fa' reminded him to resume bouncing his son, which only disturbed his pondering, momentarily.

*****

After supper that night, the summer air and excitement took their toll on John Junior. He fell asleep earlier than usual, leaving his parents time for each other. "So pleasing to see Andrew," said Lydia. "What brought him to New Grant?"

"Them Ironworks."

"Will he reside thither?"

John shrugged and took a swig.

"I pray he doth. It would quiet Goody Davis."

John's pewter cup stopped in mid-air.

"John, thou knowest how I despise gossip. It is truly Satan controlling one's lips." Lydia shook her head and continued. "Andrew hath been helping the relict, Goody Brooke?"

"Relict?" The pewter cup came down to the table, and John tapped his fingers on it.

"Goodman Brooke died, and his relict, on occasion, needs help with mannish chores. Andrew doth sleep in her barn. It's all fitting and proper, but not to Goody Davis." Lydia arose and paced. "She speaks with words improper for any goodwife to utter." Lydia grabbed her side to rein in a squirm.

"You be all right?" asked John.

Lydia dropped her hand and nodded. "Oh, the gleam in Goody Davis's eyes; ye can see Satan in them."

"Satan, a lass?"

"Satan is clever, John," said Lydia as she scowled. She winced and gripped her side again. "She carries on about the Scottish heathen and the English relict."

"And what does Goody Davis say about this Scottish heathen?"

Lydia stopped pacing. Her emotions could no longer be exorcised from her body. "Nothing," she said. "Nothing." She brought her hands to her mouth and squeezed her eyes. When they opened, they glistened. John arose and put his arm around Lydia's shoulder. He tugged her closer to him.

"It's my stepmother, Goody Draper," said Lydia, and her head collapsed onto John's chest. Momentarily at ease, she lifted it and brushed her cheek. "She must appear before The Magistrate for selling spirits to the Indians. More fodder for that evil Goody Davis." Her head sought the comfort of John's chest again. "She is in more need now that Father has departed. But she will not suffer being a pauper on Concord's dole, too fearful of what Goody Davis and others will say." Lydia raised her head off John's chest, and determination was in her eyes. "But selling drink to the Indians will bring suffering too."

"It be a foolish English law," said John. "You sell drink to MacGoon and his lot, but nae to an Indian. Guess them Indians be more heathen than we Scots," said John with a chuckle.

Lydia broke free of John and glared. "Thou knowest not what thou say," she said. "Indians with drink are Satan's animals. Certainly Goody Draper knows that." Lydia gripped her face, and John tried to rein her back.

She stepped away and grew pensive. "This Sabbath will be a dreadful burden for Goody Draper." She paused and clutched her side. Her determination returned as she said, "I must be near ye midwife."

"The midwife?" John was puzzled and wondered why the midwife had entered into the discussion. "It be summer. She be able to come to New Scotland."

Lydia shook her head.

"But you travailed without the midwife when John Junior be born."

"How would thou know? Ye were snow wandering for much of it," said Lydia. That rebuke stung John and his face reflected it. "Oh John, I am consumed with dread and speak heartless words." Lydia's remorseful look gave way to a fear-filled one. "I must have ye midwife."

"What be the matter?" asked John.

"Our son to be only squirms, never kicks, like he is struggling to live." Lydia pressed her hand against her stomach and moved closer to John. "Ye midwife resides near Goody Draper. Reverend Bulkeley and Goodman Philip Read, the physician, reside thither too, if, if…" Lydia shook her head to regain her composure. "It's God's providence that compels me to be with Goody Draper now. She doth need me." She lowered her eyes. "And I need her, too. I desire to be nigh to all of them." She peered up into John's eyes and asked, "Will thou allow me to go until thy son is born?"

"A son?" asked John. "Our child may be a lass." John's efforts to cajole lasted as brief as Lydia's smile. Even though he could not follow her logic, he said, "Thou may go."

Lydia kissed his check, and then his lips. She pulled back, and her eyes were windows into an emotionally wrecked being. John still couldn't follow her logic, but he was fearful of what he now saw. He continued gazing through Lydia's eyes at a kaleidoscope of horrific images.

Those horrors returned often, particularly at night, as he slept alone for the first time since his marriage. One image, an umbilical cord coiled like a hissing serpent with a devilish sneer, returned often. When he received word from Adam that a healthy lad was born, he hastened with his only English friend to meet his new son.

As John gazed upon Thomas, his second son, he felt a joy similar to what he had felt when he first saw John Junior. He now had two sons that would eventually help him with his chores, and later, care for Lydia. And with what was now becoming a predictable occurrence, a third son, Stephen, was born nearly two years later, on the 28th of August 1665. John's good fortune continued and seemed never-ending.

Chapter Thirty-five

September 1665

Lydia nestled the newborn Stephen close to her breast as she watched his two brothers in the field with John. His gentle suck drew in pleasant thoughts. Since marriage, her rhythm was consistent with God's providence for the chosen women – pregnancy through lactation, spanning two years. Her travails had been arduous, but less so than many, and Goody Walker's herbs had minimized most of the nuisances that pregnancy caused. Her newborns had been healthy, were still living, and, by God's grace, all sons. The staccato like beat needed for birthing was over. Now, she was enjoying the quiet interlude of a mother and newborn, her favorite part of a goodwife's two-year cycle. She would relish it as she awaited God's providence for her fourth cycle to begin.

Stephen coughed, and Lydia moved him to pat his back. John was refereeing a squabble about a stick between a four and half year old John Junior and a two year old Thomas. Lydia smiled and moved Stephen back to her breast. His warm mouth removed the chill from her nipple, and she pondered her good fortune further.

Her father's and Goody Draper's transgressions, and her guilt from her earlier experience with depravity had convinced her the Drapers had not been God's chosen ones. She attended the Sabbath meetings, but doubted she would ever receive God's grace. But since marriage, her blessings were typical of most goodwives, even though she was seldom called such.

A tingling grew from her breast to fill her soul. She arched her neck to bask for a few moments. Was this intimate feeling from the Divine? Had God sufficiently humbled her, so that now, God was willing to choose her? She straightened her neck and caressed Stephen's bonneted head as he nursed. She was certain she would have a year or so with this union, before beginning her a fourth cycle.

While the goodwives' cycles were typically twenty-four months, nature's cycles were shorter. Summer's sun, lessening each day, was now insufficient to overcome the breeze that cooled the air. Stephen's tiny lips no longer warmed Lydia's breast. The leaf fall season would bring a killing frost, and winter would suspend life until spring could regenerate it. Lydia tucked her breast into her blouse, drew her wrap close, cradled Stephen and went inside. Her view of good fortune chilled too.

*****

Early Autumn 1665

Lydia's rhythm had lost its usual pattern. When not nursing Stephen, she was cradling Thomas.

"There be plenty of porridge," said John. Oblivious to what John had said, Lydia continued to rock Thomas gently. "Aye, it be cold, me'll heat it for you."

John scooped the porridge back into the kettle, added berries and nuts and placed it on the embers. He left for more wood, and when he returned, he asked more questions that received no answers. The infant Stephen slept close to the fire, near John Junior, who sensing something was not quite right, looked often at his impassive mother.

"Come son," said John, "me have chores to do."

John Junior arose from his squat and ran after his father. The Father and son bonding eased both of them as they worked together in the invigorating air. But when they returned, it was as if they had never left, only the fire had dimmed.

The cold from the open door jolted Lydia. She pulled Thomas closer and kissed his head. "His fire still burns," she said.

"Give him more of Goody Walker's tonic," said John.

"It doth not help."

"Then remove the blanket and his clothing."

"Goody Draper said his fire will not depart until his blanket is soaked. It will help to quench his fire."

"And what did Physician Philip Read say?"

Lydia squeezed her eyes. "Thomas is in God's hands," she said.

"He be a physician, not a preacher."

Lydia returned to her rocking, and its rhythm lessened her anxieties. Her mind eased toward oblivion again. But Stephen's wail brought her back, and the rocking ceased. She nursed him, absent the pleasures of a month earlier. When she finished nursing, she took Thomas back from John.

That night, John lay close to his eldest son, near the fire. He slept fitfully and arose often to stoke it. Lydia cradled Thomas and rocked, unaware of her husband's stirrings. A crow's caw awakened John, which seemed to come too early as he was still groggy. He closed his eyes, but the grating caws continued. He staggered up and went to touch Thomas's head. His hand moved in unison with Lydia's rocking. "His fever be gone," said John.

But the drenched blankets were as stone cold as Thomas's forehead. John's legs nearly buckled with his panic, but he regained enough composure to inch his hand down to his son's chest. The rhythmic pulses were lost for eternity. Shock ripped through John, and he closed his eyes as he shuddered. But terror tore his eyelids open and filled his eyes with horror. Only Lydia's gentle rock steadied him.

"Lydia," said John as he shut his eyes and prayed for strength to finish. "Give me Thomas." John wedged an arm between Lydia and Thomas and drew him slowly away from her.

Lydia ceased rocking and yanked Thomas closer. She frowned at John.

"Lydia, please," and John tried again.

And with a violent tug back, Lydia said, "No."

John placed a hand on Lydia's shoulder and lifted her head with is other hand. His angel was in denial, forlorn and looking for answers. John's emotion-clogged throat couldn't speak, even if he had consoling words to offer. Finally, he swallowed and said, "Thomas be at rest with God."

Lydia slumped back into her chair, and John took Thomas. He swayed with him in his arms, looked heavenward, and tears streamed down his cheeks. Without Thomas to hold, Lydia collapsed into a blubbering heap. She clung to John's leg and could have clung for an eternity. His strong thigh was something to hold. It had replaced her rocking and was her new peace of mind. But John Junior stirred, and Stephen cried. Her peace of mind would have to wait.

A few days passed, and Lydia spent them cradling Stephen, regardless if he was hungry or not. The shelter was deathly quiet, but unlike John and John Junior, Lydia remained in it. A shock of light entered her gloominess as John opened the door. "Lydia, it's time," he said. She arose with Stephen cradled against her breast and followed John and their eldest son up the rise.

At the gravesite, John inhaled deeply and took in the panorama while exhaling slowly. "Me come here after me chores," he said. "Sit on that rock and admire me estate. It be peaceful, eh?"

Lydia didn't answer. John Junior moved closer to her and clung to her dress. John lowered Thomas into the grave. He arose and dusted off his breeches. "Dear God, you took me son too early. But so be it. He be with his grandfather now." John paused as finishing was going to be difficult. He surveyed his estate again while listening to nature's harmony. The always peaceful gurgle from his brook dominated the symphony. He nodded and silently thanked God for the blessing of his New Scotland. He had found some added strength. "Father watch over me lad until it's me time to come." He turned to Lydia and asked, "Do you want to offer words unto God?"

"God doth not hear my words," she said. Lydia returned to her detachment until disturbed by swishes of earth and the clank of rocks as John filled in the grave. She twitched and looked down at a clinging John Junior. She patted his head, and he smiled. He wanted more from his mother, but Lydia became distant again, lost in the rhythm of John's shoveling.

John tamped the grave and led Lydia and her two sons down the rise. He remained outside to enjoy the sunshine and soothing gurgle of the waters. Small eddies swirled from the rocks as it meandered east before blending into a gentle flow. John's mind became a gentle flow, too, and he wished it could last. But his sons, and most of all, Lydia needed him. With some reluctance, he trudged homeward and went into a cold, dimly lit home.

Chapter Thirty-six

Concord Meetinghouse
Spring 1666

Sunlight poured through the meetinghouse window behind The Reverend, which gave him a glaring backdrop, in stark contrast to the mutedly lit room. Dust particles floated, seemingly forever, and in the illumination, they shimmered. At times, the glare obscured The Reverend's face, yet his words, especially when he roared them, were always heard. "Satan is with thee who staggers home and disgorges his stomach into ye devil's inferno," said The Reverend.

A tythingman's woolen-tipped pole jabbed at the man who was the target of the preacher's concern. He snorted, opened his eyes and sat upright, exposing a "D" stitched on the chest of his sleeveless waistcoat.

"Drink is God's creation to be received with grace and temperance."

The man rubbed his eyes and nodded an agreement.

"But intemperance of drink is gluttony and Satan's damnation."

John drifted from the preacher's rant. His morning was more insufferable than he imagined. But he knew why he came. Lydia's melancholy had grown into a depression. Still illogical to John, she blamed herself for Thomas's death, and his reasoning for why it was not so was unpersuasive. Further, several days ago, Mehitable died while lambing, and Lydia, too pre-occupied with her grieving, was not there for her cherished ewe. Thus, his goodwife blamed herself for Mehitable's death too. In desperation, John thought maybe attending the Sabbath meeting with Lydia would help her. After talking with Adam, who agreed to speak with the influential meeting goers and to act as John's escort, John came to his first Sabbath meeting.

John turned to the women seated at the back of the meetinghouse. A listless Lydia sat between Goody Draper and Deborah, clutching Stephen. Her eyes were as unresponsive as they had been since Thomas fell ill. John's inattentiveness to The Reverend began to annoy the women seated near Lydia, and he turned back.

The forehead of the man with the "D" on his waistcoat glistened, and sweat beads clung above his lip. John wondered if it was from humiliation or too much drink. John enjoyed his spirits too, but he had never emptied his stomach into his hearth. All eyes were upon the verbally pummeled wretch, seemingly enjoying the preacher's harangue. As the wretch squirmed, John prayed for the man's abuse to end.

"Among ye is an outsider drawn for redemption and quick salvation," said The Reverend.

Eyes turned from the wretch, and John was quietly amused by it. *Aye, this English God does hear the prayers of a Scottish bastard.*

"Thy salvation doth not reside here. God hath predetermined who receives his grace. Thou cannot fool God with thy paltry attendance."

John had been bored and sitting on an oaken bench for three hours. But he now sensed The Reverend's word were about him. His buttocks ached and he shifted, and those on either side parted from him. The stale meetinghouse air was stifling, and John's shirt clung to his armpits. Adam eased further away, and John wondered if it was his stench.

"When our Lord wandered the wilderness for forty days, Satan tried to fool him." The Reverend pounded on his reading stand and said, "And Satan failed."

Every eye now pinned John to the bench. He was alone, lost in a Puritan wilderness. He perspired more.

"If thou chose Satan's wilderness, so be it. Stay in thy wilderness. It is where thou must reside as ye never can be saved."

John wished he could be in New Scotland now. His gurgling stream floated into his mind to soothe him until The Reverend turned elsewhere. He was now freed from piercing eyes and a preacher's scolding, yet their wounds remained.

When the Sabbath ordeal ended, John shuffled between the benches following Adam. But Adam hurried away to reunite with friends. Other pre-established cliques gelled outside the meetinghouse. John was in bustling crowds, yet alone. An older man gestured an acknowledgement, but John couldn't recall him until he saw a smirking Duncan standing to the side. Robert Blood turned back to his circle of friends, and Duncan remained outside the circle, still smirking.

Another familiar face approached John. "John Hoare, Esquire," he said. "How now, and what, pray tell, brings thee hither?"

"Me goodwife."

"Ah," and Hoare's lips pursed. "I have seen Goody Law each Sabbath." Hoare turned to Lydia, who stood to Goody Draper's side. Hoare shook his head and turned back. "Losing a son is a terrible burden," he said. "How hath thou been fairing?"

"Done me grieving; Thomas is with God and his grandfather now."

"Then thou art at peace. But my eyes tell me Lydia still grieves."

"It be harder for a lass, me think."

"Job 1, verse 21," said Hoare. "Naked came I out of my mother's womb, and naked shall I return thither. The Lord gaveth, and the Lord taketh away, blessed be the name of the Lord."

"We also lost Mehitable Thursday last," said John.

Hoare's eyes widened, and he grimaced. He patted John's shoulder. "Care for thy troubled Goodwife. Thou will need the patience of Job, my good man." Hoare ambled back to his clique. He talked with his comrades, and occasionally heads swung out toward John or Lydia. His comrade's expressions were varied, some seemed genuinely compassionate.

The children, freed from their Sabbath prison, had been running about the meetinghouse grounds. But they quieted suddenly, as John Junior had gathered several lads, seemingly to plot further mischief. A gaggle of girls waited. His animated instructions continued until the lads broke toward the girls, who screeched and ran. Their clamor sprinkled into the adult conversations. John eventually corralled his son, and after some complaining, he obeyed and trailed after his father.

"Here is my eldest grandson now," said Mary Draper. She beckoned to John Junior. "Come, meet Goody Davis."

"My so big, and how many years art thou?" asked Goody Davis.

John Junior looked at his grandmother, who answered. "He is five, born a year after his parents wed."

"Five?' asked Goody Davis. "He appears much older."

"Not possible for him to be more than five."

Goody Davis smiled. "Well, it is possible if…" and some of her cronies smiled back. "But as thou say, a mere five." Goody Davis ignored Mary's icy stare to speak to John. "Thou hast traveled from ye wilderness to join us this Sabbath," she said. "And The Reverend's preaching was inspiring, was it not?"

"T'was."

Goody Davis glanced again to her smiling friends. She returned to John. "Thou hast not answered my question. Was The Reverend inspiring or not inspiring?"

"Got me chores to do, Goody Davis."

"Chores?" Goody Davis gasped along with her clique. "Surely not on the Sabbath."

"Aye, but easy chores. Jesus did chores on the Sabbath, too." John casted an eye toward Lydia, and she knew it was time to leave.

The Laws of New Grant left Concord Center. As they walked in silence, John realized his attendance had not helped Lydia's mental state. Further, his mental state had deteriorated while sitting for hours. He wondered if anyone ever found The Reverend's words uplifting. As John pondered further, his disparate thoughts came to a conclusion. *Aye, the bastard Reverend only allowed me to come, so he could scold me.* He thought about how quickly Adam had left once the sermon was over. *Me wonder if Adam....* But his trust in Adam was too strong to think he would have deceived him. He concluded The Reverend had simply duped Adam, too.

They reached John Hoare's residence, and John paused. "John Hoare, Esquire be a good man," he said.

"Thou knowest him?" asked Lydia.

"He befriended me years ago." John had a wry smile as he said, "He told me about you."

"John Hoare hath a facile tongue. The truth doth not always find his words." John hadn't expected such an animated response, but he appreciated that Lydia still had some life in her. "He's been critical of Reverend Bulkeley's preaching in the past," she said.

"Then me like this good man even more."

"The town fathers think contrary." Lydia ceased bouncing Stephen and placed a hand on hip. "And what falsehood did he say about me?" she asked.

"He told me to do the fitting and proper thing and marry thee."

Lydia dropped her arm, resumed bouncing Stephen and smiled. Her glow hadn't been lost forever, and John savored it. But her worried expression quickly returned. "What else did he say?"

"I told him of Mehitable's passing. He was saddened." Mehitable's death was still too raw, and Lydia's unhappiness returned. John regretted his remark.

Lydia looked at Hoare's house and back to John. She looked at the ground and thought of an earlier time when Hoare had helped her. She raised her head, and a glow flickered into her unhappiness. "John Hoare, Esquire is a good man. It doth please my heart that he is thy friend."

Chapter Thirty-seven

Concord, Middlesex, Massachusetts Bay Colony
Spring 1668

John brought a clump of earth to his nose and sucked in its aroma. He crumbled it among his fingers. It was warm enough for planting. He handed his whittled stick to his seven year old son, who rested it upon both his opened palms. His eyes moved from the stick's taper along the evenly spaced notches to its blunt end. He looked up at his father, who nodded. "Laddie, push it into the soil to this notch,' said John as he pointed.

His son knelt, and while looking at his father, he eased the taper into the soil.

"Mind your notch, laddie."

His son turned from John to the stick. When the notch abutted the soil, he looked back. John nodded, and his son yanked the stick out and smiled.

"Good laddie. Now lay the stick next to the hole, and at the end of the stick push in your finger." When his son complied, John said, "Now push the stick into the finger hole up to the notch."

John Junior seemed to understand the planting procedure, and John arose from his crouch. He grabbed a bag of seed while maintaining a watchful eye. He thought of an earlier time when he was the eager student until further guidance was needed. "Keep your row straight. Uneven rows tell folks you be a slacker."

His son aligned his next bore and pushed the stick into the moist soil when his father nodded. With his son back on an even course, John straddled the row, stooped and dropped in four kernels. "Four in the hole, two to grow, one to hoe, and one for the crow," he said.

John Junior giggled. "Say it again, Father."

John complied, and his son's response was the same. After a few iterations of the saying, his son had memorized it and repeated it often. Crows cawed incessantly breaking the monotony, and John turned to the swirl of black commotion. He shook his head, and as he dropped the kernels into the hole he offered a variation. "Four in the hole, two to grow, one to hoe, and one for those God damn crows." His son's giggle returned, and John continued with an emphasis on the 'God damn crows'.

The novelty of planting soon left John Junior, and John did the boring, spacing and sowing. But his son, as always, never wandered far from his side. They worked into the afternoon, and when John paused to straighten his back, Lydia came up the rise. John placed a small stone at his stopping point and called to his son.

John Junior ceased fiddling with the soil and ran to his mother. She crouched and waited for her son to fly into her arms. But he came up short and while panting said, "Father let me use his stick all day."

"No wonder thou art eager."

"And he taught me planting words." Lydia cocked her head and John Junior continued. "Four in the hole, two to grow, one to hoe and one for the God damn crow." John Junior sniggered. Lydia was not amused, and he sobered.

As John trudged toward them with the grain sack over his shoulder, Lydia said, "John Law, thou shall not teach our son to blaspheme," John lowered the sack, confused by Lydia's remark.

She turned back to her son. "Never speaketh such words. Good men will think ye devil has thy soul."

"But Father said it."

Lydia glared at John and turned back. "But thou shall not. Now come; it's time to sup."

John Junior hugged his mother and grabbed her hand. At first, they ambled home while chatting, before clasping their hands and swinging them as they skipped. John slung the sack over his shoulder, and watching his son, became seven again. He had just finished a day with his father and was tired. He would soon eat, and after, he would cuddle with his mother, always the best part of the day.

John Junior's laughter disturbed John's reminiscing and he left it for other thoughts. His son was similar in build to when John was seven, although stockier. John thought about the many nights he had slept on an empty stomach, something his son rarely experienced. Perhaps a better diet was the reason for his stockiness. His son's hair was curlier than John's and more auburn than red, the influence of Lydia's curly brunette locks.

Stephen ventured up the rise looking for his mother. He was slender, more like Lydia than John. John wondered about Thomas, who would he have most resembled? Lydia's grieving over him had eased into reluctant acceptance, even though scars remained. Of recent, she had seemed more upbeat, and John hoped it would continue.

As he neared his home, the aroma of Lydia's cooking made his mouth salivate. John Junior's giggle could be heard from inside the house as he passed by and headed to Mehitable's shed. He stored the unused grain in the shed with the other sacks. He patted a full sack and grimaced at the thought of tomorrow. He left and headed to an excited household.

During supper, Lydia excused herself, and when she returned her cheerfulness was gone. She remained quiet throughout the rest of the meal and thereafter. Something was wrong, and John decided to wait on his questions until his sons were asleep.

Later that evening, as they lay side-by-side, Lydia broke her silence. "My monthly time has arrived," she said.

"But me thought that maybe…."

"Me too," interrupted Lydia. "It was nigh on six weeks and..." Lydia rolled away and sighed. "God's providence is still not to bless my womb with a child."

"Then we'll try some more." John pulled Lydia close and kissed her. She wasn't receptive.

"Stephen will be three this summer," she said. "He should have a younger sibling by now. And thou must have more sons to tend our fields."

"Perhaps with your grieving, God is waiting for the right time," said John.

"Or God doth not trust this womb to nourish a good child."

John had heard similar arguments before. He had tried to convince Lydia that they were baseless. Every line of tact had been unsuccessful, but he still continued trying. "Lydia, you say 'thou art a good man John Law'."

"And thou art," she said as she caressed John's cheek. "I fear it's me that is impure."

"But you attend the Sabbath meetings."

"Attending doth not effect who God hath chosen."

John rose up on an arm and moved Lydia's face to be eye-to-eye with her. "Me be an only child," he said. "So if me be a good man, then me came from a good womb."

Lydia ceased caressing John's face and thought further.

"But the Lord nae e'er blessed me mum's womb e'er again. Yet, she still be a good lass like you."

Lydia remained silent, and John eased off his arm. He had won the argument this night, yet he knew by morning Lydia would have rationalized his logic away. For some reason unknown to John, she believed she was doomed to be barren for the rest of her life.

*****

John finished his morning samp and headed to Mehitable's shed. He was unaware of his constant companion trailing after him. John put two full sacks onto his cart and looked at the third, half depleted sack. He put it on the cart, thought and removed it. John's pre-occupation left, and he noticed John Junior. "Got to pay me rent today, laddie. You stay here with your mum."

A crestfallen son looked at his father. "Please, Father." John looked back up the rise at a somber Lydia. "I'll be good," said his son.

"It be far," said John.

"I know."

John nodded an assent, and his son's face exploded with joy. He jumped up and down, causing John to laugh. John indicated to Lydia that their son would be with him for the day. Her smile was brief, and John wished he could make her explode with joy, too.

Along the way, John Junior ran from the cart to the meadow, dawdled with intriguing things and ran back. His chatter was incessant, his energy unbounded. But by the time they reached Hoare's residence, he was struggling to keep pace. John lifted him onto the cart and resumed their journey. His son leaned against the bundles facing John, too fatigued for anything else. When John paused to rest, his son scrambled atop of the sacks and faced away from John. John lifted the cart and chuckled. His son was like a potentate being carried to town by a servant.

John Junior squirmed as he pointed. "That's the grandest house of all." He turned back to his father.

"It used to be owned by Reverend Bulkeley."

"I want to be a Reverend, so I can have a grand house."

John snorted at the irony. "There be other grand houses too." His son spun forward and took in the houses lining the road. When he spun back, John nearly lost his balance. "Sit easy, laddie."

"Who owns those?" asked John Junior.

"Rich Englishmen."

"I want to be a rich Englishman." John wondered if his son would ever be anything but a poor Scotsman's son.

Concord Common was abuzz. Several carts were aligned near the tax collector, Ebenezer Clark. He was finely dressed and held a quill and parchment. He had grown more corpulent these past few years, just like Angus MacTavish. Two fat pigs, and as John neared Ebenezer he wondered who he detested more – MacTavish or him.

Ebenezer looked at his parchment and furled his brow. "Where is thy third sack. John Law?" he asked.

"Me got me family to feed."

"Ye rent is three sacks." John Junior slid off the two sacks. His enthusiasm had waned with the unsettling conversation. "This be your boy?"

John nodded.

"He seems well fed." Ebenezer turned to John Junior. "Dost thou eat every day?"

John Junior bobbed his head and sidled closer to his father.

"Just this boy?"

"Me has another at home with his mum," said John.

"Then thou should have enough corn for thy rent." Ebenezer bent over to be face-to-face with John Junior. "Is your father a slacker, boy? Doth he drink too much and work too little?"

John pulled his son back and stepped to be inches from Ebenezer. "Leave me lad be." Ebenezer pulled back, and John rapped his finger on his chest. "Do you hear me?"

Ebenezer stepped back and adjusted his cloak. "Thou till a fertile plot, John Law. Land others would dearly covet."

"Your rent be too dear, me say."

"Others, especially those not fond of drink, might not find the rent too dear."

John reined in his urge to strangle Ebenezer. Others were drawn to the argument, and John's uneasiness grew.

"Ebenezer," said a distant man, who waved to gather Ebenezer's attention. He left to converse with the man who had just summoned him.

John's son clung to his leg, and John rubbed his head. John's apprehension returned as he watched the meeting that was deciding his fate. He tried to discern an answer, but it was impossible. The conversation ended, and Ebenezer began to return.

Robert Blood, who was among the group that Ebenezer was leaving, nodded to John. John reflected to his conversation with Blood ten years earlier about paying a fair rent. Blood had said then 'trust me', and now, John hoped Blood was more truthful than Awbrey had been.

"John Law, we will treat you with leniency," said an annoyed Ebenezer as he scrawled on his parchment.

John exhaled his relief.

Ebenezer finished writing and looked with disapproval at John. "Take heed my Scottish man. Next year the selectmen may opt not to be so lenient." Ebenezer huffed and moved to another man with grain sacks on his cart.

John unloaded his two sacks. His son was now less enthusiastic than before, and John wondered if he was still shaken from the events or just disillusioned with him. Would his son still regard him with the same admiration as when they left this morning?

John Junior ran to some Sabbath friends, who welcomed him with noisy chatter. John wheeled his cart from the crowd and rested alone while his son frolicked. The curious faces had returned to their cliques. He closed his eyes and listened to John Junior's banter among his friends. On this day, his son sounded more English than Scottish, and without a trace of a brogue.

Maybe that be best for the lad. It be hard to be Scottish in an English world.

Chapter Thirty-eight

John and his son were busy in the fields getting ready for the harvest. Suddenly an eerie feeling came to John that he had not sensed since Lydia came into his life. *Could it be?* John turned around, and an Indian with hair cut like an Englishman's stood aside an adolescent. John thought it might be Nagoglancit. Yet clothed in sad colors, he appeared more honorable than the daunting savage John had met several years earlier. He thumped his chest.

Nagoglancit thumped and said, "John Law, thou still tend our lands with great care."

Startled, John Junior arose and looked to his father. He sensed his father's comfort, but still stayed away, fascinated by the adolescent with flowing raven locks.

Nagoglancit pointed at the corn tassels. "God gives thee an abundant crop."

John smiled with pride, but the feeling was brief. "Hopefully enough for me rent next spring," he said. "Me nae recognized you. You be dressed like The Reverend."

"I now follow John Tahattawan's path and John Eliot's teaching. Learn English and ye Bible. Be Christian like thee, John Law."

John smiled and thought about correcting Nagoglancit. He was not at all like the English Christians of Concord.

Nagoglancit put his hand on the adolescent's shoulder. "My son. Someday he becomes Christian too." His son brushed back his locks, and remained expressionless. "He is a man now; lived alone for one moon, west of Nagog Pond with but a knife." He patted his son's shoulder, and Nagoglancit's eyes appeared to twinkle with pride. But they narrowed as he turned to John. "Mohawks now near Nagog."

"Mohawks?" John furled his brow. "This be a new tribe."

"Mohawks come from the land of the setting sun. To be feared when they roam."

"I'm not afraid," said Nagoglancit's son, who had a confidence that resembled his father's when he was younger. Nagoglancit seem both proud and justifiably concerned. Perhaps John was having a glimpse at his future father-son relationship. He turned to his son, but unlike Nagoglancit's son, he was still skittish.

"Come laddie, meet Nagoglancit and…," John paused and looked to Nagoglancit, wanting a name.

"His Christian name is John, named for my teacher." John turned back to his son who had taken a few hesitant steps. "And also, for my Scottish friend," said Nagoglancit.

John swung back in disbelief to a straight-faced Nagoglancit as gratitude flowed through him. He wanted to thank him, but the words would not come. He grunted 'Aye', such a meaningless response, and it bothered and embarrassed John.

Nagoglancit turned to his son. "John Law hath cared for our land, and thou should be thankful."

John cheeks flushed. He didn't deserve the praise. If anything, he had deceived his friend about the land, just as the English had done to him.

Nagoglancit turned back to John. "To honor thee, I gave my son the Christian name John."

John shifted his eyes away from Nagoglancit as his stomach knotted with guilt. His naïve friend was still too trusting of him. John stepped side-to-side, wanting to end the unwarranted adulation. "Should me fear the Mohawks?" he asked.

"Mohawks take from the Indians, especially the Praying ones. But Mohawks fear the English."

Nagoglancit's words were reassuring, yet his demeanor lacked his usual resolve. John had heard various tribal names before, gibberish that he forgot as soon as he had heard it. But John sensed 'Mohawks' should be a tribe to remember.

Lydia stood on the hillcrest kneading her apron. John waved a beckoning hand. Nagoglancit and his son turned to her, and Lydia stopped kneading.

"Come meet me friend," said John.

Lydia flapped a limp wrist and hurried down the rise.

Nagoglancit gripped John's hand and stared into his pale blue eyes. He placed his other hand on John's shoulder.

"Nashobah will return one day. Care for our land." Nagoglancit looked at his son. "Someday it will be my son John's land."

An acrid gas filled John's empty stomach as the two departed. Now at ease, John Junior moved closer to his father. "Will ye land be Nagoglancit's son's?" he asked.

"Nae, me friend be confused."

"I understand. He is an Indian." John pursed his lips and swallowed an impulsive retort. "Mother says thou cannot believe what an Indian sayeth."

John grabbed his son's shoulders and spun him to be face-to-face. "Nagoglancit sayeth his truth. It be the English who deceive the Indians." And as an afterthought he mumbled, "And Scottish men too."

"But Mother said…" and John shook his son again. But upon seeing his fright, John ceased.

John marched down the rise, and his son trailed after him, wondering why his father was so upset. They both went inside the house. John remained quiet, still trying to control his shame as he sat in his favorite chair. Well aware of his father's displeasure, John Junior went to his brother and stayed near to him. Lydia was busy preparing supper, and eventually, the pleasing aromas helped to ease John's pique.

"Nagoglancit be a Praying Indian, now," he said. "His English be good. He sayeth like thou."

"Sayeth like thee, John; not thou," said Lydia. "Praying or not, he's still an Indian."

"You should have come and met him."

"I waved," said Lydia as she moved to settle a disagreement between her two sons. Her efforts were useless and her irritation grew, particularly with the instigator, John Junior. She turned back to John, yet her words were for the instigator. "John, take thy son to ye shed and use thy switch."

John arose, and quiet came at once. There would be no need for the switch.

At supper, John Junior, still suffering from his father's earlier outburst and the threat of his switch, was understandably withdrawn. For some unknown reason, Lydia's apparent distress at her son's quarreling remained throughout supper. John grew pensive and became remorseful over deceiving his friend. The silence of three self-absorbed people confused young Stephen, and he was quiet too.

After the evening meal, John filled his pewter cup and went outside to survey his estate. In the twilight, only the meandering river was distinct in the meadow. He was in New Scotland, and his moat still protected him. But smoke from John Shepard's chimney and a distant rumble from the Ironworks gave a harsh reality to his delusion. He thought of Nagoglancit and how the English had deceived him. Would he someday have a similar fate? He had no definitive answer, and he took a final swig. The twilight was gone. His moat had disappeared into the darkness, yet the gurgling reminded him that he was still in his New Scotland. He trudged up the rise. His home was as quiet as the cooling night. And Lydia, would her quiet coolness remain or could she be aroused?

He snuggled close to Lydia and caressed the nape of her neck. He rubbed her back and kissed her shoulder. An ember crackled, and light flared. His sons were asleep, away from the dim light. His empty pewter cup had stirred a passion, and the muted light intensified it.

"Should me try for another son?" asked John.

"It be of no use."

John rubbed her back. "We nae try enough." John continued to rub, waiting for a response.

Finally, it came. "God hath poisoned my womb."

Not the response John wanted. He braced himself on his forearm, caressed Lydia's cheek, and felt tears. "Lydia, what?" he asked.

Whimpers were her only response. She rolled to face John, and her lips were quivering. Her face absorbed the dim light, and contrasted against the darkness, it was the purest white John had ever seen. Yet it reflected more distress than Lydia's tears implied.

"It was so distant," she said. "But time hath not taken away my pain. Your friend hath stirred my anguish anew."

"Nagoglancit?"

Lydia nodded and looked away. John eased her face back to regain eye contact. He hovered above, looking into Lydia's reddened, tear-streaked eyes.

Lydia knew she was a captive. Her time had arrived, and she gulped. "When I was in my innocence, we lived north of hither," she said. "Day had darkened when I arrived home with Mehitable. Two Indians wandered near."

"Nagoglancit be one of them?"

Lydia shook her head no. "They were looking for Goody Draper, I suppose. Wanted spirits, but Deborah and I were alone." Tears reappeared as Lydia said, "And then…" She tried to turn her head away, but John stiffened his wrist and held her firm. "We tried to resist, but Satan gave the heathens strength that God would not allow us to overcome. They took us to Nagog Pond."

John's heart raced. He was disgusted and angry, yet aroused. His forearm trembled as he waited for more.

Lydia sniffed. "They were powwowing around a fire; oh, those dread-filled, guttural chants." She closed her eyes, and when they opened John saw their anger. "Bodies barely clad. Heathens filled with Satan's evils."

John had heard the unnerving powwowing through the years. Those chilling sounds now seemed to reverberate in the shadowy light. And with each drumbeat, a horrific image of rape flashed. His internal rage grew, which he needed to avenge on Lydia's behalf. "Was Nagoglancit there?" he asked.

"Indians were thither John; painted faces darting in and out of ye firelight. Dancing and howling in darkness. I was in the bowels of Satan's hell, and felt I could not be degraded any further." Her voice trailed off as she continued. "Then they stripped me to bear my nakedness for their pleasures. Shame filled my soul." Lydia shut her eyes, and when they opened she spoke with an impassive resignation to her fate. "The most excited among them tied Deborah to a tree and danced before her. They abused us through the night until they fatigued from drink."

John's mind had an unshakable image; Nagoglancit's face, with devilish red and orange hues streaking out from the center of it, sneered while he drove his powerful haunches into

Lydia's pelvis. He pounded Lydia with more enthusiasm than his father's prize ram had ever pounded a frightened ewe. His black eyes, vindictive and paying John back for years of deceit, were looking at him.

"Was it Nagoglancit? Me will slay him."

Lydia rushed her hands to her face. "I truly know not," she said. "I have tried to forget those faces. Is it important?"

Nagoglancit was still thrusting, and his smile broadened with each thrust. John needed an answer to make his nightmare end. But badgering Lydia was futile and only causing her further pain. There was no definitive answer. John would have no closure this night. Lydia's still questioning face needed a response. John resigned himself to his situation. "It nae be important."

Lydia's questioning face left. Now, embarrassment, guilt and regret swept across her, and like a fallen angel in the night, she lowered her eyes. Her quiet was brief, and she raised her eyes again. "I threw my burden unto ye Lord, and he heard me. One among the devils stood watch and never slept. When all was quiet, he untied Deborah and hastened us not to tarry."

John kissed Lydia, and her face reflected an ease from finally unburdening her self-imposed guilt. She smiled, and John hoped it would last for an eternity. But it left immediately. "Father said not to speak of ye devils' madness," she said. "But Satan hath his ways. Words from the gossipers' lips came forth. Oh that Goody Davis, she is Satan incarnate." Lydia shook her head to rid her pique. "John Hoare. Esquire was the Lord's only voice of reason, trying to quell the investigation."

"Investigation?" asked John. His arm trembled again, and he reclined.

"A midwife came from Charlestown. Goody Davis and another goodwife came too. They made me disrobe. Naked was I before the gossipers, and I was as doleful then as when I was before the heathens." Lydia's resolve was cracking. She brushed her eyes and continued. "The midwife probed and kept uttering, 'Oh my fair child'."

John's heart raced, and his head was dizzy. He thought of the night under a tree with Andrew Adams. *"Maybe all we get is the wenches."* He closed his eyes and grimaced. *It nae be her fault.* He inhaled and let the air slowly seep out. His emotions slowed too. "What did they find?" he asked.

"I told them I was penetrated not, that I was still pure."

A thrusting Nagoglancit with horns like Satan danced in John's head. Andrew Adams' words echoed, and a fallen angel laid aside him, longing for forgiveness. John's emotions had never ranged so far and with such intensity before this night. He rose back upon his forearm.

Lydia whimpered. "'We know my fair child' is what they said. But their eyes, filled with Satan's lust, belied their Godly words." Her anger returned. "Hypocrites, all of them."

John still had many questions that needed answers. Was Lydia just abused or was she penetrated? Was Nagoglancit an abuser? What did Goody Davis know?

Lydia tried to speak, but her lips trembled and she couldn't. She sniffed until her trembling ceased. "Dost thou believe me?"

John's unanswered questions swirled, and a kaleidoscope of images spun to answer each. He didn't know where to begin as his wife awaited his response. Suddenly, the swirl halted, and the most important image in his life remained. He kissed Lydia and said, "Thou art me Goodwife."

He started to ease off his forearm, and Lydia grabbed his face. "Let me see thy eyes. Let me see God's forgiveness in them. Dost thou believe me?"

"Me does," he said, and their eyes remained locked for a seeming eternity. John prayed Lydia saw truthfulness in his eyes.

Lydia broke eye contact and rolled away from John. He pulled her close, and her warmth melted over him. Her cheeks had a warm softness he hadn't felt for a long time. Slow and rhythmic breathing came to his angel, and it eased him too. He started to doze.

Unexpectedly, Lydia turned and held him tightly. She kissed him with an ardor he had not known for years. John's blood surged with new found vigor. Lydia's passionate kissing was unrelenting, which only increased his throbbing. John raised Lydia's night shirt and caressed her breast. She arched her back, and whispered, "Firmer." Her breathing grew more rapid, and she said 'firmer' repeatedly.

John now cupped both of her breasts, and he paused his caressing to gain control over his passions. But Lydia grabbed his hands and forced them between her now open and warm thighs. John fingered Lydia's moist warmth, which was more inviting than her previous kisses. He lowered his breeches and mounted an eagerly awaiting Lydia. She was unburdened and rolled her head back and forth in seeming delight as John drove into her. Her pants increased with each of John's thrust, and eventually she reached a climax. Then her breathing slowed and became rhythmic again. Her eyes had seemingly drifted to a distant and much needed, peaceful place. Only the flickering of her eyes told John his angel hadn't completely left him.

He rolled off of Lydia, and his breathing eventually slowed and became rhythmic too. His added burdens that nagged for answers had drifted far away. Emotionally satisfied, he slept peacefully.

Chapter Thirty-nine

Late winter 1669

Lydia and Stephen walked on frozen snow cover away from Goody Shepard's house. Lydia occasionally broke through the crust, and a four year old Stephen shuffled on top of it, slipping every once in a while. When he did, Lydia picked him up and brushed the snow off. After several falls, she hugged and consoled him until his tears ceased. His cheeks were scarlet, and stringy mucous hung under each nostril. Lydia quickened her pace, and Stephen whined for her to walk slower. Eventually, after much cajoling, the two reached home.

John was weaving aside the hearth. John Junior stood near, watching and listening to his father's occasional comments. Lydia removed Stephen's wrap, wiped his nose, and ushered him to the hearth.

"Goody Shepard's children's ague has departed," said Lydia. "She is blessed to have so many children. But when they all ail, she doth need help. I know she is thankful for my visit." Lydia removed her wrap and hugged John Junior. "And I am thankful too. God's way of giving me more children."

John squinted and continued weaving another strand into the loom.

"Goody Shepard said Captain Thomas Wheeler will be our new neighbor. He hath traded with the Indians for years. He's quite well to do, you know. Having a Captain in New Grant will protect us from the heathens."

John and Lydia locked eyes, each knowing there was deeper meaning to Lydia's words. John nodded. "Me suppose John Hoare had his say on the matter?"

"Truly not, my fears are too trifling. They gave Captain Wheeler land, north of the Shepards, where thou dost gather wood, not far from…"

"Gave him land?" asked John, and he ceased weaving.

"Truly, to tend dry cows."[32]

"So meadowland, and nae me woodlands?"

"Ye woodlands are not thine, dear."

John pointed to where Stephen was rubbing his hands. "What burns in me hearth? What warms me sons?" he asked.

Lydia fiddled with the top of her dress and stepped closer to Stephen. She pulled him near and kissed the top of his head. "Still cold, dear?" she asked. Lydia turned to John who was still waiting for an answer. "Well I don't rightly know," she said. "Goody Shepard just said land. But I doubt she meant thy woodlands."

John nodded and returned to his weaving. Stephen turned to face the fire, and John Junior moved next to him. They jostled for the warmest spot.

---

32 *Dry cows are those that have entered a period in their lactation cycle where they no longer produce milk. Thus, they need less attending than other cows and can roam with minimal care.*

"It's pasture land for sure," said Lydia. "Captain Wheeler will receive two shillings for each dry cow."

"Me could tend dry cows," said John. He stopped his interlacing and looked up. "Hoot mon, me would tend them for farthings."

"Dear, thou art a shepherd, and a good shepherd," said Lydia.

"Me have tended dry cows too," said John.

Lydia arched a doubting eye.

"In Scotland, with me father."

Lydia's brow wrinkled.

"For a few shillings, me would learn," John said, and he returned to his weaving.

"I know thou would. But Captain Wheeler's lease is for over a hundred dry cows, far too many for thee to tend."

"Over a Hundred," said John as he arose. "Me God, who gave Wheeler all this?"

"Ye town fathers. Goody Shepard said it is all fitting and proper."

John moved away from his loom while muttering, "Fittin' and proper."

"Hast thou seen ye Town Common? It is dreadful, littered with animal droppings. The good men of Concord need more pasture land."

"English bastards always be caring for their own."

"John, the children," said Lydia, and she moved to them. They had ceased their jostling and had turned out from the fire, intrigued by their parents' discussion. "Thou are not on Doon Hill. Chase the devil from thy lips."

John ceased his pacing. His family was huddled together, and his sons were anxious.

"Dost thou realize I am, as thou say, 'an English bastard'?" John lowered his head, and Lydia pointed to her children. "And what then art thy sons?"

John returned to his loom, but his muttering continued. "A pike thrust on Doon Hill would be better than the many me gets here." He sat down and continued to mutter. Lydia moved from her children, and they turned back to the glowing fire. John looked up from his loom. "Remember when it be us. Me be king, and you be queen of New Scotland. And me moat protected us?"

"And me with a fertile womb to bless thee with sons." Lydia turned to her sons and back to John. "God hath burdens for each of us, doth he not?" She smiled and said, "But we know not what God's providence will bring. For me, Captain Wheeler's presence is a blessing."

John's muttering was now barely audible.

"My dearest John, surely thou dost not believe New Scotland would be all ours forever?"

"Aye, me did." His children were still jockeying, and John smiled briefly. "For me sons too." He returned to his weaving and added, "And their sons." The embers crackled, and John looked up from his loom. "First Shepard, now Wheeler. They get the land, and me grovel for farthings."

"Thou hast bartered with vigor. Thou art prosperous too." Lydia moved around the loom and hugged her husband. He looked up, smiled and returned to his weaving. Lydia kissed him and moved to her sons, who were still captivated by the fire. She put an arm on each of them. They didn't react. She pulled them close and looked back at John. His muttering had ceased, but his sadness remained. He would need more therapy than a smoky home could offer. Lydia knew winter would soon free him and hoped toiling in the brisk spring air would brighten his spirits.

Chapter Forty

Spring 1675

John had mellowed these past several years. He accepted the questionable transactions involving the town of Concord, Shepard and Wheeler. Further, other English had trickled onto his land, which John rationalized as the English caring for their ilk. He now acknowledged he did not own all of the land Awbrey originally promised, but he still owned a substantial part of it. Other unsettled areas were nearby, and with the Indians scarce, additional lands were available further west, which John rationalized could be used to compensate for what he had lost.

Having the Shepards as neighbors was a benefit to Lydia. She and Sarah Shepard had developed a deep bond, similar to what many goodwives of Concord proper had developed. They attended the meetinghouse each Sabbath and, on occasion, met during the week. Unlike Lydia, Sarah had maintained her womanly two-year cycle. Lydia had not been so blessed because of her transgressions in her youth. She had unburdened her shame to John and now willingly accepted God's providence. Yet her innate desire for children remained, and helping Sarah with her seven children tempered Lydia's desires, allowing her to feel like a blessed goodwife, too.

John envied the financial arrangement Captain Wheeler had received and was predisposed to dislike him. But he met him once, and his prejudice lessened. Wheeler was a proud, accomplished man, and his sons had many of his positive qualities. John saw a parallel; his sons, particularly his eldest, were a lot like him. As John reflected further, he understood the significance of Lydia's comment that his sons were half Draper, and thus half English. His sons would have more advantages than a Scottish man. Perhaps one day his heirs would carry a moniker, such as 'The Laws of New Scotland', a sign of their acceptance, instead of John's current one, 'The Scottish heathen of New Grant'.

With Wheeler residing near, Lydia's Indian fears had eased. She had become calmer, yet John had become more ill at ease with the Indians. His familiarity with them stemmed mainly from his dealings with Nagoglancit. He had helped John in understanding the land, and without his support, John's early years would have been more difficult. John inferred his positive feelings about Nagoglancit to all Indians. Moreover, John identified less with the English than with the Indians. They, like John, were outcasts and subjected to the English impulses and manipulations.

But Lydia's ordeal had shaken John's confidence and frayed his ties to Nagoglancit. He had persuaded himself that Nagoglancit had not been a participant in the rape. Like Lydia, John still had occasional nightmares. His unease, though, was driven by guilt. John was now less trusting of Indians and readily accepted as fact any rumor of Indians committing horrific acts. Consequently, having this 'English bastard Wheeler' nearby was reassuring to him, too.

*****

John couldn't believe his eldest son was fourteen years old. It seemed like just yesterday, he was teaching him to sow the fields. But John Junior had learned through the years and now did many chores on his own or with Stephen as his helper. This particular morning, John and his eldest were repairing a fence rail, and Stephen was nearby, fertilizing the garden. Lydia was down the rise, taking advantage of the breeze to dry some clothing. John Junior had roughed out a rail, and John had honed it further. John eyeballed the taper, and they maneuvered it between two posts. A nine year old Stephen watched with dung pail in hand.

"Well done laddie," said John.

Stephen looked at his pail. "I'm finished too," he said.

"Keep slinging laddie."

"But it's too hot," said Stephen as John's eyes narrowed. "I need water, Father."

"Have your drink and then get back to your work," said John. Stephen ladled some water from the bucket and dawdled a while before heading back to the plowed field.

"Greetings, my friend," said a familiar voice.

John turned around and, by instinct, began to thump his chest. But he stopped on the second thump and glanced down the rise. Lydia had finished hanging the washed clothing and was inside. John thumped a third time.

Nagoglancit raised the Bible he was carrying and said, "I confessed my sins unto ye God and have been baptized as one of God's own."

John bobbed his head and turned to check on Stephen. "Get on with it laddie, or it'll be a birch branch for your backside." John turned back to Nagoglancit.

"Water was poured upon me," he said. "A cross was etched on my forehead. I am forever sealed and protected from Satan."

"Aye," said John as he turned to check again. Stephen was slinging dung, and John turned back.

"It's an honor to be one of God's children."

"Aye, truly," and John glanced over at Stephen. "So why the Bible?" asked John.

"I teach ye Okommakamesits[33] the Lord's ways."

"Okie make sit," said John. He thought for moment. "Ah, Marlborough."

Nagoglancit smiled, appreciative that his friend had connected the tribe to a town. "I also teach ye Hassanmesits, Makunkokoags, and Chabanakongomuns."[34]

John closed his eyes and shook his head. "And where be they from?" he asked with a sigh.

"They arrive from the land of the setting sun. They fled to the Okommakamesits for safety."

John arched an eye. "Safety?"

"Nipmucs,"[35] said Nagoglancit.

---

33 *A tribe that dwelled in what is now the town of Marlborough*

34 *Tribes that dwelled in what are now the towns of Grafton, Ashland, and Webster, respectively*

35 *Nipmucs were a Nation from Central Massachusetts, consisting in part of Hassanamisco Nipmuc, Chabanakongomuns Nipmucs, and Natick Nipmucs.*

John was being inundated with tribal names, which meant nothing to him, except the one he still feared. "Are Mohawks coming too?" he asked.

"No Mohawks," said Nagoglancit, who was momentarily befuddled by John's question, "just Nipmucs. Unlike Concord, no great river protects Marlborough. English and Okommakamesits live together and build defenses for protection." Nagoglancit continued jabbering about the praying and non-praying Indians, sprinkling in more tribal names as he did.

When Nagoglancit expounded on the problems caused by the English and Indians being closely corralled together behind a stockade, John thought, *Me God, me would rather die than be in a stockade with Englishmen for even a day.* But as Nagoglancit rambled more, John detected an uncharacteristic nervousness to his voice. "Laddie," interrupted John. "Why do Nipmucs cause trouble?"

"Ah John Law, big problems; Metacomet say Plymouth English poisoned his brother Wamsutta many moons earlier. But Plymouth English say Metacomet killed John Sassamon and placed his body in Assawompset Pond."[36]

John was lost again in a fog of foreign sounding names. "Seems like Plymouth has a problem, right laddie?" He turned to check on Stephen.

"Metacomet very powerful," said Nagoglancit.

When John turned from Stephen, he noticed a wide-eyed John Junior. John smiled and said, "Easy laddie."

---

36 *Assawompset Pond is within the current southeastern Massachusetts towns of Lakeville and Middleboro, approximately twenty miles southwest from Plymouth.*

"Old sachems ignore Metacomet. But not so with young braves. They roam, cause mischief."

"But a Plymouth problem, right?"

"John, the English know Metacomet as King Philip."

John's stomach roiled. He was now as wide-eyed as his son. "Me have heard of King Philip," John said as he rubbed his hands on his breeches. King Philip was nothing but trouble, and with Marlborough close to New Scotland, it was not just a Plymouth problem. If the Nipmucs had joined King Philip, would the Mohawks do the same? Other menacing thoughts pre-occupied John, and his anxiety increased when he spotted Lydia. Fortunately, she was out of earshot.

"Fare thee well, John Law," said Nagoglancit.

John muttered a reply to his departing friend. John Junior had grown wide-eyed again, and John flashed a dismissing hand. "These Indians always be squabbling with each other." He jabbed his son's shoulder and chuckled. "Be like you and your brother." His son smiled, but it didn't entirely mask his worry.

Once Lydia went inside, John said to John Junior, "No need to be alarming your mum with these Indian squabbles, eh?" The two moved toward the house. Stephen dropped his dung pail, and sprinted to catch up. John jostled his eldest, and his stone face eventually broke to a smile. "Now, nae a word," said John.

Chapter Forty-one

July 1675

The Laws of New Scotland had their own Sabbath ritual, unlike any other in Concord. John Junior was mature enough to lead his mother and brother to the meetinghouse. Along the way, they would stop at the Shepards and proceed from their house together. While his family was gone John would do chores, albeit light ones. Upon their return, Lydia would relate the latest social news; important to her, often mind numbing to John. On the Sabbath, John's grace was lengthy and sprinkled with remembered childhood phrases. His 'so be it' was always emphatic.

On this particular Sabbath, Lydia prepared the meal without her usual chatter, and when 'so be it' came, she busted open. "The goodwives couldn't stop talking about King Philip this day. His heathens attacked Mendon[37] and drove us English east."

John grunted and continued to inhale his pease porridge.[38]

---

37 *On July 14, 1675, early violence in King Philip's War took place in Mendon, with the deaths of multiple residents. Mendon is approximately 25 miles southwest from Concord*

38 *A savory pudding dish made of boiled legumes, which mainly consists of split yellow or Carlin peas, water, salt, and spices, often cooked with a bacon or ham joint.*

His sons, who usually were more ravenous than John, scooped infrequently while watching their mother. "They burned abandoned houses," said Lydia. "It's terrifying." She clasped her hands in front of her mouth. "I pray Mendon had no stragglers." She dropped her hands and gazed. "No women stragglers."

John looked up from his bowl. "How far be Mendon from New Scotland?"

"Oh, I do not know John, but close enough."

John nodded and continued to eat.

The boys had barely eaten, and Lydia waited impatiently for more of a reaction from John. Nothing came, and she became frustrated. "John, we must remove until King Philip is captured."

John looked up and shook his head. But soon the prolonged silence began to unnerve him. "We stay," he said. "We be safe, the Mohawks nae be with King Philip."

"Mohawks?" asked Lydia. She looked with bewilderment at each of her sons. "John what art thou saying?"

"We be among Nashobahs. They be a friendly lot."

Lydia glared, and John wished he could have inhaled those words. "As thou knowest, ye Nashobah are not a friendly lot."

John had rekindled the past, and feigning nonchalance was no longer an option. "Me knows, but they be Praying Indians now," said John. Those words did little to comfort Lydia. "Nagoglancit carries a Bible. Do you believe he would harm you?" John pointed to his sons, "Or John Junior or Stephen?"

His sons appeared as concerned as their mother. His rationale wasn't working, and he was outnumbered. He returned to his dinner. Only his periodic slurping broke the quiet, which soon became maddening. John thumped the table, jolting the three of them. "We can nae leave," he said. "If we did, me home would be in ruins." His outburst ceased. "Just like Mendon."

"I care not for thy earthly possessions. Our safety is my worry."

The three bowls were still nearly full, and John's outburst had frightened his family. "Me be worried, too," said John. "But we nae be alone in New Scotland. Shepherd be just over the brae."

"Goody Shepard is as troubled as I."

John grimaced. "And is her husband?"

"No, he's like you."

John smiled an 'aha', and resignation momentarily settled into Lydia. She took her first scoop of porridge. John gnawed his brown bread, and dropped the hard pieces of it into his bowl. He stirred them until they softened. "Captain Wheeler be in New Scotland, too," said John.

"No, he hath left."

John ceased stirring and stared at Lydia.

"He and his son have gone with Captain Edward Hutchinson of Boston to meet with the Nipmucs."

"Aye, see," said John as surveyed the table. He nodded to his eldest. "Wheeler and his lads will take care of these Nipmucs." John Junior ripped a piece from the loaf and dropped it into his bowl. Stephen followed his brother's lead.

"Perhaps thou speak truly," said Lydia. "Captain Wheeler hath experience with Indian matters." But as Lydia thought further, her angst returned. "But Goody Shepard asked when we would remove across the river."

Stephen stopped eating and asked, "Mother, are we leaving?"

"Not yet, but thy father may not wish to tarry too long."

"How long must we tarry?" asked John Junior.

Lydia had reignited her sons' fears, and was now besieged with questions. She tried responding without alarming them, but many answers needed to come from John.

John slammed his fist on the table, and the commotion from the back and forth ended. "It be me land and me homestead. Nae King Philip, nae the Nipmucs, nae the Mohawks shall chase me from it." The discussion ended, but worry still etched Lydia's face. John wiped his mouth on his sleeve. "Me'll speak with John Shepard tomorrow," he said. A brief smile crossed Lydia's face, and she resumed eating.

*****

The following morning, Lydia watched John amble across a well-worn path, which she and her sons had often traveled. She knew John only blusters when he is concerned, at a loss for words or torn by a dilemma. Offering to talk with Shepard confirmed to her the depth of John's concern.

"To what do I owe this rare occasion?" asked John Shepard.

"Me wife, she be afraid."

"As is my Goodwife Sarah," said Shepard. He ceased picking his teeth with a straw reed. "Goody Davis hath stirred the goodwives of Concord yet again."

John drew his lips tight. "Goody Davis."

"She prattled on about Indians ravaging Mendon's goodwives in ungodly detail. Truly Lydia told thee."

John shook his head no.

"That's surprising. Lydia's countenance was as though horror had seized her soul. Sarah eased her worries on our journey home, yet they seemed to return as she departed."

"Me had nae idea," said John.

Shepard tossed his reed to the ground and straightened his posture. "If thou came to meetinghouse, then thou would know."

John had dreaded coming to see Shepard, but he did so for Lydia's sake. On his walk to Shepard's, he had rationalized that Shepard was a wee bit different than the rest of his lot. But reality now set in. Shepard was just like every other haughty Englishman. "According to Lydia, your Goodwife Sarah said you will remove to Concord soon," said John.

"Thought about it."

As John gestured his arm from Shepard's lush crops, past his straight and unbroken fence rails, to his two-story home, he asked, "Leave all this to the heathens?"

"It is a problem."

"But we be safe. Captain Wheeler will see to it."

"Well if thou were at ye meetinghouse…"

"Me know," interrupted John. "Me nae need to be at the meetinghouse to know Wheeler's gone with Captain Hutchinson."

A chagrined Shepard turned to the direction of Wheeler's homestead. "Giving Wheeler the land was fortunate. Ye Selectmen possess wisdom and are truly guided by God's providence."

"Aye, good men giving me New Scotland to every Englishman they know."

Shepard turned back, massaged his maimed arm and glared.

John lowered his head and kicked at a dirt clump. "Well, me will be staying here."

"My Goodwife Sarah will be thankful to know Lydia is nigh." Shepard's glower hadn't eased, and John turned to leave. "And thy Goodwife Lydia, will she be thankful that Sarah is nigh?"

"Aye, Lydia will be fine."

As John trudged back home, he pondered his departing comment. His stomach had a burning discomfort, and his heart fluttered. His homestead came into view, modest in comparison to Shepard's or Wheeler's, but all his. Protecting what he had amassed through the years was paramount, and his discomfort eased. But when Lydia emerged from the house, John doubted she would be fine.

Chapter Forty-two

Some news is so horrific it travels without the weekly Sabbath chit-chats. Captain Hutchinson's expedition had been ambushed near Quabaug, a village far from Concord, but now close to its heart. Concord's Samuel Smedley had been killed, and Captain Wheeler and his son wounded.[39] Lydia had grown quiet again, despondent over the news. Another piece of John's argument for remaining in his New Scotland had crumbled. Worse, Wheeler was not just a defensive pillar that Lydia viewed as a protector, but a man who John admired.

Last night, John's nightmare was his mutilated sons lying near the Great River with a pleading Lydia tied to a nearby tree as war painted heathens howled in delight. Even as John toiled this day, the images of last night's trauma were still vivid.

"Lydia, laddies, it be too hot to toil," said John.

John's sons ran to him, and Lydia paused her cultivating. She dropped her hoe, wiped her forehead and moseyed up to John. The family moved to the hillcrest where the air was breezier. John and Lydia sat beside one another as corn tassels

---

39 *The ambush also known as Wheeler's Surprise, and the ensuing Siege of Brookfield, was a battle between Nipmuc Indians and the English in August of 1675. Quaboag is some 60 miles west from Concord.*

swayed. Sweet summer fragrances and their sons' joyful chatter rode upon the southwest winds. John draped his arm across Lydia's shoulder and tugged her near. She was surprised at first, but smiled. He brushed some dirt from her cheeks, and she tucked some dangling tresses under her bonnet. She was older, but still as pretty as a teenage angel, and John pecked at her cheek. They tumbled back onto the soft meadow and rested.

Leaves rustled in the uplands and meadow grass swished with each gust; birds chirped, crows shrieked and the boys bantered - a soothing summer symphony. John's noon day meal had settled in, and his eyelids grew heavy. A contented Lydia snuggled close to him. His raspy inhales and occasional snorts when he stirred added to Lydia's symphony. The nape of her neck was perfectly fitted to John's bicep. Her body seemingly fused into his side. She was as peaceful as her husband.

But soon unnatural sounds, indistinct commands, yelling and occasional laughter disturbed their tranquility. John lay with eyes closed, listening while his heart pounded, trying to decipher the noises. His breathing abated and his body tightened as the disharmony grew. With John's unease, Lydia's peace vanished. She sat up, and her sons drifted near. Their joy had left too.

The rumble rekindled John's distant past, and his eyes flew open. He rubbed them as he thought, *Be me below Doon Hill, or be me in New Scotland?* He arose and looked into the sun. Lydia arose and pulled Stephen near as John Junior moved closer.

"What is it, John?" she asked.

John cocked an ear as dust billowed above the horizon, followed by horsemen and two rows of men, spaced apart, walking single file. John moved off the rise toward the road.

"Where art thou going?" asked Lydia.

John didn't answer, and John Junior ran to catch up with his father. Once he did, he matched his father's pace. Lydia brushed off the meadow grass that had clung to her breasts and stomach and flapped her dress to free more of it. Stephen put both hands around his mother's waist and squeezed. Even though he was ten, he was only a head shorter than his petit mother. They moved together as one toward John.

People appeared out of the dusty haze. John Junior often looked back and forth between his father and the approaching men. Indians, roped by their necks in chain-like fashion, trudged deliberately in fear they might cause a pinioned comrade to stumble. The captives were weary and quiet while riders shouted and occasionally cursed, seemingly for their enjoyment.

As the horses neared, John stepped back from the road. John Junior matched his father's move. Stephen, who was still several yards away, squeezed his eyes and clung more firmly to his mother.

"Halt ye heathens," said the lead man. The rumble quieted. All but one Indian obeyed until his neck snapped back. His vacant face grimaced, and he reeled. "Dost thou have water on this hot afternoon?" asked the lead man.

John shook his head. "Nae."

"Oh, a Scotsman," he said as he turned to his comrades. "And thou won't offer water?"

John's mind returned to when he was held captive by pompous English asses. His blood pounded, and he had many impulsive retorts, but he corralled them. "Down the road be a river," he said. "There be water for you and these men."

"Men?" asked the lead man. He turned to his comrades with a smug look. "These are but lowly dogs." He laughed, and his men, like well-orchestrated sycophants, joined in.

The tattered hides barely covered the Indians. Some were bare-chested, most were bare foot and their copper skin was peppered with crimson welts. John was unsure if they were from the sun or the lash. Grime caked their lips, dust coated their bodies, and where their sweat combined with the dust, mud oozed. Unlike Nagoglancit's eyes, these eyes peering over raised cheek bones were communicative. John immediately identified with what they were signifying as he had been one of the subjugated, years earlier. "Aye, but they seem thirsty," said John.

"Scotsman, I am Captain Samuel Mosely, entrusted to bring these massacring cowards to Boston." Mosely's eyes were unwavering and upon John. "They murdered the God loving people of Lancaster,[40] innocence murdered by the Godless." Mosely eased his stare and turned to Lydia. "Hast thou heard of Lancaster?"

Lydia drew back. She had hardly looked at the near-naked Indians since they evoked too many horrors, and had kept her focus on Mosely. She was grateful for this man of authority. Her delicate dress fluttered in the breeze, and Mosely savored the sight. He rose up in his saddle, and its leather creaked. He arched his back, squirmed in his saddle and leered over his horse. "Art thou a goodwife?" he asked.

Lydia gathered her dress close and nodded. Mosely was now making her more uneasy than the Indians, and she looked at the ground.

---

40 *Lancaster, Massachusetts is a town approximately 20 miles due west of Concord*

The breeze quieted, and Mosely turned back to John. "So Scotsman," he said. "Ye heathens thirst for many delights." The breeze freshened, and Mosely became distracted again. Lydia shrunk and pinched in the few fluttering edges of her dress as Mosely watched. The breeze lessened and Lydia ceased struggling with her dress to pull Stephen's head to her bosom. Mosley turned back to John. "They thirst for blood, particularly when it comes from a God fearing goodwife."

Mosely's sweaty horse snorted and stirred. Foam circled the horse's mouth near the bit. His horse was as bedraggled looking as the captives. Mosely clicked, and his horse stepped. Others clicked, the ropes tugged, and the Indians jerked forward. Dust rose up, perfectly positioned for the Indians to walk through. As Mosely neared Lydia, he leaned out from his saddle for another leer. Lydia pressed Stephen's head closer to her bosom, which now moved in unison with her nervous breathing.

Mosely eased back into his saddle and turned back to John. "Scotsman, take heed. Remove thy family to Concord."

John shut his eyes and swallowed. When they opened, Lydia's eyes were begging him to act on Mosely's orders. She looked back to Mosely and kissed the top of Stephen's head. Mosely doffed his cap without turning back, and Lydia released her hold on Stephen's head. The riders and their captives grew smaller as they proceeded further down the road to Concord Center. Eventually, the dusty haze obscured them.

Lydia turned to John. "We should remove as Captain Mosely hath ordered."

John didn't respond, but thought, *he be just another English bastard taunting those nae of his ilk.*

Chapter Forty-three

The terror of King Philip's War was relentless, no longer ebbing and flowing with sporadic encounters. Before the war, many Concordians, unlike Lydia, had had limited contact with the Indians. Now, the consensus was clear. Every Indian was a heathen. But the Indians' leader, King Philip, was more discriminating than the English. To him, the friendly Indians, particularly the Praying ones, were the most loathed. He regarded them as traitors. Thus, the Nashobah were rightly apprehensive of him.

In the fall of 1675, two English brothers were killed near Nagog Pond, and their sister was taken captive. That news reignited Lydia's personal horrors, and her nightmares returned, more vivid than ever. As John consoled her on those nights, she asked him to remove to Concord yet again. But he remained steadfast against it; asking was futile.

The Nashobah were alarmed and left Nagog Pond and erected their wigwams on Concord Common. When the news reached Lydia, she no longer asked John but begged him. John's doubts about staying were increasing too. But being cooped up with the English and having his home torched overruled them.

Contrary to Lydia's pleadings, he believed he was caring for his family and, by protecting his wealth, was ensuring their future.

A few months later, Captain Wheeler's son died from wounds he had incurred near Quabaug. This was the closest the war had come to John. His son was the first white male born in New Scotland, and Wheeler's son was the first white male to die in New Grant. The coincidence haunted John. He had lost young Thomas and identified with Wheeler's grief. John prayed he would never have to experience losing an adult son. He still doubted God ever heard him, but praying was all he had. As he rationalized further, he wondered if he was closer to God, perhaps God might hear. That illogical belief coupled with fears for his family's safety on their Sabbath journeys drove John to the meetinghouse.

But nothing had changed. The sermons were still unbearable, the stares as cutting as before and the gossip never ceased. At times, it escalated to the irrational, which created hysteria and petrified the timid. John now appreciated why Lydia was so unnerved each Sabbath when she returned home. The Sabbath worship was an irritant, but John had his way to endure it. He blocked out the sermon and reflected with his God on his fears. He still doubted God ever heard him, but wondered, if someday, he could achieve a lasting inner peace that Nagoglancit had seemingly achieved.

*****

On a Sabbath in February 1676, John waited outside the meetinghouse, apart from any pre-established cliques. He perused each clique with his usual disdain. But envy came when he realized he simply didn't belong in any of them. One group was especially intriguing. Several men, with concerned expressions, huddled away from the other groups. A head rose

The Immigrant

up, looked about and turned back. Moments later, another head lifted and surveyed the meetinghouse grounds. The doors opened, and the congregants bustled to their usual seating areas. John's intriguing huddlers arrived late and dispersed to their usual seats.

John continued to wonder about these men as The Reverend preached on. Why were they meeting apart from the other groups? He thought about their occasional furtive looks and wondered what they might be plotting. He sat, encased in iciness, seemingly alone, waiting for the sermon to conclude. 'Amen and so be it,' was John's favorite phrase, which he longed to hear. The Reverend rambled and, several times, seemed to be reaching an appropriate time for the sermon to conclude, but he diverted to more bombast. John squirmed and thought, *Me God, when will this suffering come to an end.*

His answer abruptly came when the back door rumbled and a chill entered. The congregation turned to the back of the room, and several men stormed in. Captain Mosely strutted out from the group and spoke. "Ye good men of Concord, the Godless still remain among thee. John Hoare's custody[41] of them is no longer sufficient to keep thee safe."

Aye, this Mosely is up to nae goot, thought John as a few congregants grumbled.

"I hear thy fears and sense thy dread. God's providence demands me to remove these savages to Deer Island in Boston Harbor, isolated and far from this God fearing congregation."

---

41 *After the Nashobah had moved onto Concord Commons several months earlier, the town grew increasing hostile to them. John Hoare decided to become the Nashobah's guardian, and removed them from the Commons to a dormitory that he had erected especially for them.*

The room quieted and Mosely continued, invoking the Lord's name several times. He strutted, paused occasionally for drama, and when he concluded, he returned to his scruffy looking men.

A congregant arose and parroted Mosely's proposal. Then another arose; and another. Each was part of the late arriving huddle. The last speaker asked, "Doth any among thee object to Captain Mosely's generous offer?"

"Amen and so be it," said The Reverend.

John's favorite phrase came so quickly no one could respond. Mosely stormed out with his men as a congregant stumbled over John in his haste to follow. John remained on the bench and pondered. *Aye, the bastard Reverend be part of the scheme, too.* His anger changed to fear as he thought of when he first met Mosely. Then, John identified with those desperate wretches who were in circumstances similar to when he was an adolescent. Now, Mosely was preparing to take his long-time friend Nagoglancit, and he would have to suffer what John had once endured. John's anxiety grew, and he bolted off the bench.

Lydia was outside with her usual cluster of women. Her sons were with other boys, teasing the Shepard girls. As John hustled out of the meetinghouse, Lydia broke from her group to meet him. "God hath sent Captain Mosely to save our blessed Concord," she said to John. But he was focused on the now distant, still clamoring crowd and ignored Lydia. "Where art thou going?" she asked

"To John Hoare's Indian dormitory," said John. Lydia excused herself from the goodwives, corralled her sons and followed after John.

When John arrived, Hoare was questioning Mosely's authority as he invoked the Lord's name in support of his actions. Nagoglancit was among many apprehensive Indians who were watching the discussion. The Indians were motionless as they shifted their eyes between the two debaters and the ever growing crowd.

Mosely ceased debating and beckoned to his ruffians as the Indians gathered closer together out of fear. He strutted about the perimeter before moving closer to his intended victims to eyeball several of them. He strutted back to the gathering crowd. "Ye good men, it is ye Lord's Day. We will honor it, but my guards will remain here. John Hoare, Esquire agrees to have his Indians removed for their and thy safety."

Hoare stepped forward to speak, but Mosely's hooligans stepped in front of their Captain and blocked Hoare's path. Hoare dropped his head and moved back while muttering. Resignation came to John too, as he felt as powerless as Hoare seemed.

The clamor from the good men and goodwives increased, and Mosely raised his arms. "Attend to thy Sabbath, for I, Captain Samuel Mosely, will remove these heathen goats from Concord's blessed flock of sheep." The din rose to a supportive rumble as many heads nodded. "Go and pray unto ye Lord." The crowd quieted and dispersed.

On the way home, Lydia strode with her head up as her sons mimicked what they had heard. She offered occasional comments championing Mosely's cause. But John was silent and tried to control his anger. His thoughts often drifted to Nagoglancit. His captivity would be agonizing, and he feared the worse for his friend. He was powerless to help, which added to his frustrations. The family chatter eventually became exasperating, and John stopped walking. Lydia and her two sons stopped, too. Lydia furled her brow, wondering why the abrupt halt.

John glared at John Junior who continued to babble. "Nagoglancit be among those that your Captain Mosely will drag to Boston. Did Nagoglancit attack Lancaster?" The meadow was now quiet. John Junior was frozen in place by his father's demeanor. "Or kill those brothers at Nagog Pond?" His son looked away as steam from his nostrils now billowed out his seething anger. "Your Captain Mosely be more a coward than Nagoglancit."

John shifted his eyes to Lydia. She was relieved that her son's verbal pounding had ended. "And Nagoglancit be more a man of God than that suffering bastard, The Reverend."

Lydia gasped. "John, cease thy blasphemy from thy lips." She gathered her wrap tight to her shoulders and stared at her husband.

John muttered and the Sabbath procession recommenced. The journey was silent, except for the rustle of meadow grass and occasional pants of weariness. Even though the chatter was gone, John's frustrations continued to grow.

*****

The night added to John's worries. When he did doze, it was fleeting. Each time he awoke, his heart pounded, and he struggled to rein in the chaos in his mind. By early morning, he had targeted his emotions. *Me should have done more.* Still weary, John left for wood, returned and rekindled the fire.

As he left again, Lydia rolled to her side. When John didn't return, she wrapped his bedding covers about her for added warmth. They were a poor substitute for what John could have offered. His silent departure was troublesome.

While Lydia worried alone at home, many had gathered at Hoare's dormitory, shuddering and rubbing their hands. A few were vocal, but most were somber, perhaps still drowsy on this early morning. Mosely's men were taking clothing, shoes, dishes; anything they could grab from the helpless Indians. Hoare's misgivings had returned, and he pleaded with Mosely to reconsider. But Mosely squashed further discussion under the banner of God's providence.

Nagoglancit was shoved forward, and John moved toward him. Two of Mosely's thugs blocked John's path, and he attempted to break through them. They shoved John back, and he point to Nagoglancit. "He be me friend."

John tried to break through again, but was grabbed. Each of Mosely's men put an arm under John's armpit, lifted and carried John back several yards. "Scotsman, if thou persist, we'll chain thee to thy friend."

John remembered when he was chained to Andrew Adams as they marched from Durham Cathedral twenty-five years ago. He never would have survived the journey without Andrew. If only he could now be chained to Nagoglancit, his journey might be easier. John shook his head, such a foolish impulse. Lydia and his sons needed him. *Aye, but if only*, thought John as he looked between the shoulders of Mosely's men, which now framed his friend.

Nagoglancit's raven hair was streaked with gray, and his opaque eyes receded into darkened sockets. He was barefoot and shirtless. He drew a deerskin tight to his shivering torso. His forlorn look pierced through John's heart. If only, but John was powerless to embrace or soothe his friend. He wrung his hands while muttering, "God, me beseech thee, ease his burden."

Nagoglancit's eyes regained some life. His deerskin drooped to one side to reveal his Bible. He quickly concealed it and nodded to John. John slowly thumped his chest thrice while wondering if God had heard his supplication. Nagoglancit returned the thumps before shuffling with the others onto the road that led to Boston. The horses prodded some fifty Indian captives to move quickly and to close ranks. Saddened Indian women and their children followed. A few wails pierced through the rumble of hooves.

Away from the crowd, Hoare sat on the dormitory step, head in hand, moaning. He raised it to watch until his guardians disappeared around the bend on the road. John moved near and placed his hand on Hoare's shoulder. Hoare looked up and cocked his head. His quizzical gaze remained.

"Nagoglancit be me friend," said John.

"Ah Nagoglancit," said Hoare. He slumped and bobbed his head. He looked up and smiled. "Squaw Sachem's favorite."

John turned to the road. Some women and children were returning, not knowing whether to follow their men or remain; but remain where? One woman clutched an infant and swayed in unison with her sobs, just like an oblivious Lydia had done as she rocked a dying Thomas. John squeezed his eyes to erase the horror. It eased, but didn't leave completely.

Hoare brushed the fatigue from under his eyes. "Mosely doth not know what he hath wrought. More will now be driven to Metacomet. He will have his vengeance." John gulped and more horror flashed. "Thou should be with thy Goodwife Lydia and caring for that fair child."

John placed his hand on Hoare's shoulder again. He looked up and said, "I'll be safe, but my entrusted guardians, oh how I fear for them." He shook his head while saying, "That braying ass Mosely."

As the now awakened crowd grew more boisterous, John continued to stare at a beaten man. "Boston or the wilderness, but do not tarry in Concord, squaw," said a goodwife.

"Ye wilderness bitch is where thou belong; and take thy bastards with thee," said one obscured in crowd of good men.

Hoare looked to the stinging insults coming from the rabble. "I am safe, but now I must endure the good men and goodwives of Concord." Hoare looked back at John. "God doth have burdens for each of us, doth he not?"

Such an odd phrase, these English use, thought John. He reflected upon the first time he heard it. *T'was the Reverend Bulkeley.* John had been terrified about ever meeting Bulkeley, but when he spoke those words, his fears eased. John was coming to understand the English better. And now, his torrent of horrific images was abating too. He was surprisingly calm. He bobbed his head, and with a renaissance twinkling in his eye he said to Hoare, "Aye, God dost."

Hoare's smile this time was not fleeting, and John was heartened to see it. *What joy did me cause this Englishman?*

"John, if thou persist to speak like an Englishman, ye should sayeth God doth, not God dost."

Chapter Forty-four

22 April 1676

A gray cloud drifted among budding tree limbs on a southwest breeze. As it neared, the smoke grew pungent. John heard a distant clamor, which awoke him from his now recurring lament of Nagoglancit's unjust fate and his inability to help. But he had left his lament, went outside and looked to the sound. A red glow illuminated the horizon where the gray cloud now drifted. The strange sounds had also awakened Lydia. John had told her the clamor was nothing, but he doubted she believed him.

Because his fields needed tending this morning, there was no time for worrying. He trudged up the rise. But he was weary from another fitful night, and his fears wouldn't leave this day. As he stared at the unplowed field, he wondered if his crops would still be standing by the summer. The advent of spring always lifted his spirits, but not so in the spring of 1676. King Philip's War was omnipresent. *Why should me even bother?* And John headed back down the rise.

The door creaked, and Lydia emerged. She twitched her nostrils, looked at the cloud and to John.

"Sudbury, me thinks," said John.

She shut her eyes, folded her hands and mumbled as John neared. She opened them and looked to the heavens.

"King Philip and the Nipmucs be moving east from Marlborough," said John.

"And ye town next to Sudbury?" asked Lydia. John grimaced, and Lydia answered her question. "Next to Sudbury is thy New Scotland."

John put his arm around Lydia's shoulder. She smiled to acknowledge his thoughtfulness. But her face quickly became as impassive as before. "Our providence is with God. I pray our death, if God so deems it, will be swift." Lydia had grown inured to the war, but not as resigned as she was now. Her eyes welled, and she drew her hands to them. "I prayed last night that God's providence for Mary Rowlandson is swift."

"The captive of the Lancaster attack?" asked John.

Lydia nodded. "Mary and her three children."

"But it be nigh on two months. They must be dead by now." Lydia raised an eyebrow and stepped away. "That second Lancaster attack be revenge for your Captain Mosely. Aye, for sure, John Hoare foretold of it."

Lydia flashed a dismissive hand. "I doubt John Hoare foretold anything. Since Mosely, the attacks have been endless. Even a village simpleton would appear a wise man for saying they would come."

Lydia looked at the ground as she stepped. "Mary is alive, but her burdens are never ending. She hath died many times." Lydia flicked her eyes, looked to the heavens and back to John. Emotions now carved her face. "My ordeal was but a night, but

Mary's," and Lydia rushed her hands to her face. Pain now poured from her eyes. "Maybe God's providence will end her ordeal soon?" Lydia watched the smoke drift, turned to the rising sun and inhaled. She scuffed at a sod clump. "Goody Davis said…"

"Aha, Goody Davis. Why do you listen to her mistruths?"

"Goody Davis may be a gossip, but God hath blessed her with eyes that see from the back of her bonnet. She knows of what she speaks." John considered debating Goody Davis's worth, but decided to let it go.

Lydia ambled away from the cloud, alternating her gaze between the ground and the sunrise. "Goody Davis said Mary is to be ransomed. The goodwives of Boston are holding a public subscription to raise money as we speak." She turned back to John. Terror now filled her eyes. "I carry her burden and live her ordeal each night."

John closed his eyes. Lydia's restlessness had increased these past few months. She would lay quiet for hours, as if in a trance. When she dozed, she often awoke with a jolt. She would crawl into his embrace until her panic climaxed and her trembling ceased. She had said nothing, but now John knew the cause of her increased trauma.

The sunrise shimmered on the dewy fields, the early morning fog was dissipating, and songbirds' pleasing trills were peppered with annoying caws. Lydia's head hung low as she continued to worry about Mary Rowlandson. She ceased meandering and looked to the sky. "Mercy, those crows." She turned back to John. "We have chores to do this morn. I will awaken thy sons." And Lydia marched back to the house.

Chapter Forty-five

Princeton, Massachusetts, Massachusetts Bay Colony
2 May 1676

Maybe God's providence is that I shall be bounded into captivity like Joseph to the great Pharaoh, thought John Hoare. His two Indian escorts reflected similar doubts. Hoare's eyes moved from his escorts, past several young natives to the gathering Sagamores.[42] The young natives seemed to reflect more loathing than the wise council of Sagamores, which was deciding the fate of two lone English, Mary Rowlandson and himself.

He studied the Sagamores further and thought. *I know the Indian mind so well, and how to deal with them.* He ceased his study and rubbed his forehead. *Beware the barrister so full of his bounty, for he will yield nothing.* Hoare moved back to his limp satchel. *But I will not fail.*

When Hoare arrived two days earlier, the satchel had teemed with ransom for Mary's release. Such a welcoming; gunshots whistled under his horse, accompanied by ear curdling whoops and eye shocking gestures. Hoare thought then the offer of negotiations was but a ruse. But if it had been, he would be dead and the entire ransom would be gone. No, the

---
42 *Sagamores are similar in rank to Sachems, subordinate chiefs among the Indian tribes of North America.*

welcoming was just the opening salvo. But Mary, upon hearing the commotion, must have believed her hope of release had been snuffed out before the negotiations started.

Most of the ransom, tobacco, trading cloth and twenty shillings, had been stolen in the night. Hoare wondered again if it was a ruse, or just an Indian custom of immediately enjoying the rewards of negotiation. The Sagamores were still discussing among themselves, a few utterances were decipherable, but reading expressions was useless. The only certainty was there wasn't unanimity. Mary's captor would hold the most sway, and he had to be convinced to release her.

Her captor had dressed for the feast the night before in a Holland shirt with silvery buttons and white stockings. Shillings jangled from his garters and wampum rattled from his chest as he danced in the night. His squaw danced too in a kersey coat, red stocking, and wampum girdles from the loin up, with jingling bracelets and swaying necklaces. The Indians drummed on kettles throughout the night to sustain the frivolity.

As twilight moved in, Hoare slipped his hand into his satchel. He pushed aside a protecting cloth and fumbled for the feel of glass. It was his last hope. He looked back to the Sagamores, who were in animated discussion. He glanced skyward and thought. *Am I Daniel in the lion's den? Is it thy providence for an angel to shut these savages' hungry mouths or will they devour me once they've tasted Satan's evil?* He slipped a glass flask into his waistcoat and was led to the wigwam of Mary Rowlandson's captor.

As he entered, her captor arose and stood, unsmiling and seemingly still fatigued from the night before. Hoare offered him the spirits as negotiated earlier. He gulped and then shuddered.

"Thou art a good man, John Hoare," he said. His good English dialect, which he had previously learned from missionaries before leaving them, was still prevalent. He sat on the ground and motioned for Hoare to do likewise.

Hoare's rheumatism had returned during the ride from Concord, so sitting, ankles crossed, would be difficult. But not to comply might foil the negotiations. He struggled to the ground, pulled his ankles together, and splayed his legs. The intermittent gulping continued, and Hoare's doubts increased with each swig. The quiet was unnerving and finally Hoare broke it. "Where is Reverend Joseph Rowlandson's Goodwife?"

Mary's captor raised the flask, and Hoare hoped it meant in due time. Hoare's Indian escorts had assured him Mary would be released if he offered alcohol to him. He trusted them, but the gulps were now savoring sips. *Were the spirits taking hold?* thought Hoare. "I demand to see Mary Rowlandson, before thee take another swig," he said.

"Thou art a rogue, John Hoare," and the Indian eased the flask to his lips. He licked the rim and sipped. His head lunged forward, and Hoare recoiled. Several more menacing gestures came, followed by a laugh and another sip. As the Indian muttered, Hoare waited with the patience of Job. "Thou should be hanged John Hoare. Thou art a rogue."

Hoare wrung his hands and shifted his bottom to ease his knotting leg muscles. The flask was emptying, and once gone, indeed, maybe he would be hanged. The Indian's muttering turned to shouts in his native tongue. As his rant continued, Mary and his squaw entered the wigwam. The pint was pointed in Mary's direction, and the Indian's words slurred forth. "Thou hast served me and my squaw well. Thou art a good woman."

Mary stood trembling, and turned to Hoare. She wanted a nod or any sign of assurance from him. But Hoare had none to give as he was as uncertain as her. Mary's captor continued to talk, now with civility, and her trembling eased. After another sip, his squaw spun away and left the wigwam. Mary's captor struggled while arising. He steadied his teetering and weaved out of the wigwam. Mary and John remained quiet, listening to the commotion from outside, occasionally looking to one another and allowing their facial expressions to be their communication.

The commotion ended, and Mary said, "Ye spirits have certainly had an effect."

"Ye spirits were given in good faith," said Hoare.

"I know, but there are so many to please; King Philip, the Sagamores, my master, my mistress. I sold the tobacco you brought to please Philip."

"My satchel is nearly bare. Thy ransom hath all but been consumed. I know not what comes with the morn."

"As with every morn, John Hoare, Esquire, God's divine providence will come."

"Thy words are apt. They could only have been spoken by the Goodwife of an honored Reverend." Hoare and Mary spent the rest of the night wondering if their ordeal would end.

The next morning, Hoare's Indian escorts came with two horses. John Hoare's most difficult negotiation of his life had been successful. Two English people rode through the wilderness and reached Lancaster by sundown. Mary's infant child had died while in captivity, and her two older children had been separated from her. Lancaster, which lay deep in the wilderness, and where her husband came to be its first Reverend, was now an unoccupied rumble of ashes – more of God's divine providence. Mary's one consolation was her husband had been in Boston when the attack occurred eleven weeks earlier.

*****

As news of Mary Rowlandson's rescue swept across the Colonies, a sense of triumph came to Concord. For Lydia, who had lived Mary's ordeal, it was liberation from her self-imposed anguish. John now was re-energized and undertook his annual spring chores readily. His sons sensed their parents' optimism and renewed enthusiasm, and their outlook changed too. Stephen's nightmares ended, and John Junior no longer had to pretend to be a brave older brother.

As summer set in, the Colonists were winning the war. Local authorities were garrisoning vulnerable towns, and defensive forces were being deployed. Colonial soldiers were now skilled in fighting like Indians, and military units were making offensive sorties, helped in part, with valuable scouting and combat support from friendly natives

Chapter Forty-six

On August 17, 1676, Lydia and the boys were dressing for the Sabbath. "John, will thou be attending with us?" asked Lydia.

John didn't respond, so Lydia glared to force an answer. "Got me corn to pick," he said.

"Thou hast tomorrow for ye corn harvest."

"Must be done today. Tomorrow me harvests me hay." Lydia's stare persisted, and John said, "King Philip has all but vanished. John Junior will protect you." John turned to his fifteen year old son, "Aye laddie, when me be your age, me be a pikeman fighting for King Charles."

"It's not protection my heart doth desire, but our family as one on the Sabbath," said Lydia.

John frowned and headed to his fields.

Lydia had grown accustomed to her family attending the meetinghouse each Sabbath, an odd benefit of the war. But she had heard the gossip too. John had endured much, and she was sympathetic to why the corn absolutely had to be picked this day. Most likely, future Sabbaths would bring other chores John absolutely had to do. Though disappointed, she understood and left, comforted by the thought she had married a really good man.

John Junior shouldered his father's musket, just as he imagined his father had shouldered his pike years ago. He stepped with pride as he led his mother and brother on the path toward the Shepherds. John stopped picking his corn to watch his family depart. As he watched his eldest son leading the family, he scrunched his shoulders as shivers shot up his spine. *Aye, me lad be a man this day.*

Throughout the day, the sky remained cloudless, and John paused often to wipe his brow. By mid-afternoon, he was finished. He slung the sack of corn over his shoulder and headed down the rise. After storing it in the shed, he stripped and, with energetic anticipation of what he desperately needed, bounded into the river. He splashed around until the shock of the cold water wore off. He dunked, ran his fingers through his gnarled hair, and treaded water to remain in the cool current. But eventually his arms tired, and he floated into the reeds. His fatigued muscles were now soothed, and the sun warmed his face, providing a welcome contrast to his submerged body. *Aye, what a glorious Sabbath it be.* He thought about crossing back to the riverbank closer to his home, but he was too comfortable and stayed put.

"John, what a glorious Sabbath it is," said an excited Lydia as she and her two sons suddenly appeared on the bridge.

Startled, John inched further into reeds and submerged to his chin

"Thou will not believe the good news." Lydia ran across the bridge to the riverbank across from John. "King Philip is dead.

Shot down in Miery Swamp near Mount Hope[43] on Wednesday last. Praise the Lord."

"Aye, praise the Lord," said a still crouched and self-conscious John.

"Our burden hath ended. Praise the Lord indeed." Lydia now wondered why John's response had been halfhearted and why he was still crouched in water. Her eyes widened, and she moved her fingertips to her mouth. "Mercy John, thou art like the baby Moses in ye reeds. I will tarry no longer, so thou can come hither." Lydia ushered her sons up the rise.

John inched out of the reeds and called out. "Lydia, can you fetch me breeches?"

---

[43] *Miery Swamp is in present day Bristol, Rhode Island, 50 miles southwest from Plymouth, Massachusetts. At the intersection of Tower Street (at milepost 0.7) and Metacom Avenue (Rhode Island Route 136) in Bristol is a marker to commemorate where King Philip fell on 12 August 1676, which was place by the Rhode Island Historical Society in 1877.*

Chapter Forty-seven

Fall 1676

King Philip's War was seared into the Colonists' consciousness. Prior to the War, most had limited exposure to the Indians. But now, even those who had escaped any horrific encounter with them knew someone who had been less fortunate. King Philip had become the universal image for all Indians. The prejudice John had witnessed several months earlier at Hoare's dormitory had grown more hostile, even though the Indians were no longer a threat. Many Indians had died in the War, others were removed, and some were sentenced to death or died while in custody. Much like what happened to John twenty-five years earlier, the young and potentially dangerous ones were sold as slaves, including Metacomet's nine year old son.

The Colonists now journeyed from their settlements with confidence. Whenever they encountered an Indian, the contrasting body languages reflected who had won the war. The English had a swagger from which the Indians now cowered. John, unlike most Colonists, had varying images of the Indians, disdain for King Philip and admiration and respect for Nagoglancit.

People traveled through New Grant more frequently than before. Some settled in it. John still disliked the increased interaction with the English, but Lydia welcomed it since it provided additional sources of news and more contact with women. Whenever someone visited the Laws, John often had a chore that absolutely had to be done. He worked in his fields and avoided the chit-chat.

With the onset of the leaf fall season, the winds cooled, which was nature's prompt for John to gather firewood. His woodlands were being slowly depleted, and someday they would be bare, which would be a hardship for Lydia, his sons and their heirs. To delay the inevitable, John, on occasion, would fell trees away from his house. But with increased traffic, gathering wood unnoticed from wherever he pleased became more challenging. Further, hauling it from distant locations in low light or at night fall was more laborious now that John was in his early forties.

Several fallen hardwoods, ideally dried by now, lay on the edge of Wheeler's woodlands. As John went to gather them, he passed a Concord resident returning home. They nodded to one another, and he stared at John's axe, but said nothing. John worried the passing stranger would inform the town's wood reeve.[44] Paranoia crept in as John entered the woodlands to follow his previously marked path. His temple scar throbbed, and John wondered if it was God's reminder to be careful when chopping? He eventually amassed enough wood to fill his cart, which he would haul later, under the cover of night.

As he popped out of the woods, three people were moving in the meadow. John hadn't heard them and was startled. He lingered at the edge of the woodlands, under the browse line created by feeding deer. His eyesight wasn't as keen as when he was younger, but they seemed to be Indians. When they spotted John, they paused and stared, before moving ahead.

---

44 *Wood reeves were appointed at the annual meeting to police the proper cutting of timber.*

John squinted in the dimming light and thought Nagoglancit was among them. He bolted out from under the browse line, and the Indians froze. "Nagoglancit," said John as he thumped his chest thrice. But it wasn't Nagoglancit, it was his son. John slowed to an amble. When he was close, he asked, "John Nagoglancit what brings you to me New Scotland?"

The Indians grunted and relaxed. Nagoglancit's son stepped forward and said, "Good evening, John Law."

"How be your father?" asked John.

Nagoglancit son's raised his head and crossed his arms in the front of his chest. His face was as dead-panned as his father, revealing very little. He held his father's dog-eared Bible in one hand. The two older natives muttered to one another in their native language, and John's heart pounded. Their icy stares increased his anxiety. Finally, one stepped forward and said, "Nagoglancit left us several moons ago."

John sensed bad news might be forthcoming, but never this. He shook his head back and forth.

Nagoglancit's son moved from the group to be face-to-face with John. "Father walked barefoot in the cold," he said. "He was bare-chested, but for his deerskin. Soon, he was stricken ill, and ye English put him with sick Nashobah and Okommakamesits." He gestured and said, "Kattansett was with Father when he died and saved his Bible." Raising it he said, "Father is with his English God. May God grant my father everlasting peace."

"Your father be a good man," said John. Guilt rushed into John's soul. He hadn't done enough for his friend. John Nagoglancit was the image of a man who befriended John twenty years earlier. Nagoglancit would have been proud of his son this day. As John thought further, he wondered if he would be as equally proud of John Junior someday. An epiphany came unto John. *Life after death – just like The Reverend sayeth, just like Jesus sayeth.*

Kattansett moved aside Nagoglancit's son and spoke. "Nagoglancit is with Glooskap, with Nashobah ancestors, and not with the English." His eyes were seething. They remained locked onto John until he turned to the other two, and they continued their journey to Nagog Pond.

John wandered home wrapped in philosophical thought. What would John Nagoglancit do – follow his father or Kattansett? What would John Law Junior do after John was gone? When John arrived home, he didn't bother with his cart. He went inside the house and contemplated further. He didn't say much during supper. On this night, he relished just being among his family. Whenever he looked at John Junior, more thoughts about what he might become fluttered in his head. He lamented for Nagoglancit, muttering inaudibly whenever he did. Only two words were distinct among his mutters, 'English Bastards'.

Nagoglancit's needless death continued to haunt John. He wasn't King Philip, or a Mohawk, or a Nipmuc. He was Christian and more devout than John. This gloomy effect of King Philip's War lingered until another shocked came. In December of 1676, Captain Wheeler, like his son, died from wounds suffered at the Quabaug ambush. Nagoglancit and Wheeler, two good New Grant men were now dead, which brought another epiphany unto John. He was not immortal, someday he would die too.

Chapter Forty-eight

Concord, Middlesex County, Dominion of New England
Summer 1684

It had been eight years since King Philip died, bringing peace to the Colonies. On a hot summer afternoon, a nearly fifty year old John dunked his head into the water as he knelt on the bridge. He held his face submerged until his breath gave out. His face flew out of the water, and he gasped. He brushed the water from his face, combed his thinning hair back with his fingertips and squeezed his matted mane, allowing the wet ends to drip down his back. He splashed handfuls of water onto his face and cupped his hands to drink. He heaved a sigh, grabbed the bridge's side post and arose. He brushed the dirt from his knees and patted the bridge post. "Me laddies done good," he said.

Time had not only taken its toll on John, but also on the bridge that Nagoglancit constructed nearly thirty years earlier. John Junior and Stephen rebuilt it this past spring. John continued his deep breathing and thought further. The new bridge should last another thirty years, most likely more than John's remaining lifetime. "Aye, it will be me lads' problem," he said with a chuckle.

He headed up the rise, pausing often to admire his homestead. It was now a grand home. Not the grandest in Concord or even in New Scotland, just two stories with a cellar hole for storage, glass in the window openings, a pitched roof and a stone chimney.

He paused in front of his house to catch his breath again. John Junior was in the fields instructing Stephen. Those earlier sibling squabbles over who was in charge had been resolved with the passage of time. Stephen nodded and headed to where his older brother had pointed. The sun would not set for a few hours, but his sons would finish his remaining chores. John went inside with a full heart.

"Where be yah mum?" he asked his seven year old daughter Elizabeth.

"In the meadow with the ailing lamb."

"What ailing lamb?"

"The one that walks oddly," said his daughter. "Mother said she stepped on a chestnut burr."

John reached for his pewter cup. "Me suppose your younger brother Samuel be with her too."

Elizabeth grinned. "Of course," she said. John dunked his cup into the vat. "Mother says it may be too watery."

John gulped until the cup was empty and then burped. "Watery be best," he said. "The heat hath taken much out of your father this day." Elizabeth couldn't follow her father's logic, but she smiled and giggled. John dunked his cup again and took a sip. "The first cup quenches me parched throat. This one be to ease me head." John smiled at his daughter as he drank. He had hoped for another son, but soon appreciated the delight a daughter gives. He raised his empty cup to his daughter, and her ever present smile widened. He saw Lydia in Elizabeth's sweet, young face.

John handed the cup to Elizabeth as he left the house. He paused at the cradle in the shade next to the house. His two year old son lay diagonally across it. He stooped and rocked it gently. He stopped rocking and caressed the cheek of his sleeping son. "Thomas, me be heading up where the breeze freshens to see ye namesake."

The grave marker, which had been placed some twenty years earlier for the first Thomas, was now gone. But John didn't need it. He knew every stone and sod clump there since the gravesite was also his favorite resting spot.

When he reached the hillcrest, he lowered his buttocks onto his favorite rock, and seemingly by John's command, the breeze freshened. With his lower body nestled perfectly into the rock, muscle memory was triggered, and he leaned against the tree behind him. John inhaled deeply as Awbrey's words echoed in his head. *"Find the choicest spot and settled on it. The land will all be yours."*

"Me sure did ye English bastard," said John. But Shepard's house came into view, which soured John's outlook. "Aye, it still be the choicest spot for resting just the same."

His eyes shifted from Shepard's house to where Thomas was buried. Lydia, unlike John, never found solitude here, even more after Thomas died. Perhaps the spot was a painful reminder of Thomas's death. Or perhaps she knew John relished sitting upon his favorite rock, in solitude, and didn't want to disturb him. On occasion, John Junior would join John on the hillcrest and be regaled with tales of how he had developed New Scotland. 'Someday it all be yours, laddie' always completed those stories. His other children didn't have the same bond that John Junior had with his father. They never felt comfortable joining John at his favorite spot.

John dozed until the sound of his snort roused him from a catnap. He rubbed his eyes and looked to his fields. John Junior and Stephen were heading out of them toward home. John knew someday those lads would be responsible for an aging Lydia and younger siblings. John yawned and thought. *Hopefully the good Lord ain't through with me yet.* Lydia was holding five year old Samuel's hand as they neared the shed. He was looking back at the limping lamb, which followed after them. *Me wonders about me wee lad, he be so close to Lydia.*

John slowly arose from his rock, stretched and took a few stiff legged steps. Coming down the rise was now hard on his knees, and he gimped. His face was flushed from the effects of sun and ale, yet he still shuddered in the cooling breeze. Thomas was stirring in the cradle, and John paused, looked down at him and back to the grave site. Young Thomas squawked, and Lydia came around the corner of the house.

"He be hungry too," said John.

Lydia knelt down, slid her hands underneath Thomas and removed him from his cradle. She rested him on her protruding stomach and bounced him gently. "Soon, thy sister can have thy cradle," said Lydia.

"Sister?" asked John.

"Or brother," said Lydia with a smile.

"And what does your twisting stomach be telling you, a lad or a lass? Lasses always know."

'Poppycock, John." Lydia squeezed Thomas close and looked toward the gravesite. "I pray God's providence is for another healthy child." She kissed Thomas, and he squawked. "Mother knows, come let's sup before we all faint from hunger."

*****

A sumptuous evening meal, several cups of ale and toiling the day in the heat had been too much for John. He dozed off right after supper. Lydia left him and her four eldest children for the twilight and refreshing air. She sat upon a bench and rocked Thomas while resting her other hand on her belly. Her natural womanly cycle had returned. Soon another child would replace Thomas in the cradle.

With mixed emotions, she reflected how her life had changed after her brother's death shortly following the War. She was in shock and grieving then, but Adam's widowed wife, Rebecca, needed help in caring for four young children. She spent several months helping Rebecca to cope and to get her shattered life back in order. Curiously, soon after, Lydia's womanly cycle had returned to normal. She sighed and thought. *Adam's death brought new life to my womb, God's providence indeed. Life truly is everlasting.*

Thomas squirmed, and Lydia ceased her rocking. Would he fall back to sleep? His lips quivered as if he was sucking on her bosom. *So precious*, and Lydia resumed a gentle rock. He thrashed his hands about his face and nestled to his side. Lydia hummed, and after a while Thomas's squirming ceased.

She thought about the painful burden of her barren years between the deaths of her son, the first Thomas, and Adam.

God had to humble and punish her for her transgressions when she was a captive for a night. But now God deemed her fully repentant. She reflected on what had become her favorite verse from the Bible. In unison with the rock of Thomas's cradle, she recited John 3, verse 3 from memory: "Verily, verily I say unto thee, except a man be born again, he cannot see the kingdom of God."

Lydia ceased rocking, and with Thomas now asleep, she arose. The moon was rising as she pondered God's providence further. A cool blend of autumnal scents filled the night air. Lydia extended her arms, turned her palms up and raised her head to the heavens. "I have humbly repented and ye, O God, heard my supplications through the years. Blessed be thee who hath removed the poison from my womb."

Chapter Forty-nine

Concord, Middlesex, Dominion Of New England
Autumn 1686

The Puritan theocracy that governed Massachusetts was losing more power. King James II,[45] an Anglican, appointed Edmund Andros Governor of the Dominion of New England, an amalgamation of Massachusetts Bay Colony, Plymouth Colony and surrounding areas. One of Andros's actions was to limit local rule and restrict each town to a single annual meeting, which roiled Concord's good men. When Andros decreed previous town actions invalid, particularly the grants of land, the citizens were infuriated. Governor Andros was now the main discussion topic at the meetinghouse. The good men of Concord objected to the loss of their autonomous rule and felt powerless to act. The Law lads were uneasy too, and Stephen urged John Junior to discuss their concerns with their father.

At the supper table, John Junior and Stephen lingered as John picked his teeth. "The talk last Sabbath was about land grants," said John Junior to his father. "Governor Andros hath decreed them invalid."

---

45 *James II was the last Roman Catholic monarch to reign over the Kingdoms of England, Scotland and Ireland from 6 February 1685 until he was deposed in 1688.*

"Aye, about time Shepard and his lot with all their mysterious dealings get their comeuppance."

"But what about your grant, Father?"

John leaned back from the table. "Me nae got a grant," said John with a contented smile. "Awbrey gave me land."

"But thy Awbrey still remains a mystery to ye selectmen."

"Aye, he be as slippery as the alewife in me weir. He slithered away years ago, the snake."

"And Andros hath decreed Indian purchases invalid, too."

John ceased picking his teeth and grabbed his cup. "Go on lad."

John Junior looked to Stephen, who had seemingly shrunk from the table. He turned back to his father and rubbed his hands. "Concord purchased New Grant from ye Nashobahs," said John Junior.

His father stared while nodding an 'aye'.

"And since Indian purchases are invalid, Concord never had title to New Grant."

John furled his brow and his stomach tightened. He sipped while he pondered. John Junior glanced at Stephen, who had eased some from his cower. Lydia came into the room to listen. None of them dared break the silence. John lowered his cup and smiled. "Nae laddie, both Shepard and Nagoglancit told me about the purchase of New Grant. They both be there when the grant was signed."

"Father, you speak of a second purchase, of lands closer to Nagog. The first purchase occurred when thou were at the

Saugus Ironworks. Some believe the first transaction for New Grant was not a purchase, but a lease."

"Lease," said John. But as soon as he had roared the word, he thought of Squaw Sachem. She had a similar one word response. John twitched as the image of Squaw Sachem would not leave. He rubbed his stubble. "What'll the town do? Give me land to the Nashobahs? What about Shepard's and Wheeler's land?"

John Junior didn't answer, but was unshaken by John's bluster. Stephen shrunk back from the table, and Lydia fumbled with the top of her dress and waited for more. John took a sip and thought further. Squaw Sachem repeatedly saying 'lease' wouldn't leave his mind. *Maybe the old squaw be right?* John glared at his eldest. "Me have been on me land for thirty years. It be mine, and someday it be yours."

"We know, but ye town fathers fear Andros."

"Laddie, ye town fathers fear their new Sovereign, King James," said John. He took another swig. "Aye, there be no Cromwell to protect them now." John stared at his mug while his thoughts swirled in an effort to get Squaw Sachem from his mind. Finally, he smiled. "Laddies, there be no worries. Me fought Cromwell for King Charles II, and now that he be dead, his brother, James, be king. Aye, and without me, Andros would nae be Governor. Me land be me just rewards for what me did at Doon Hill."

John was pleased he had recalled Andrew Adams' twisted logic. He sipped contentedly while his sons remained flabbergasted. They knew of their father's war experiences, but had never heard until now that their father was a renowned crusader for King James and the Anglicans.

*****

John continued to display nonchalance about his land ownership, but inwardly the scuttlebutt and the image of Squaw Sachem saying 'lease' had shaken his self-assurance. After a few days of anxiety, he needed more than third hand information.

"Me'll be leading the family this Sabbath, laddie," said John.

Lydia ceased bouncing young Mary in her arms. "My heart doth beat with such fervor. All the Laws of New Grant will be going to ye meetinghouse this morn."

"That be the Laws of New Scotland," said John.

A confused John Junior moved between his father and Stephen as John led the family east. Lydia carried the infant Mary while Elizabeth, Samuel and Thomas clustered around her. When Lydia's arms grew weary, Elizabeth relieved Lydia until her numbness left. As the Laws strolled along the main road leading to the meetinghouse, several heads turned toward them. Lydia reflected to an earlier time. Heads turned then when the Drapers of Concord approached the town common each Sabbath. Some of the silent expressions now were similar to those earlier ones. How ashamed she felt back then for her transgressions, but not now, she was just another goodwife with her family, honoring the Sabbath.

Once at the meetinghouse grounds, the family dispersed. John Junior and Stephen went to a crowd of young lads. Lydia and the other children headed toward the gathering of goodwives, which left John standing alone. The Sabbath journey had tired him, and he leaned against a tree to survey the clusters of townsfolk. John Junior was regaling some young men with Stephen close to his side, re-enforcing his brother's comments.

The Immigrant

Unlike John, his older sons had been accepted by their peers. Lydia was engaged in conversation as Elizabeth listened while holding Mary. Thomas and Samuel seemed bored. John wondered what those two younger lads would become when full grown. But surveying the gathering was not providing information that John wanted, and he moved closer to a group gathered near the pillory stocks.

"I have yet to verify William Taylor the junior's claim to his land," said Goodman Wylie.

"Impossible, like all eldest, he received a double portion of his father's land with his relict having a life interest," said another.

"Indeed, but it is Goodman Taylor's original grant that is in question," said Wylie.

"My memory hath fogged, but I do remember the day we approved his grant." He pointed and said, "Thither, in the meetinghouse."

"Me too," chimed in another.

"As do I," said Wylie. "But the grant was never recorded."

"Then draft a new document," said Goodman Stow.

"That would not be fitting and proper," said Wylie.

Goodman Stow stepped back, and with both hands, tugged on the inside of his cloak. He raised his head, and his eyes didn't flinch as he responded to Wylie. "My good man, our records are most untidy. Our Governor's actions, despicable as we may deem them, compel us to remove such clutter so we can bear witness to ye truth." Wylie shied from Stow's stare as a few sidled closer to Stow. "It is most assuredly fitting and proper to bring order to ye town records." Stow turned to his recently formed audience. "The day will arrive when the honorable Governor is summoned back to England."

"Oh if only thy words could be God's providence," said one standing near.

Stow nodded and continued. "We must resolve the muddle Concord hath wrought." Stow lowered his hands from his cloak, and the eavesdropping John gloated as he thought. *Good to see these bastards squirm.*

"And then there is New Grant," said Wylie.

"New Grant hath too many issues for now, and ye meetinghouse door doth beckon," said Stow.

The group dispersed, as did John's smirking. He pondered what Stow meant by 'too many issues for now'. Was one of those issues what Squaw Sachem had called 'lease'? Beneath John's bluster, he knew his title rested solely on the word of Awbrey. But Awbrey was gone. Possibly Blood, or his servant, Duncan, could vouch for Awbrey's word? But Blood had died, and no one would believe the word of the Scottish Duncan. And another thought now added to John's worry. Maybe there would be no double share to his eldest, and no life interest for Lydia. But John always had a solution whenever he fretted too much about his land issues. *God damn it. Me have been on me land for thirty years, it be mine,* thought John as he entered the meetinghouse to sit in a sea of English bastards.

Chapter Fifty

Concord, Middlesex, Dominion of New England
April 1689

Lydia dashed across the meadow from the Shepard's farm with her young children trailing behind. Elizabeth and Samuel helped their two younger siblings to keep pace. As John closed the door to the shed, he wondered what Lydia's news would be. He moved toward them as a gasping Lydia neared. "Thou will not believe what Goody Davis told Sarah," said Lydia.

John cocked his head slightly.

"Riots in ye streets of Boston."

John raised his eyebrows.

"William of Orange drove King James[46] and the popery from the throne."

"Aye, so why the Riots?" asked John. "Me would think Boston would be rejoicing."

---

46 *When William of Orange, a protestant and a son-in-law and nephew to James, invaded England from the Netherlands in the Glorious Revolution of 1688, James fled England and thus was held to have abdicated his throne as of 13 December 1688.*

"Ye rioters captured Andros. He doth reside in ye Boston jail. John Shepard is so thankful that God's providence hath prevailed."

"Thankful for what?"

"He hath worried Andros would take his land."

"I doubt that."

"Well no matter, our land is now safe from Andros too. He will stand trial and possibly be hanged. Not that I wish such a fate."

"If he be sent to England, he will be hanged. He nae be of William's ilk."

"Ye good men of Concord control our destiny again, as it should be." John wrinkled his lips and headed back to his house as Lydia continued. "Ye selectmen are drafting a listing."

John spun back. "What listing?"

"Of men entitled to vote. John Shepard is on it."

"And is John Law on it?"

"Well, I don't know." Lydia thought further. "But thou hast never attended ye town meetings."

John knew the listing was more than just voting privileges. It also confirmed land ownership. He pondered further, not listening to Lydia's rambling until she said, "John Shepard believes April 19th will be celebrated for years to come; a day Concord shall never forget." John scratched his head and stared at Lydia. "The 19th is the day of the riots," said Lydia.

"Shepard be daft. April 19th will always be just like any other day in Concord."

Lydia's excitement continued through the evening meal. Like his father, John Junior had concerns over the listing's existence, and he questioned his father about it. His answers were predictable; bombastic at first, slurs against the English and the familiar refrain, 'it be me land for years, laddie'.

*****

At the next Sabbath, knowing his father's bluster would be insufficient to prove title, John Junior mingled with the elders, listened and occasionally asked questions. The selectmen had indeed compiled a listing of land proprietors. John Shepard was on the list, and John Law was not. John Junior was determined to resolve the problem.

Over the summer, he spoke with several selectmen. Since they viewed him as his father's surrogate, he had to endure the vitriol intended for his father before he could even ask questions. However, Thaddeus Blood, a retired selectman, was unlike the rest. He was tall and gaunt, which gave him a commanding demeanor. His crop of bushy white hair and extended white side burns accentuated his countenance. When age had fogged his mind, he retired as a selectman. Yet his influence remained. John Junior found Thaddeus welcoming.

On a cheery, autumn Sabbath, John Junior waited for the meetinghouse doors to open. He was watching the good men conversing with Thaddeus Blood while trying to determine how to interrupt the group. After a few minutes, he marched toward them as his heart pounded in fear. "Grand Sire Thaddeus Blood, may I speak with thee?" he asked.

Startled, Thaddeus turned out from his circle of friends. The interruption annoyed the group, except for Thaddeus who remained unruffled. He nodded and excused himself from his friends.

"Might we speak thither?" asked John Junior. Thaddeus paused for a second, looked back to his friends, and relying on his walking stick, followed John Junior.

Once John Junior felt comfortably out of earshot from the group, he stopped and turned to Thaddeus. "Grand Sire, ye Selectmen's listing of land proprietors hath brought great concern to my mother, Goody Law."

Thaddeus knitted his bushy white eyebrows. John Junior's heart raced again, and he twitched his fingers. He hoped invoking his mother concerns, even though she had never expressed them, would be better than mentioning his father's name. He waited for Thaddeus to break the silence. Maybe it was a mistake to mention his mother? Maybe he should correct it? Thaddeus's eyebrows finally eased. "Ah, ye listing. What doth trouble Goody Law?" asked Thaddeus.

"My father's name doth not appear."

"He must be on it. He's a land proprietor is he not?"

"For over thirty years."

Thaddeus stepped back, centered his walking stick and placed both hands on it. John Junior regretted his enthusiastic response. Thaddeus stared, and John Junior twitched his toes inside his boots. "Ye selectmen discussed all proprietors last spring," said Thaddeus. He removed a hand from his cane to stroke his hair. He toyed with a sideburn while he thought. "Thy father is a free man?"

"Truly," replied John Junior.

"We discussed all New Grant residents; thy father, John the Shepherd, Wheeler, my kin of course." Thaddeus ceased toying and looked skyward. He faced John Junior directly. "Art thou sure?"

John Junior wasn't sure, but nodded anyway.

"Oh me, thy father should be on the listing."

The selectmen's meeting finally came to Thaddeus. The meeting had become bogged down with the John Law controversy. The chairman deferred the discussion and continued with other less contentious proprietors. Either because of oversight or by design, the chairman never returned to discuss John Law. Thaddeus now pondered how best to correct the situation. "Much has happened this past year, hath it not young Master Law?" he asked.

John Junior creased his brow and nodded in agreement.

"William of Orange overthrew that Anglican. Andros will stand trial for his crimes. And while he was a misguided, headstrong Governor, he did awaken us to Concord's failings."

John Junior's shoulder's sagged as he wondered where the conversation was going.

"We truly had neglected our duties. But with God's guidance, we began recording a fitting and proper listing of proprietors." He placed both hands on his walking stick and peered out from a snarl of white eyebrows. He was as clear eyed as a hawk readying to strike. "Young Master Law, I will ensure ye listing will be amended for thy father's and for his Goodwife's sake."

John Junior's mouth dropped, stunned by the abrupt change in Thaddeus's demeanor. Then Thaddeus's hawk eyes left. "I shant this year, ye warrant hath been determined," said Thaddeus. "But I will next year."

John Junior wondered if the Grand Sire was merely placating an exuberant youth. "But Grand Sire, I…"

"I know thou art eager," interrupted Thaddeus. "Let thy questions rest. Thou hast my word. This unintended misdeed will be set right."

"I am truly thankful as will be my mother," said John Junior, even though doubts still nagged at him. His father had heard similar words throughout the years. Thaddeus's demeanor suggested their conversation was over, and John Junior moved back toward his mother and siblings.

"Pray remember me, Master John Law." Thaddeus spotted Lydia and made a slight hand movement to her. He nodded and mouthed, "Goody Law." Lydia acknowledged Thaddeus's graciousness with a smile, and Thaddeus ambled back to his friends.

"I say, I did not know John Law the junior and thou were acquaintances," teased one of Thaddeus's friends.

"I ask thy forgiveness for departing in such haste." The chuckling ceased as Thaddeus continued. "As thou knowest, my cousin, Robert Blood the elder, departed several years prior." The group became sober. A few bowed their heads. "It was odd, but on his deathbed he beseeched me to ensure John Law be treated fairly. John Law can be a rascal, but his eldest son is not of the same temperament."

"He hath Draper blood," said one. "Not the most decent blood, but more so than the Scottish blood that doth flow in his father's veins." One sniggered, and a few nodded.

Thaddeus was with another thought, oblivious to the slights. He came back to the conversation. "Fondness doth grip my heart for young Master John Law. He doth remind me of my eldest." Those in the group looked furtively among one another as every head bowed.

Thaddeus went back to his thoughts, looked skyward and ambled alone, leaning upon his walking stick with every other step. Others moved to the meetinghouse as the doors would soon be opening.

Chapter Fifty-one

As the spring of 1690 warmed into summer, a fifty-five year old John Law paused yet again under a cloudless sky, removed his hat and wiped his brow. His breeches clung to his sweaty thighs. He and his sons were cultivating Lydia's garden not far from the house. He leaned on his upright hoe and reflected. His relationship with his eldest had evolved over the years. At first, he had been the teacher and his son the dutiful student. But John Junior grew less compliant, questioning more than obeying as he became more independent. John's father had died early in John's life. Thus, after early adolescence, John lacked reference points for the ever-changing father/son relationship. At times, John viewed his son's independence as disobedience, which caused him to worry their relationship had been irreconcilably damaged. But as his son aged, he evolved from a rebellious youth to a confident young man. John now considered him to be a worthy heir to his estate. His frustration had evolved to admiration.

John scrapped at a few weeds and paused again. John Junior was now stronger and more energetic than him. John's aches had grown to constant pains, his energy was sapped by mid-day, and while he naturally tended to procrastinate, chores weren't done now, simply, because he couldn't do them. He smiled inside with the thought that Lydia now forgave him for leaving some chores undone. The decision he made thirty years earlier to marry her was a good one. As still air freshened, John closed his eyes and stretched his neck toward it until John Junior disturbed him. "Father rest. Ye noon day sun is most fierce."

John grumbled and returned to his hoeing. His son lacked a Scottish brogue and spoke like an Englishman, traits from Lydia. He was more tolerant of the English than John, and was more readily accepted by the English. John had disliked those aspects of his son, at first, but now he was envious, realizing his son had community standing where his was lacking.

He paused again and surveyed his estate. It had been a long trek from Doon Hill, and he had endured many burdens along the way. But he had finally arrived at a mountaintop where he could envision the rest of the journey. One day his eldest would assume his role, and Lydia and the rest of the children would be secure. Stephen would continue to follow his older brother, and while still young, so would Thomas. Those three lads would easily maintain his estate. On the other hand, Samuel was a different sort, more content to be with Lydia than with him. Samuel's inclination to care for the livestock continued to develop. Lydia was convinced Samuel would be a physician someday. John couldn't envision a Scottish lad ever achieving such status, but he respected Lydia's judgment and hoped she was correct. And of course, the two girls would help Lydia, no doubt marry, hopefully men of importance, and continue to care for their mother in her twilight years.

*****

The chill returned on an autumn breeze, and an unpredictable early, cold snap blanketed the fields with a killing frost. As the sun glistened in the meadow, John fretted this winter would be ruthless. Gathering firewood now became his single focus. The woodpile expanded until an Indian summer welcomed in November. John's sense of urgency abated, but returned when a slate-colored, herringbone sky brought blustery winds and a brief snow shower.

As John sat one morning regretting his procrastination, John Junior came into the house cradling a stack of wood. "Laddie, be too much," said John.

"Mother doth shiver, and Mary's lips are purple."

"Nae be winter yet."

"After breakfast, Stephen and I will gather more."

"Can I go too?" asked an eight year old Thomas.

"I will hear none of this. Thomas is too young," said Lydia as she came into the room wiping her hands on her apron.

"He nae be too young to learn," said John.

"It is cold, even the sheep huddle nigh," said Lydia. She moved to John Junior and hugged him. "Tomorrow may be better, dear."

"Be colder tomorrow," said John.

"Father is right," said John Junior as he moved away from his mother's clutches. "Thou and my sisters are cold. We must gather more wood before winter sets upon us."

Lydia clutched her apron, admiring her son's sense of duty, and left for the other room.

"Stephen, fetch ye cart and axe," said John Junior. He turned to Thomas. "Finish thy porridge, and thou can come too." Thomas scooped quickly and scrambled out the door after his older brothers.

The winds were constant and gusted, at times, rumbling through the house. When John stepped out for more wood, he looked toward the hills where his sons had gone. The herringbone sky had morphed to solid granite, blocking the sun. The gusts were now bone chilling. John shuddered and went inside.

"Hast thou seen them?" asked Lydia.

"Nae, be too early."

"John, darkness hath arrived."

John stared into the fire while Lydia asked him more questions. He responded with mutters. Samuel and Elizabeth drew near to Lydia and hugged her. They pondered the fire in silence too until a rush of cold air startled them. Thomas bolted through the door and stood, shaking and blowing on his hands. Tears ran down his reddened cheeks.

"He is too young to be so long in such a cold wilderness," said Lydia. She ran to him and smothered kisses on his tear streaked cheeks. She glared at John. "Much, much too young."

Stephen and John Junior staggered into the house. Stephen's arm was around his older brother's waist and John Junior's arm drooped over Stephen's shoulder. Lydia shrieked, and Thomas jumped and squeezed his eyes. More tears oozed out of them. With the commotion, the other three children came into the room. John struggled out of his chair as panic surged through him. His heart raced, and his temple scar throbbed as it had over thirty-five years earlier.

John Junior continued to cling to Stephen's shoulder as he was led to John's chair. His head was bloodied, a welt was near his temple, his shirt sleeve was tattered, and his arm dangled by his side. His face was seemingly drained of blood. He released his arm from Stephen's shoulder, and his brother used both arms to help him to slump onto their father's chair.

"Mother, do not worry; a mere mishap," said John Junior. He closed his eyes. "We were felling a tree, and my axe became stuck." He inhaled and opened his eyes. "I wandered away. But the wind shifted, and the tree fell and struck my head and shoulder."

A still teary Thomas looked up at his mother. "I yelled but ye winds were too strong."

"He never heard us," added Stephen.

The three lads continued discussing the accident, and the shock eventually ebbed away. For Thomas, it took added cuddling from Elizabeth to settle him. But for John, guilt now replaced shock. His doggedness for wood had driven his sons into a dangerous, near death encounter. His temple scar continued to throb.

What wasn't discussed was John Junior lay unconscious while a distraught Stephen shook him. Thomas wailed, believing his brother was dead. When John Junior regained consciousness, the two eldest realized they had averted a disaster. Once they calmed Thomas, John Junior made him promise never to tell anyone that he had been unconscious.

Emotionally drained, the family slept through the night, except for John who was too guilt laden. With one wind gust, he thought he heard the door open and his son leave. But Doon

Hill taught him that winds always deceive a troubled mind. He nodded off and awoke again, a disrupting cycle that occurred throughout the night.

The next morning, when John stepped outside for wood, several clumps of vomit lay on the ground. His son had indeed left during night. John's temple scar throbbed anew, and he grew woozy. *Why did me nae arise?* He looked heavenward. *You let me pretend to be on Doon Hill?* He thought about cursing God, but didn't. *It nae be your fault, it be me.* He looked at the door. *Lydia will nae see this.* He kicked the clumps to disperse the evidence. But kicking only dispersed the vomit and not the guilt piling upon his troubled mind. John went back inside.

Lydia was re-examining John Junior's shoulder and arm as Samuel looked on. Turning to Samuel Lydia said, "His bones do not appear broken. Yet his arm droops and a lump remains on his shoulder."

"And the lump on his head?" asked John.

"The potato from the cold cellar hath lessened it," said Lydia. John Junior eased the potato from his temple. John didn't notice any difference from the previous night.

"No dear, keep it thither," said Lydia. She went to the hearth and took the wooden spoon from Elizabeth. She stirred the kettle, and using her apron, removed it to the table. "Goody Draper's elixir. Once it hath cooled, I will give thee a ladle full."

*****

Over the next two days, John Junior's welt receded as did John's guilt. But his son still had limited arm movement and no appetite. When a clump of discolored fluid greeted John in the early morning of the third day, his worry intensified. Lydia brewed several more concoctions, but their effects, if any, were unnoticeable.

On the fourth day following the accident, Stephen led Lydia and his younger siblings to the meetinghouse while John stayed with his eldest. "Here son, sip," said John. John Junior struggled up, sipped, grimaced and crashed back down. "Me knows, but yah mum said ye must."

John Junior's eyes were closed as he rolled his head from side to side. "Father, this potion is most foul," he said. "But don't let mother know." His head ceased rolling, and his breathing abated.

After a few minutes, John said, "Laddie," and by habit, John Junior's eyes flew open upon hearing his father's voice. John was relieved. His son had responded. "Laddie me nae should have…"

"Father, I was the foolish one," mumbled John Junior as he closed his eyes and lay still. The fire crackled, and John waited, hoping his son would say more. The wait seemed endless, and the silence was unnerving. John Junior rolled his head. "Thou told me often about thy mishap." He soon fell back to sleep.

John Junior's few words were insufficient for John. He was beginning to sense something dreadful would soon happen. John Junior's snort and a pop from the hearth were the only sounds in the otherwise, deathly quiet house. John clenched both of his hands into fists to calm his trembling. John Junior snorted again and thrashed his head back and forth. John opened his fists, and his eyes widened.

"I should have listened," said his son with his eyes closed. He coughed and chuckled. "Thou say me nae listen."

John shook his head. "Perhaps when you be young, but nae now."

"Nae, you be right, Father. Me nae listens."

His son's breathing was now rhythmic, which soothed John. Perhaps the worst wouldn't come. But John's relief from his ultimate fear was brief. He had to speak. "You be me eldest son. You be me heir. You be…" John couldn't continue, yet he still had more to say. He wanted to tell his son how he admired and loved him, but he couldn't move the words out of his swollen throat to his dry lips.

His son's breathing was no longer peaceful, but rough gasps. John's blood pounded so hard he thought his temple scar might explode. The fire popped, and smoke drifted, creating a whiff from the distant past when John lay on the floor of Durham Cathedral. Then, the smoke had been tinged with death, and John wrung his hands. But it was futile as the pungent reminder remained. He lowered his head, cupped his hands and whispered in a dry rasp. "God, me doubt thee ever hears me. Father, Mother," pleaded John, "please someone hear me this day."

Angus MacTavish appeared in John's guilt ridden mind with a bloodied spindle from the alter rail in his chest, as did the stained glass window of Jesus with inviting palms. "Jesus, me did nae kill Angus. He already be dead. God, you must believe me."

John's appeal to God had risen in volume, which startled John. His son's rhythmic breathing returned. His chest rose and fell like a soothing sea. John returned to a whisper. "I beg thee God, do nae take me lad. Me be too old to bear another burden, nae one that be so heavy." His throat tightened further as his eyes welled. Whispering was now difficult as he said, "Me heart would break. Me would nae make it."

He still had doubts about God hearing him, but continued his entreaties anyway, unsure if he muttered, or just thought them. He emptied his heart, hoping something would strike a chord with the divine. Then a commotion from outside broke into his soliloquy. He scurried to the door as it was opening. "John Junior be resting," he said.

"Ah," said Lydia, and she raised her hand to quiet her children. In a forced whisper she said, "Physician Reed was not at the meetinghouse. He is to arrive in Concord Thursday noon. But Goody Eaton hath given me yet another elixir."

"Nae elixirs. Let the lad rest."

"But perhaps later."

John hoped this elixir would be more palatable than the last one he had given his son. More importantly, he hoped it would have an effect. Elixirs and the remote chance God had heard him were all he had until Thursday.

Lydia went inside, and her children followed. As Stephen passed by John, he grabbed his shoulder and steered him to the side. Stephen's face reflected his usual fear whenever his father singled him out. John rubbed Stephen's shoulder, and he eased from his cringe. "Thou know I love thee," said John.

Stephen's worry now turned to bewilderment. He knew John Junior was his father's favorite, understandable since he was the eldest. He sensed his father's love, but never thought he would hear him say it. His father looked different. These past few days had aged him by years. Strain was etched deep into his father's face. "Surely, Goody Eaton's potion will cure John Junior," said Stephen.

"Aye, surely," John said. But their eyes belied their nodding heads.

*****

John Junior now slept peacefully, and only awoke when urged to swallow the elixir. For John, waiting for Thursday to arrive was a seeming eternity. Since the accident, the weather had been unseasonably warm, which added to John's guilt – wood gathering could have waited. By Wednesday, he had to relieve his despair and spent the morning splitting wood with Stephen. Thomas joined them, confident he was old enough to split logs. But Thomas's first few axe swings were useless. Frustrated, he brought the axe over his shoulder, and when he swung it, he lost his balance. The axe head missed its target, and the handle creaked as it hit the side of the upright log.

John spun around, and panic swept through Thomas as his father approached. John grabbed the axe to check the handle. It wasn't cracked. He put his arm around Thomas's shoulder. "Laddie, stack the wood and let your brother do the splitting." Thomas hurried to the woodpile, relieved he wasn't scolded.

Waiting inside the house for another day to come was an eternity for Lydia too. She thought another dose of Goody Eaton's cure would help. She tapped on her son's good shoulder to awaken him. She nudged him gently, and he still didn't stir. She kissed his forehead. It was cold, and her eyes widened with surprise as she drew back. Panic shot through her, and she gripped John Junior's face. It was as cold as his forehead. She grabbed his head and pressed it against her bosom much as she had done with Thomas, years ago. "First Thomas, and now John Junior."

Her resignation to her fate was brief. She pushed John Junior from her bosom and shook him. But reality returned when he didn't respond. She released her grip, sagged to her knees and sobbed. After several minutes, she looked heavenward, spread her arms and turned her palms up. "Is this thy providence? Have mercy upon us." She looked to the door and squeezed her eyes. "Have mercy upon John." She thought further about what had just occurred. With a sense of resignation, she wiped her eyes, arose and left to tell John.

As Lydia came outside, she didn't have to say a word. Her face said it all. John slumped, reeled toward the woodpile and collapsed upon a stump. Stephen lowered his axe and placed his hand on his father's shoulder. John was too bereft to acknowledge the gesture. Tears trickled down Thomas's face as he stood holding several split logs. Samuel and his sisters raced up from the shed and slowed as they neared. They sensed what had just occurred. Samuel went to his mother and rubbed her shoulders. Elizabeth stayed with six year old Mary, draped her arm across her shoulders and pulled her close. Mary looked up at her sister wanting an answer. But the only answer was Elizabeth's tears, so Mary cried too.

On an unseasonably warm Wednesday of December 6th in ye year of ye Lord 1690 John Law Junior left New Scotland for an eternity.

****

The unseasonable warmth continued, and a few days following John Junior's death, John labored up the rise with his family toward the gravesite. He had walked this path many times, usually in anticipation of sitting on his favorite rock and relaxing. The lone exception had been when he buried two year old Thomas. Then, it was a heavy laden trek as John was burdened with the memories of Thomas's short existence, knowing there would be no more to come. Now, John had thirty years of memories to carry with him and also the loss of all his futures aspirations for his family. John sensed the weight of this burden would soon crush him. His thighs grew heavier with each step, and he was forced to rest before reaching the gravesite.

Stephen left the family standing at the gravesite and came to help John up the rise. When he put his arm around his father's waist, John shooed him away and trudged alone to the site. Stephen returned to the family and stood next to the grave that he had dug earlier; thankful the ground had yet to freeze completely. He said a few words as John stood numb, oblivious to what was being said. The stimulating sound of the bubbling waters and the peaceful vistas were as they had always been for John when he came to relax. But John didn't hear or see them. After Stephen finished speaking, the family waited in silence, hoping for John to speak. Finally Stephen asked, "Father, would you like to offer a few words unto God?"

"God nae hears me," said an impassive John.

A teary-eyed, somber Lydia went to John and rubbed his back as Stephen filled in the grave. John didn't acknowledge Lydia's sympathy. His only sensations were the sound of earth being swished into John Junior's grave and the feeling of a stake being driven deeper into his heart with each swish.

Chapter Fifty-two

January 1691

It was on a cold January night, a month after John Junior's tragic death, when Thomas asked his mother, "Can Mary and I go and seek?"

"Yes, but bundle thyselves," said Lydia. Thomas and his younger sister grabbed a woolen cover and raced toward the door. "Stay nigh, my children," said Lydia. She was unsure if her scampering children had heard her.

Outside, Thomas paused and looked skyward as the woolen cover he was holding drooped onto the ground. Mary looked east, above the Great River and toward Concord Center. She spun back to her brother. "He's gone," she said.

"No, he hath just moved."

The northern lights dazzled Mary as she pivoted around. "There are too many," she said.

"You have to look with diligence." Thomas dropped the covering and rotated his head from the east toward the north as his eyes scanned up and down the sky.

"I'm cold," said Mary.

Thomas continued his slow turn. "There he is," he said. "How do you fare, my brother?"

"I don't see him," said Mary.

Thomas sidled to his sister, and while still looking at the sky, he pointed to the big dipper. "I still don't see him," said Mary.

Thomas put his hands on each side of Mary's cheeks and pivoted her head. He pointed again. Her eyes grew as bright as the twinkling stars. She jumped up and down while saying, "Johno, Johno." Thomas picked up the woolen cover, swung it over their shoulders and drew Mary close. "I miss you, Johno. So does Thomas."

Meanwhile inside the house, Lydia placed her sampler on the chair and moved to her still grieving husband. She rubbed his shoulders. "Can I refresh thy cup?"

The empty cup hung from John's hand. Lydia rubbed again and broke John's trance. "God nae hears me," said John.

"God hears us all. But he must humble us first, so we can hear him."

"He hath humbled this wretched Scotsman all me life. Gives me a farthing and takes a shilling in return."

"We still have been blessed."

"Me eldest be gone."

Stephen looked up from the Bible, and Samuel paused from helping Elizabeth with balling the yarn. Lydia smiled at them and returned to massage her husband's shoulders. "Thou still hath an eldest and four others," said Lydia. The dancing flame had regained John's attention, and Lydia ceased massaging. "I best be checking on thy two youngest." Lydia threw her cloak over her shoulders and headed for her children.

As Lydia came outside, Thomas was graciously listening to Mary's chatter. When Mary turned to Lydia, the delight in her eyes was infectious. Lydia's mood brightened. Mary broke from underneath her brother's arm and raced to her mother. "We found him this night," said Mary.

Lydia crouched to greet her daughter. "Of course you found him." Lydia scanned the sky and continued, "The heavens are so clear. Oh look at that moon, dear. Why it's the full wolf moon this month isn't it?"

Mary looked up at the moon and shook her head. "No, thither Mother," she said as she pointed away from the moon.

Lydia arose from her crouch to marvel at the big dipper. "Ah the Great Plow," she said.

"Do you see Johno sitting in its cup?" asked Mary.

"I do."

"Mother sees him too, Thomas," said Mary as she jumped up and down again.

Lydia absorbed the night, focusing on the moon, the stars and one particular group of stars. The air chilled her face, but she was warm, basking in the wonders of God's universe. The three stood mesmerized until Lydia urged them to move inside. Mary held Lydia's hand, and they paused near the door for a last look at the big dipper.

"Pray remember me, Johno," said Mary.

Lydia squeezed her daughter's cold hand. "Pray remember me too, Johno," she said. The sky had now captivated Lydia as much as the flickering flame had captivated John. She sighed and whispered, "Mother, Father, pray remember me." The glow in Mary's eyes reminded Lydia of God's blessing she had received after helping her brother's widow. She murmured, "Adam, my beloved brother, I miss thee too."

Mary remained standing, enchanted with the big dipper and chattering away with her 'Johno'. Lydia tugged on Mary's hand. It was time to go inside. Lydia took a step toward the house and abruptly stopped. "Thomas, my precious Thomas, I have not forgotten ye. Pray remember me, my son."

Mary giggled and pointed. "Mother, Thomas is hither, standing next to you."

Lydia moved to her son and rubbed his head. "Of course Thomas is hither." She turned back to Mary and said, "Sometimes mothers forget." As the children scampered inside, Lydia took a last glance up the hill toward the gravesite. "But mothers should never forget."

Chapter Fifty-three

John wanted to flee anywhere to escape the painful reminders of his eldest son. But they were all-pervasive. He rarely went outside, and if he did, he couldn't look at the woodpile without seeing John Junior. Mostly, he languished at the hearth and stared at the glow, just as he did when tending the charcoal pits along the Saugus River. The images were not, however, fond reminiscences of his mother, but the horrors of his new existence. He mumbled often and apologized for what he had wrought.

He stumbled to bed and lay awake, too fearful to close his eyes since the horrors grew more vivid at night. Sadly, when sleep came, it brought a swaying gnarly-limbed tree, a broken body and a writhing son crying for help as fiends derided John for what he had caused. He would bolt up and eventually ease back down, hoping for morning light so he could return to his hearth and less horrific images. Melancholy engulfed him and blocked his soul from offering any relief.

Unlike John, Lydia's grief eased with time. She still wept, quietly so as not to add to John's worry, even though she sensed he was too self-absorbed to hear her. She accepted God's providence, dreadful as it was. God had humbled her in the past, and she endured it. She would endure this burden, too. Getting out of a smoky house each Sabbath was therapeutic for Lydia. The walk in winter's chill tired her and ensured a restful night sleep. She sat in the meetinghouse with her thoughts and blocked out the sermon whenever it drifted to hell and damnation. She was sure of one thing; Thomas and now John Junior weren't with Satan, but were with her family and God. She listened to the conversations, thanked those who offered condolences and, over time, engaged in conversation. Talking about her grief with the goodwives helped to heal her pain.

*****

One Sabbath in late winter, Lydia and her children returned from the meetinghouse. They found John sitting in his chair, unaware the fire was but embers. Stephen and Thomas dashed outside for more wood. Samuel and his two sisters moved to the back room.

Lydia drew close to John and rubbed his hand. "Dost thou know Grand Sire Thaddeus Blood?" she asked. John flinched at her touch, but still concentrated on the smoldering embers as Lydia answered her question. "Surely, everyone knows him – a tall stately man, bushy eyebrows and dazzling blue eyes."

"Me knew a Robert Blood," said John while still staring at the fire.

"No doubt they are kin." Lydia grabbed a stool and sat to be face-to-face with John, blocking his view of the hearth. "He offered his condolences and spoke about John Junior, so glowingly you'd think we were kin."

Stephen returned and, like always, was putting too many logs on the fire. But John didn't bother to correct his son. Lydia rubbed John's hand again to get his attention. "He offered his thoughts and prays for thee," said Lydia.

A few embers flared and crackled, and John shifted back to the fire.

Lydia settled back on her stool and, after several minutes, spoke. "Thaddeus lost his eldest son, too. He said his heart was torn from him and his soul was filled with bitterness. But bitterness left, and God's sweetness returned to the blood in his veins. David's Psalm lamenting Absalom's death was Thaddeus's salvation."

"Me nae know an Absalom Blood," said John.

Lydia eased forward and patted John's hand. "Absalom, King David's son," she said. "Truly thou knowest the story."

The fire was losing its allure, and John turned from it to shake his head.

"Absalom rebelled from his father, just like John Junior when he was young. Their struggle never ended. It grew to a battle, and when Absalom was fleeing, a tree ended his life." Lydia ceased rubbing John's hand. "His tresses became ensnarled in branches, and he hung there until God's mercy ended his agony."

"A tree killed David's son?" asked John.

"And a tree killed thy son too." Lydia's eyes widened with hope. Perhaps John would continue to draw the analogy. "Can thou fathom King David's grief?"

John didn't respond, but eased forward from his chair.

"David's most heartfelt Psalms lament the loss of his son," said Lydia. "O my son Absalom, my son, my son Absalom would God I had died for thee, O Absalom, my son, my son."

John's eased back in his chair and thought. *God take me tired body, and return to John Junior's his youthful one.* He reflected further and shook his head. *Such a foolish plea, nae wonder God doesn't listen to me.*

"Grand Sire gave me the verses that eased his pain." Lydia removed a rolled parchment from her pocket. "Goody Davis told the Grand Sire she doubted we owned a family Bible. So he scrolled them for thee. Oh that gossip. Even though she is dead, she still torments from the grave."

Lydia held the parchment far from her eyes and moved it until the words came in focus. She read Psalm 55: "My heart is sore pained within me; and the terrors of death are fallen upon me. Fearfulness and trembling are come upon me, and horror hath overwhelmed me. And I said, oh that I had wings like a dove, for then would I fly away, and be at rest. Lo, then would I wander far off, and remain in the wilderness. I would hasten my escape from the windy storm and tempest." Lydia lowered the parchment.

Like King David, John realized his constant lamenting to flee was a not an escape at all. He was trapped and would have to endure his burdens. Tears flowed over John's cheeks as he thought further. *"God doth have burdens for us all"* Aye it be what Reverend Bulkeley said. Even though Stephen and Thomas were near, John let his tears remain on his cheeks. He squeezed his eyes and more tears fell.

Lydia closed her eyes and thought how bitter John's tears seemed. Lydia prayed sweetness would return to the blood in his veins. She opened her eyes and rolled up the parchment. She arose, moved behind John and stared at the blaze. She brushed her tears and kissed the top of John's head.

"I will leave David's Psalm on the table. Grand Sire Blood said he read it often." Lydia left for another room and its solitude. There, she wouldn't have to fight back her tears.

Over the next few days, John read the Psalm often. His melancholy receded with each reading, making room for more than sorrow in his life. His soul was now able to bring forth its many experiences of when a father loses a son. John was slowly finding ways to move past the horror he had been mired in these past few months.

Prodded by Lydia and with encouragement from Stephen, John began participating in the normal spring cycle routines. Toiling released therapeutic endorphins, and with each day, John toiled more. He said little and never complained about his aches, preferring to remain with his thoughts. They were cheerier than before, offering hope and not gloom. He was physically drained by night and slept less fitfully. His demons were gone; perhaps for an eternity.

*****

Springtime, the period of renewal, was throughout Concord. The townsfolk were sowing their fields and travelling about, visiting neighbors. They were upbeat until a sad note resounded. The town's eldest statesman, Grand Sire Thaddeus Blood, had passed away. On the Sabbath following his death, the preacher had a lengthy oration. Not to be outdone, each selectman spoke at the annual town meeting. The lengthy speeches delayed the conclusion of the town meeting until late evening. John Law Junior and Grand Sire Thaddeus Blood were dead. So too was their article amending the proprietor's listing of land owners, which no one noticed, not even John Law.

Chapter Fifty-four

March 1698

In 1655, the Commonwealth granted to Concord 5,000 acres of land across the river from the town, which became known as New Grant. Ten years later another 5,000 acres was granted, adjoining the initial tract. Consequently, New Grant had grown to be half the size that Concord had originally been and larger than some neighboring towns. The granted land was initially held as commons by proprietors, most of whom were initial settlers of Concord. The proprietors' understanding was the common land would eventually be parceled into private land for their heirs.

In 1697, a special committee was tasked with compiling a complete listing of proprietors. After several months of researching town records, the listing was complete. Through the years, a small section of New Grant became densely populated and known as Concord Village. Following the 1698 Concord annual meeting, Concord Village held a special meeting to present the listing.

The meeting commenced with Goodman Noyes, one of the committee members, standing to the side of the committee, holding a list and facing Concord Village's good men. The meeting was well attended, but John, like always, was not there.

To him, it was another excuse for the English to parcel the land among themselves.

Noyes cleared his throat and said, "Ye first New Grant resident was John Shepard, Senior. He is ailing, so John Barker the junior will act on his account."

The committee chairman nodded to Noyes, scanned the crowd and, seeing no apparent objections, gaveled. "John Barker the junior, upon ye account of John Shepard the senior, one share." He gaveled again, and a hand shot up from the audience. The chairman thought about ignoring it – who could possibly question John Shepard's ownership? But Goodman Marion was now standing and still waving his hand. "The gavel hath sounded," said the chairman. "Thou will be out of order if thou questions John Shepard's share."

"It is thy listing that is out of order," said Marion.

Several villagers gasped, and the chairman gaveled to quiet the room. "Art thou questioning Goodman Noyes's veracity?" he asked.

"The first settler was not John Shepard, but John Law," said Marion

The chairmen looked to Noyes, who shrugged.

Marion continued standing. "John Law hath resided hither over forty years, much earlier than when Shepard came to his land."

Another attendee sprung from his seat. "That lazy Scotchman believes he owns all land west of Concord Center. He's without bounds; cuts wood, plants crops and grazes livestock wherever he pleases." The murmuring had grown to distinct grumbles. The impromptu speaker still had the floor, and he pointed to one of the grumblers. "Thou knew my father, God rest his soul. He paid dearly years ago to have John Law tend his sheep." He turned and pointed to another. "But Goodman Samuel Parsons never paid Law a farthing."

The aged Parson arose. "Not a farthing, but plenty of malt and grain."

The Chairman gaveled, but to no avail as another voice shouted. "John Law is filled with the avarice of Satan; shiftless, stubborn, and his sons…"

"My esteemed chairman," said Marion. The murmuring and gaveling ceased with his shout. "I believe I was speaking. Truly John Law is stubborn. But he is a proud, God fearing man." The murmurs returned as did the gavel. "Brought here a mere boy, forced to work in servitude and now a family man with a Goodwife…," Marion paused to scan the room, "and a land proprietor."

"Land proprietor, who doth sayeth?" asked one in the room.

The crack of the gavel resounded through the room. The clamor quieted, and Marion sat down. The chairman turned to Noyes. "Continue with thy recitation."

Noyes tugged at his collar. "Second on ye listing," he cleared his throat, "is John Law, one share."

The chairman grimaced as the clamor returned. He gaveled until the disorder quieted. With the lull, he gaveled and said, "John Law, one share." The shouting began anew. Only gaveling and the threat of barring the doors to keep everyone until the entire list was recited brought decorum.

It took forty years, but on 7 March 1698 John Law was recorded as a proprietor. He was no longer deemed a mere inhabitant, squatter or worse. The issue had been resolved, but the John Law controversy would continue.

*****

The following morning, John Shepard's son-in-law, John Barker, Jr, walked along a well-worn path to John Law's house. Stephen and Thomas were working near the property line. Barker told them the results of the meeting the night before, and relief came to both of them. With their father confirmed by the town as a proprietor, the land would pass to them according to John's direction upon his death. Their lingering doubts had finally been resolved.

John was sitting near a slowly dying fire with a woolen wrap around his upper body. He was in the midst of his usual morning catnap when Stephen and Thomas disturbed him. "Father, a glorious day, Ye New Grant proprietors' listing was approved at ye town meeting," said Stephen.

John rubbed his eyes and pulled his wrap closer. "Aye, another listing to parcel out me New Scotland."

Stephen ignored his father's cynicism. "John Shepard is listed first with one share, and second is John Law."

John leaned forward. "Can nae be." He stared at his sons and wondered. He rubbed his eye, and struggled up from his chair. His wrap fell off of him, and he gimped about the room. "Can nae be." His confused sons looked at one another as John continued to gimp. John ceased moving and stared at his sons. "Shepard arrived after me."

"Surely," said Stephen. "But you are finally recognized as a proprietor."

John scowled. "Laddies, me nae need a list." He shuddered, moved to the hearth and stirred the embers. He placed the poker to the side of the hearth and rubbed his hands. He turned back to his sons and said, "Ye list nae be glorious."

Steven looked at Thomas, who shook his head.

"Me land always be mine." John took a step closer to his sons. "Aye, just like the snake Awbrey said." He moved to be face-to-face with them. "And someday it be yours." He pulled them from their napes toward him, "Eh laddies?"

Chapter Fifty-five

Late autumn 1698

Lydia bid her 'fare thee well' to Physician Jacob Read, who had come yet again to visit. She closed the door quickly to block the cold draft. She moved quietly to the fire and rubbed her arthritic hands. But the cold awoke John from his nap in his heavily padded chair. He lowered his covering and raised his head off of the backrest. "Did Physician Read leave?"

Lydia nodded and moved to sit with her back to the fire facing John.

John yawned and rubbed his eyes. "Samuel be studying that physician book some more?"

Lydia, seemingly deep in thought, simply nodded.

John smiled. "Perhaps you be right. Maybe someday our Samuel will be a physician, too." John stretched his arms up, drew his covering near and sagged back into his chair. "Nice of that Read lad to takes such an interest in Samuel."

Lydia straightened up on her stool, looked around the room and finally spoke. "I think the young Physician hath other interests than just tutoring Samuel."

John cocked his head.

"Elizabeth."

"Aye, me sensed the lad visited often and with more on his mind than Samuel."

"Elizabeth's heart doth beat with ardor whenever he draws nigh." Lydia folded her hands and sighed. "I know how she feels." She smiled her sweet remembrances of her courtship. "Physician Read may soon do the fitting and proper thing and ask your blessing for their marriage."

"Elizabeth be of age," said John as he stirred in his chair to become more comfortable. "A Scottish lass marrying a physician," and John thought further while chuckling. "Would Goody Davis say Elizabeth be marrying into a high station?"

"Goody Davis died years ago."

"Then what would the other goodwives say?"

Lydia unfolded her hands. "John, Elizabeth is half Draper and, thus, half English. Times are not like when we married. And even though Jacob's father is a physician too, he doth not possess the esteem accorded most physicians. He is a man enamored by hard water."

"Every man has drunk hard water."

"And he is a blasphemer. He once said his patient's illness was caused by Reverend Edward Bulkeley's lengthy preaching in a cold meetinghouse."

"Aye, Physician Read spoke the truth." John yawned again and said, "His son comes from good stock." John pulled his covering close and shut his eyes.

"Physician Read was fined and banished for his blasphemy."

Elizabeth wandered into the room behind her father and made eye contact with her mother. Lydia shook her head quickly, and Elizabeth left. Lydia waited for John to open his eyes, but after a few minutes she sensed he might be nodding off. "So John, if Physician Jacob Reed doth speak with you," said Lydia hoping for John's attention. "Would thou give thy blessing?"

"Me suppose," said John with his eyes still closed. As he thought further, his eyes flew open and he leaned off his back rest. "But if Elizabeth be married, you would only have Mary for your chores."

"It is no bother. Elizabeth's mind has not been on her chores of late."

John nodded and closed his eyes until another thought came. "What about her dowry?" He reflected on Lydia's dowry and how Adam had been helpful in changing his then shelter into a home. "Me be too old to build. And me lads be too busy with their chores to help."

"We have items we can spare." Lydia thought about all the possessions she had accumulated over the past forty years. "We have been truly blessed, have we not?" She arose and kissed John's forehead. "Thou hast been a great provider to thy family."

John snuggled into his chair, closed his eyes and smiled. *Aye me hast.*

Chapter Fifty-six

November 1707

The rap at the door startled Lydia. She arose from the seat opposite John and placed her sampler on the stool. She drew her shawl close and shuffled to the door, tucking a few dangling white tresses back under her bonnet. She flexed her hand and rubbed the sun-spotted, weathered back of it.

"What cheer Goody Law, this frosty morn."

"Samuel Buttrick, Esquire, do come in. Mary's brewed some tea. It will surely warm thee."

Lydia took the lawyer's heavy coat and hung it on a peg. She ushered him into the main room where John sat in his chair, sipping tea. Lydia motioned to Mary, and she brought the teapot with a cup and saucer. John arose from his chair and shuffled, hunched over, until he regained enough balance to stand erect.

"Goodman Law, no need to arise. Please sit and rest."

"Just being fitting and proper," said John as he shuffled back to his chair.

"Can I add sugar to ye tea?" asked Mary as she poured. "Or perhaps some spirits?"

"Just tea will be fine." Buttrick took a sip and said, "Ah, splendid; nice and hot to warm my soul."

"A taste of spirits would warm you more," said John.

Buttrick waved a cautioning hand. "It still be early morn."

"We will leave ye two good men to thy duties," said Lydia.

Buttrick remained standing until the two women left. He sat down at a small table across from John. "On my journey hither, I was dazzled with the beauty of your land; sun glistening off the dew, truly a spot of paradise." Buttrick took another sip of tea.

"Aye, be the best in all of New Scotland," said John.

Buttrick lowered the cup from his lips and thought further. He had heard several names through the years for the area known as New Grant, but never heard New Scotland. He also had heard John Law could prickly and decided to not ask further questions about the name. He took another sip. "Um yes, the best spot in all of Concord."

"Me nae need any documents," said John. "But me wants to be fitting and proper for me Lydia and me sons. A lad's word be good enough for me. But nae for a scoundrel like Awbrey. Aye, that Awbrey be so…," and John paused, "he be so English."

Buttrick tightened his lips and again decided not to respond. "Then fitting and proper it shall be," he said. He removed some parchment and ink from his satchel and placed them on the small table. He took out a quill and nodded.

"Aye, let's be on with it," said John.

"John Law art thou of sound mind?"

"Me body be broke, but not me mind."

"And when thy time arrives, will thy body be decently buried to obtain resurrection?"

John gulped as the image of MacTavish with a dagger in his chest and Jesus with welcoming palms flashed in his mind. He shook his head to erase the image. "Aye."

"Dost thou commit thy soul unto the Lord Christ for his judgment?"

"Aye. Me hopes me redeemer hears me."

The scratch of Buttrick's quill and a hissing from the fire accompanied John's thoughts. Did God ever hear him? Would he spend eternity with his parents, his sons and Lydia? He looked at his hearth. Or would he descend into Satan's fire? Buttrick left the room to inventory the contents of the house. John continued pondering. Like always, he had no definitive answers. But he continued wondering until Buttrick came back into the room.

Buttrick sat and began to scroll again. "The Lord hath given thee much. How dost thou propose to dispose of it? Household goods to Lydia, land to thy sons, with a double share to the eldest."

"Me eldest died."

Buttrick's face reddened. "My sincerest apology. My mind was elsewhere when I spoke."

John waved a dismissive hand. He struggled off of his chair and pointed northwest. "Stephen gets me land toward Nagog Pond." He pointed over his shoulder. "Samuel gets me land to the east in the uplands across from me brook. And Thomas gets me land to the south." John paused, waiting for Buttrick's scratching quill to cease. "And me meadows…"

"I say Goodman Law thou hath amassed a large estate."

"Nae be easy, but me have. Me meadows be for Lydia until she passes. Then they will be me lads."

"And thy barn?"

"Me lads, but the livestock is Lydia's." Buttrick paused with quill in hand, seemingly perplexed. "Lydia be fond of the animals, particularly me sheep. She gets me orchard too. She makes the best cider in all of Concord." John rubbed his eyes to stop them from welling. "Aye, Lydia be the best goodwife in all of Concord."

Buttrick smiled an acknowledgement. "And the entire household belongs to Lydia?"

"Aye, and when Lydia passes, Mary will get everything." John thought further. "Except for the brass kettle, Mary should get that now."

"Such a valuable good to be giving to a daughter."

"Mary does all the wool boiling in the brass kettle. Only fitting that it be hers now."

"And Elizabeth?"

"She married Physician Read and be in Connecticut."

"Surely, and a physician is a man of means. No need for bequests to Elizabeth."

"Nae, me needs to be fair to me daughters, too." John rubbed his face. "But me lasses can nae be sharing a brass kettle."

Buttrick took a sip of tea while he waited.

"Me will give twenty shillings to Elizabeth as her share of me kettle. Does that seem fair?"

"Most surely, but dost thou have twenty shillings to bequeath?"

John leaned forward. "Me have plenty of shillings. Keep some in me pewter cup. The rest be elsewhere." He settled back. "Me have pounds too." He folded his arms in front of his chest. "You be paid when me goes. Me be a man of me word."

"Goodman Law, I was not suggesting anything to the contrary."

"Me lads will pay you a fair wage."

Buttrick remained embarrassed, but decided to let the misunderstanding rest. "Among thy belongings, I noticed a finely woven, embroidered jerkin flared at the waist with shiny buttons. Hath it ever been worn?"

"Hasn't."

"And who doth own such finery?"

"Me."

"And never worn?"

"Such finery be important in me youth. Me was going to be like Awbrey." John struggled up from his chair, and his tired eyes regained their youthful fire. "But when would a Scottish man e'er have reason to don such finery?"

"Well, I suppose to meetinghouse or to….."

John snapped his hand, interrupting Buttrick. John settled back and asked, "Aye, Buttrick, do you want me jerkin?"

Buttrick waved his hand and shook his head 'no'. "It would not be fitting and proper." Buttrick arose and began putting his notes and ink into his satchel. "I will duly complete your bequest, and then thou can make thy mark."

"Me can write."

Buttrick cheeks reddened again. "Surely, I meant to say."

"Me can read too."

*****

As Buttrick left the Law residence and walked back to Concord Center, he reflected. He had been forewarned that 'John Law was prickly, filled with avarice, stubborn and proud'. Buttrick chuckled. *He most certainly was prickly.* He thought about the lengthy list of items in John's estate. *Only a greedy man of such humble beginnings could amass such an estate.* But reflecting further, his opinion softened. John had been determined to be fair with Elizabeth about the brass pot, and unlike many of his other clients, John didn't try to haggle over his fee. He simply agreed to pay a fair sum.

Buttrick paused at the bridge to look back at the Law homestead. John Law had certainly amassed much more than Buttrick thought possible for any Scottish man to achieve. Buttrick had many clients who parceled their estate in a pre-determined manner. This was not the case with John Law. He had a deep loving concern for Lydia that was quite apparent. When John talked of his sons' future land holdings, Buttrick saw the pride in his eyes.

A chill grew within Buttrick, and he turned back from the Law homestead. He knew he had an hour or so of daylight, and he hastened. After several minutes, Buttrick was warm, and he paused to catch his breath. He looked back. The vivid western sky was streaked with reddish and orange hues. But lower down on the horizon, the brilliance darkened, lost its color and became blue-black just below the treetops. The meadows were a ghostly slate gray, with only hints of color. A curl of smoke rose from John Law's chimney to provide a unique contrast to the dramatic sunset. A cow lowed, and the waters bubbled around the bridge pilings. *If I owned such an estate, I might forego the ado of Concord Center and be a recluse too.* Buttrick shuddered and continued his journey home.

Chapter Fifty-seven

4 January 1708

A shivering Thomas came into the house with an arm full of wood. The cold air blasted across John's face, and he opened one eye to see snowflakes float into the house. *Aye, it be a bonny day.* John closed his eye until Stephen came in, bringing another cold blast. John opened an eyelid again. *Plenty of wood; me laddies have worked hard.* Lydia and Mary mumbled to one another, indecipherable to John, but he didn't care. He closed his eyelid and returned to his interrupted dream.

In his dream his lads were no longer shuttling wood. It was summer, and they were in the cornfields. John wandered closer to them. They said nothing to him as they cultivated the fields. The cornstalks were the tallest, leafiest and most verdant John had ever seen. The amber tassels, held high by sturdy stalks, dazzled as they swayed in a warm breeze. The swaying ceased, and John picked up a handful of earth. He clenched the rich loam hard enough to feel its moisture. He smelled it, turned his hand and eased his pinky finger open. Rich granules fell from his hand like refreshing rain. As he eased his grip more, the breeze freshened to create a stream that fell close to his feet. With a half emptied fist, John tightened his grip and the stream ceased. He threw the remaining soil onto the ground. *Aye, this earth will provide for me family for an eternity.*

John's fantasy shifted to the barn. A blood and slime covered Lydia assisted ewes with their birthing. Samuel stood at Lydia's side and helped. The births were endless, and Lydia tended to each as quickly as it came. John moved closer. Mother and son worked in silence; even the ewes' bleats were soundless. The air was sweet, lacking any trace of the stench of afterbirth. What should have been pandemonium was amazingly serene.

John was suddenly in the house where the kitchen table teemed with fruit. Mary placed preserve jars into a massive, fully-stock cabinet. Even though it was jam-packed, Mary continued to stock it. She worked in silence. When she looked up and saw John, she smiled and held out a jar in each hand for him to see. She remained motionless, holding the jars and smiling.

The dream's grainy milieu left, and bright lights filled the voids, causing Mary fade out. Dazzling rays shot out from the white backdrop, and tranquility swept through John. He relished it, and did not want to be disturbed. He rested until the rays faded and his senses were overcome with a familiar odor.

John opened an eye and Mary returned, hovering over her brass pot and boiling wool. To her side, Lydia hummed as she worked the spinning wheel. Mary dropped more fleece into the pot, and the odor intensified. John raised his head and looked toward the odor and humming. *Lydia's yarn will fetch several shillings this spring. Aye, she be fine.*

Mary looked at John while she worked and smiled. "How do thee fare, Father," she said.

John's facial muscles couldn't react to smile. He conjured a response, but couldn't move it to his lips. He was frustrated with his inability to respond, but it eventually left. He was too weary, so his response remained trapped within him.

Lydia stopped spinning, came to John and caressed him. "How do thee fare, my dear?"

John basked in the warmth of Lydia's hand. Impulses to respond flickered, but John was unsure if he spoke them. He was drained and wanted his tranquility. Lydia continued to caress John's face. She brushed back his wet matted hair from his cheek, kissed him and talked gently.

John shut his eyelid, and the white glow returned with its tranquility. He was enthralled as images now sprinkled the white canvas. When a familiar looking man appeared, John was startled until he said, "Aye laddie, it be a long while since me have seen you." John wanted to respond to his father, but he was unsure if he did. He didn't care, peace had returned. He exchanged his thoughts about his life with his father. Images appeared with each thought, which he and his father enjoyed. Even the awful ones in his life, Doon Hill, Durham Cathedral, the bowels of the *Unity,* had lost their horror.

The exchange was replaced with another voice. "Me son, praise you Lord." As John exchanged thoughts with his mother, images from his youth came. The MacElwees joined his parents, and John thanked them for the care they had given his mother while he had been away. John had never experienced such bliss.

Another voice came, "Father, you are finally at peace with me." The sound of his son's voice was heavenly, and John's bliss expanded as John Junior beckoned him deeper into the white canvas. The two walked together, joined by John's parents and the MacElwees. With each step, John's tired, worn out body grew more restful. He was almost freed of its burden, and when he was, he sensed he would float with his family for an eternity.

Beads of water suddenly trickled on John's cheeks, and he wondered if he was crying. The droplets interrupted his peace, and he thrashed to drive them away. But they now streamed, the white canvas ebbed, and the grainy backdrop reappeared. Lydia was wiping his face with a wet cloth, still cooing, but John barely heard her. Mary, Thomas and Stephen with anxious faces huddled above Lydia, but soon faded out. Thoughts flickered in John's mind, and he wanted to express them to Lydia. But he lacked the energy to move the thoughts from his mind to his lips. He longed for the tranquility of those who had departed the world before him.

God, give me enough strength to force me ears to hear nae more, and me mind to nae think.

Throughout John's life, he wondered if God ever heard him. Now, in this fleeting wisp of eternity, God did. John Law had endured enough, and his supplication was granted. There was silence. The white canvas sprinkled with pleasing images returned, and John's tired body bathed in a sea of tranquility.

Lydia wept. She put her lips on John's cheek and held them there as tears fell from her cheeks onto John's. She gathered herself and wiped her tears away. She bent down and closed John's eyelid. He seemed so peaceful, and Lydia was truly happy for him. She turned and entered her children's embrace. "This is truly God's divine providence. So be it," said Lydia.

*****

On 4 January 1708, John Law left his New Scotland to his descendants to return to an eternal peacefulness with his ancestors.

Chapter fifty-eight

The rule of primogenitor dictated that John Junior and the first Thomas should have received most of John Law's inheritance. But they had preceded their father in death. Stephen was the next male in line and, thus, maintained the family homestead for Lydia. Lydia died in her 94th year on 6 January 1733, two years before Concord Village was incorporated as Acton. Stephen married soon after his father's death, but had no children. He died the same year as his mother on 25 November. His nephew, one of Thomas's sons, inherited the Law homestead.

Samuel sold his home, which he had built east of Law's Great Brook, became a physician and moved to Connecticut. He married Martha (Wigglesworth) Wheeler, relict of Dr. Joseph Wheeler, following his father's death. In 1727, Samuel died in Groton, Connecticut from a dose of fresh, but probably contaminated, laxative he had received from Boston. Mary married Samuel Davis in 1710, kin to Elizabeth's husband, Dr. Jacob Read. Thomas married, and since Stephen was childless and Samuel had left the area, his progeny would be the Laws of Acton, although such a worthy sounding moniker was not often spoken.

Thomas and his wife Sarah had three sons: John, Titus and Stephen. Several of Thomas's descendants would serve in the Revolutionary War, including Reuben Law, who was born 22 October 1751.

*****
Acton, Middlesex, Massachusetts
September 1776

Reuben Law looked across the family acreage at the brown, slowing dying corn stalks and thought about this year's poor crop yield. He again offered to help his eldest brother in return for housing and a share of the crop yield. His brother had been reluctant to accept help since he didn't need it, but he eventually relented. The truth was now obvious to Reuben. There were too many Laws for their worn out acreage.

Reuben's Uncle Titus owned most of the family's modest estate. Reuben used to wonder why, but he eventually found answers. Reuben's father, John, had died before his sons had become adults. Thus, Uncle Titus never viewed Reuben's eldest brother as his father's peer. He was a nephew, and Uncle Titus had no qualms in favoring his sons over his nephews. Reuben's father was the eldest male, and his sons should have had priority when the land passed down from the previous generation. But Titus got it. It might have been different if Reuben's father was still alive. Certainly Uncle Titus's overreaching would have been curtailed.

Reuben turned away from the fields and wandered home. He wondered about his great grandfather's thoughts when he first settled in New Grant some 120 years earlier. Still pondering, he stooped and picked up a handful of earth. He stared at the grainy soil, before clenching it. It was dry as dust. He rotated his fist and relaxed his pinky finger. Grains trickled out, like sand through an hourglass. A breeze freshened, and the trickle grew to a stream that fell far from his feet, just like dust in the wind. When his fist has half emptied, he tightened it and rotated his hand back. He opened his fist and was momentarily lost in thought. He shook his head, reared back and threw the sandy soil onto the ground.

"This worn out, overused earth will never provide for me and my family."

He pondered his outburst. He was unmarried and had no children, no land and no money. He was twenty four years old, and he had to get on with his life.

*****

January 2009

A Jaguar sedan sped along Route 2 with a map of old Acton laying on the passenger seat for reference. The driver was researching the past of John Law, his distant ancestor, trying to pinpoint where he settled some 350 years earlier. This direct descendant had spent his youth twenty miles west of Acton and frequently traveled Route 2 into Boston. The Concord rotary was an approximate midpoint between Boston and his home. The road used to change noticeably at the rotary. To the west, there were rural towns and a divided highway, and to the east, suburbs and an undivided highway, littered with stoplights and congestion. The farmland just west of the rotary had changed little since he first saw it in his youth. No matter how often he passed by the farmland, he always had peculiar sensations. Often those sensations reminded him to adjust his speed. If he travelling east, slow down and endure the congestion, and if travelling west, open it up and look out for cops.

Those sensations, which he hadn't felt for quite a while, returned as he turned south onto School Street, the last street in Acton before the Concord rotary. He drove between open farmlands, portions of which were now soccer fields. As he drove further, the road carved into the woodlands. He went down a hill, around a curve and arrived at a T intersection. A green road sign with white lettering that read 'Laws Brook Road' was across the road from him. He parked his car on the shoulder and got out. He was struck by the solitude, and those peculiar sensations intensified. He wondered if those sensations, all along, had never meant for him to adjust his speed, but for him simply to stop for something important. The whirl of Route 2 had ceased once he descended the hill. The gurgling of Law's Brook was now ubiquitous. There were scattered houses in the wooded lands. An occasional car whizzed along Laws Brook Road and across a small bridge. But he didn't see or hear them. He was no longer in 2009.

RESOURCES

My professional career was spent attesting to the facts and forming a conclusion. "The Immigrant" is historical fiction, but 'is riveted to history and tempered with plausibility to elevate an insignificant being, as envisioned by an author with a few drops of his blood'. For those of you who want more on the Scottish Prisoners of War, Colonial times, historical characters and/or John Law, listed below is a partial bibliography that was useful for me.

Not listed are the enumerable searches that were performed on the online data bases of the New England Historic Genealogical Society (NEHGS) at http://www.americanancestors.org/home.html. Those searches coupled with numerous visits to their 99 Newbury Street, Boston location provided added insight on the historical characters and helped me in developing the purely fictional ones. If researching Colonial New England is your passion, you must become a member of NEHGS.

Descendants of Scottish Prisoners of War from the battles of Dunbar and Worcester on 3 September 1650 and 3 September 1651, respectively, have a website, teeming with information, at www.scottishprisonersofwar.com

Books

Carlson, Stephen P. *The Scots at Hammersmith* Saugus, Massachusetts Eastern National Park & Monument Association in Cooperation with Department of the Interior National Park Service – Saugus Ironworks National Historic Site 1976 Reprinted in 1979

Conforti, Joseph A. *Imagining New England: Explorations of Regional Identity from the Pilgrims to the Mid-Twentieth Century* Chapel Hill, North Carolina University of North Carolina Press 2001

Copplestone, J. Tremayne *John Eliot and the Indians (1604-1690)* Portland, Oregon Powell's Book 1998

Cronon, Walter *Changes in the Land, Indians, Colonists and the Ecology of New England* New York, New York Hill & Wang, a division of Farrar, Strauss & Giroux 1983

Donahue, Brian *The Great Meadow: Farmers and the Land in Colonial Concord* New Haven, Connecticut Yale University Press 2007

Fisher, David Hackett *Albion's Seed: Four British Folkways in America* New York, New York Oxford University Press, Inc. 1989

Fletcher, Rev. James *Acton in History* Boston, Massachusetts and Philadelphia, Pennsylvania J. W. Lewis 1890

Hartley, E. N. *Ironworks on the Saugus* Norman, Oklahoma University of Oklahoma Press 4th Edition 2001

Hudson, Alfred Sereno *The History of Concord, Massachusetts* Concord, Massachusetts The Erudite Press 1904

Jennings, Francis *The Invasion of America - Indians, Colonialism, and the Cost of Conquest* Published for the Institute of Early American History and Culture at Williamsburg, Virginia London, England and New York, New York W. W. Norton & Company 1975

Phalen, Harold R. *History of the Town of Acton* Cambridge, Massachusetts Middlesex Printing, Inc. 1954

Philbrick, Nathaniel *Mayflower. A Story of Courage, Community and War* New York, New York Viking Press 2006

Rowlandson, Mary *A True History of the Captivity and Restoration of Mrs. Mary Rowlandson* initially published 1682 available via Google Books

Shattuck, Lemuel *History of the Town of Concord* Concord, Massachusetts Russell Odiorne and Company 1835

Thompson, Roger *Cambridge Cameos* Boston, Massachusetts New England Historic Genealogy Society 2005

Ulrich, Laura Thatcher *Good Wives – Images and Reality in the Lives of Women in Northern New England 1650 – 1750* New York, New York Vintage Books A Division of Random House, Inc. 1991

Walcott, Charles H. *Concord in The Colonial Period* Boston, Massachusetts Estes And Lauriat 1884

Wheeler, Ruth R. *Concord Climate for Freedom* Concord, Massachusetts The Concord Antiquarian Society 1967

Articles

Anonymous 1651: "The Battle of Worcester" www.british-civil-wars.co.uk

_____, "Battle of Dunbar (1650)" via the internet from Wikipedia

Beck, Steve "The Battle of Dunbar – September 3, 1650" Via the internet

Bell, Dennis "Battle of Dunbar – 1650" Burnaby, B. C., Canada 1998 www.scotwars.com

Butler, James Davies "British Convicts Shipped to American Colonies" Citation American Historical Review 2 12- 33 HTML by Dinsmore Documentation added May 13, 2002. Via the internet

Choate, Isabella V. and Conant, Elizabeth S. "The Clerk's Book of the Concord Village Proprietors – presentation to the Acton Historical Society January 23, 1994" from the Acton Public Library

Houghton, Marion E. H. "Acton's Forgotten Man – The First Settler" www.colonial-acton.com

Nylander, Robert H. "The Iron Work Farm in Acton, Inc." [SN 1966] Acton Public Library reference 974.44.A188

_____, "Upon Which His Descendants Live In Independence" Assabet Valley BEACON Thursday, June 28, 1973

_____, "History of the John Law House" copied by his wife, Barbara Nylander from his notes.

Parziale, T.C. "Prisoners on the John and Sara 2000" via the internet

Rapaport, Diane "Scots for Sale: the Fate of the Scottish Prisoners in Seventeenth-Century Massachusetts" via the internet

Woollacott, III, Alfred "John Law of Acton, Massachusetts, and Reuben Law of Acton, Massachusetts, and Sharon, New Hampshire", published in two installments by Massachusetts Society of genealogists in their Spring and Summer 2011 editions of MASSOG, available at http://www.myfourleggedstool.com/john-law-of-acton-massachusetts.html and http://www.myfourleggedstool.com/reuben-law-of-acton-massachusetts-and-sharon-new-hampshire.html , respectively.

www.ingramcontent.com/pod-product-compliance
Lightning Source LLC
Chambersburg PA
CBHW032024290426
44110CB00012B/652